Battlecry of Freedom

Ngakma Nor'dzin

Aro Books WORLDWIDE

2019

Aro Books WORLDWIDE
PO Box 111, Aro Khalding Tsang,
5 Court Close, Cardiff,
CF14 1JR, Wales, UK

© 2019 by Ngakma Nor'dzin

All rights reserved. No part of this book may be reproduced in any form or by any means, electronic or mechanical, including photocopying, recording, or by any information storage or retrieval system, without permission in writing from the publisher.

First edition 2019

ISBN: 978-1-898185-46-8 (Paperback)

Slogan cards with a card for each slogan and full-colour backs, available from:

https://makeplayingcards.com/sell/arobooksworldwide

 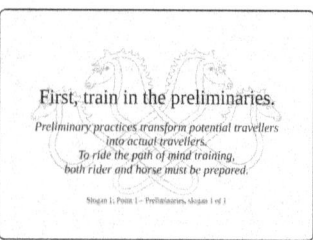

*'Oh yah! You must ride! A ngakpa must ride!
A ngakpa must be like Ling Gésar!
We are warriors of Ling Gésar's army!
We must ride to overcome the savage 'thom yors
who harm others – and ... you must teach your
students to ride.'*
Ngakpa Chögyam quoting Kyabjé Künzang Dorje Rinpoche
– *Wisdom Eccentrics*, p. 272.

Contents

List of slogans		vi
Part I – *overview*		3
	1 Battlecry on Horseback	5
	2 A Brief Historical Background	11
	3 The Seven Points of Mind Training	17
Part II – *the slogans*		29
Part III – *practising Mind Training*		279
	1 Progression through the Seven Points	281
	2 How to Use the Slogans	301
Part IV – *appendices*		305
	1 The Bodhisattva's Garland of Jewels	307
	2 The Heart Sutra	311
	3 Commentary Comparisons	313
Glossary of Buddhist terms		345
Glossary of Equestrian terms		353
Bibliography		361

List of Slogans

1	First, train in the preliminaries.	30
2	Consider all phenomena as dreamlike.	36
3	Examine fundamental unborn awareness.	40
4	Even the remedy self-liberates into its own natural condition.	46
5	Remain in the dimension of kun-zhi, the essence of the path.	50
6	Everything that arises in daily life is illusory.	54
7	Train in alternately sending and receiving; fix these two on the breath.	58
8	Three objects, three poisons, three roots of goodness.	62
9	In all activities, train with slogans.	68
10	Begin the sequence of sending and receiving with oneself.	72
11	When the world and life is full of malice and bad circumstances, transform it into the path of awakening.	76
12	Drive all blames into one.	80
13	Practise gratitude to everyone and everything, everywhere.	86
14	Meditating on the delusions as the four spheres, emptiness is unsurpassable protection.	90
15	Apply the four highest methods.	94
16	Immediately join whatever you meet with meditation.	98
17	Apply the five perfect powers.	102
18	The five powers are the only crucial manner of conduct.	106
19	All teachings agree at one point.	110
20	Embrace the primary of the two witnesses.	114
21	Always be joyful.	118
22	If you are capable even when distracted, you are well trained.	124
23	Continually train in the three general principles.	128
24	Be determined to practise transformation, but remain natural.	132
25	Refrain from talking about weak limbs.	136
26	Do not dwell on the opinion of others.	140
27	Train with the strongest afflicted emotion first.	144
28	Give up all expectation about the fruit of practice.	148
29	Abandon poisonous food.	152

30	With a good nature rely on the root text.	156
31	Do not be agitated by past grievances.	160
32	Do not wait in ambush.	162
33	Do not bring out others' secret state.	166
34	Do not put a dzo's load on an ox.	170
35	Do not hurry to reach the summit.	174
36	Do not pervert the meal.	178
37	Do not turn gods into demons.	182
38	Do not look for happiness in others' pain.	186
39	Practise all the teachings with a single intention.	192
40	Reverse all misfortunes with a single intention.	196
41	Both first and last, two things to do.	200
42	Whichever of the two occurs, practise patience.	204
43	Guard the two, even at the risk of your life.	208
44	Train in the three difficulties.	212
45	Embrace the three principal causes.	218
46	Practise so that the three do not deteriorate.	222
47	Keep the three inseparable.	226
48	Train without prejudice in all areas, deeply and pervasively, and once perfected, cherish everyone and everything, everywhere.	230
49	Always practise with whatever makes you boil.	234
50	Refrain from being influenced by external circumstances.	238
51	This time make practice the priority.	242
52	Refrain from falsifying and perverting.	246
53	Refrain from being sporadic.	250
54	Check how much you are gripped by training.	254
55	Escape duality through investigation and analysis.	258
56	Avoid boastful behaviour.	262
57	Avoid being constricted by jealousy and frustration.	266
58	Refrain from practising just a little.	270
59	Do not wish for thanks.	274

Battlecry
of
Freedom

Part I
overview

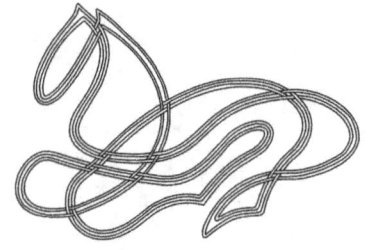

1 – Battlecry on Horseback

A battlecry[1] is the shout of confidence and solidarity of warriors entering a combat. It is a vocalised assertion of the shared purpose of those involved in a campaign. The battle that is engaged by the heroes and heroines of Mind Training is to overcome the domination of personal identity. The campaign that is tirelessly embraced by the heroes and heroines of Mind Training is to fulfil the needs of everyone and everything, everywhere.

Mind Training is presented through pithy, succinct phrases of teaching. The Tibetan for these is *tshig*. There is not an English equivalent of *tshig* which means *word, talk, expression, sentence, line, saying, speech, phrase, term, name, utterance*. *Slogan* is the most common word that is used in presentations of Mind Training, and it is entirely apt. *Slogan* has Celtic roots and refers to a war cry, or battlecry.[2] The yell of the heroes and heroines of Mind Training is a *Battlecry of Freedom*.[3] They gallop into awakening.[4]

---

1. This is usually written as two words—*Battle Cry*—but for this book I am using it as a single word to encompass the sense of energy and the call to action that is encouraged by the slogans.
2. *Slogan* is an Anglicisation of the Scottish Gaelic and Irish word *sluagh-ghairm* – *sluagh* meaning *army* or *host*, and *gairm* meaning *cry* – ref: https://en.wikipedia.org/wiki/slogan.
3. The title *Battlecry of Freedom* was suggested by my teachers, Ngak'chang Rinpoche and Khandro Déchen, the lineage holders of the Nyingma Aro gTér Lineage. As an author, Ngak'chang Rinpoche is known as *Ngakpa Chögyam*. The Aro gTér is a lineage of the non-celibate householder tradition – gö-kar chang-lo (*gos dKar lCang lo*). I have been an apprentice of Ngak'chang Rinpoche and Khandro Déchen since 1983, and was ordained as a *ngakma* (*sNags ma*) in 1989.
4. Awakening—Tib. chang-chub (*byang chub*, Skt. *Bodhicitta*)—is the purpose of Mind Training. It is the realisation of the nonduality of emptiness and form, self and other, existence and non-existence.

Mind Training is a translation of the Tibetan word *lojong*.[5] *Lo* means *mind, intellect, consciousness, wisdom, awareness*, and *intelligence*. *Jong* means *training, refining, purifying, cleansing, studying*, and *practising*. Therefore Mind Training encompasses refining and purifying the mind, as well as training.

I first received teachings on Mind Training at Lam Rim Chö Ling in Raglan, Wales in the 1980s. On these courses we were sometimes encouraged to invent our own slogans as an aid to being present and aware in everyday life. When leaving home, think: *I will walk the path of practice*; or when closing a door: *I am closing the door to the lower realms;* or when opening a door: *I am opening the door to a kind heart*. Such reminders can be most valuable, but do not compare to the richness and depth of the 59 slogans of Mind Training, which express the full depth and breadth of Buddhist practice.

The teachings of Buddhism are presented through the medium of *vehicles*.[6] A vehicle is a complete path of practice, and has a base, a path, and a fruit. The base is the starting point; the path contains the methods of practice; and the fruit is the destination and result of practice. In *Battlecry of Freedom* I refer to the vehicles of practice from the perspective of Dzogchen. These are the three vehicles of Sutra, Tantra, and Dzogchen. Sutra is the path of renunciation and its primary form is monasticism. The base of Sutra is the experience of dissatisfaction, and its fruit is the discovery of emptiness.[7]

---

5 *bLo sByong* – the *j* in lojong is pronounced as in the English word *jam*, rather than as the *j* in the German word *Junge*, or the French word *je*.

6 Vehicle – a path of practice. (Tib. thegpa (*theg pa*), Skt. *yana*). The three vehicles (Tib. *do, gyüd, Dzogchen* (*mDo, rGyud, rDzogs chen*), Skt. *Sutra, Tantra, Mahasandhi*) will be referred to as Sutra, Tantra, and Dzogchen in this book.

7 Emptiness (Tib. tongpa nyi (*sTong pa nyid*, Skt. *shunyata*) – the womb of potential from which everything—form—arises.

Tantra is the path of transformation, and employs visionary practice and Lama'i Naljor[8] as its primary method. Its base is emptiness, and its fruit is the recognition of the nonduality of emptiness and form. Dzogchen is the path of self-liberation. Its base, path, and fruit are nonduality.

Slogan 22 of Mind Training says: *If you are capable even when distracted, you are well trained.* My pithy commentary to this slogan is: *If you stay in the saddle of Mind Training even when the mind shies through distraction, you are a skilful rider.*

Reading this, my teachers, Ngak'chang Rinpoche and Khandro Déchen, suggested that I could use my horse riding experience as an analogy throughout the book, rather than just for this single slogan. This is how the manner of presenting Mind Training in *Battlecry of Freedom* was born.

> *'Kyabjé Künzang Dorje Rinpoche—and his Sangyum, Jomo Sam'phel Déchen Rinpoche—were keen to watch the Li-thang races on video when the opportunity arose – and it was delightful to be in their company as they enjoyed the spectacle.'*
> Khandro Déchen — personal communication

Horsemanship is a highly regarded skill in Tibet, particularly in the eastern regions of Golok, Kham, and Amdo. Tibetan skill on horseback predates Mongolian prowess in the saddle, and the daring military combats of Tibet in the 8th century were achieved with a well-trained cavalry. The Tibetans also used horses for communication across their vast territory. In Kham the tradition of skilled equestrianism continues with the summer Li-thang Horse Racing Festival. Riders demonstrate their skills in the saddle with high-speed races, acrobatic tests of horsemanship, and archery target practice on horseback.

---

8   bLa ma'i rNal 'byor (Skt. *Guru Yoga*) – unifying with the mind of the Lama (spiritual teacher) through visionary practice.

I learned to ride as a child. My parents regarded it as a hobby they could not support financially, so I had to pay for it out of my pocket money. I never had the opportunity to have private lessons, but received instruction as part of a group at various different times in my life.

In my teenage years I was asked to exercise a six-year-old gelding[9] called *Whiskey*. He was the first horse that I had a real relationship with, and for several glorious school summer holidays we were inseparable. Later I was asked to exercise another horse, *Bobby*. He had a particularly uncomfortable saddle, so I used to take him out riding bareback. I fell off quite a lot, but this was itself useful experience.

I was in my fifties before I was finally able to own my own horse. This was *Dee* – a thirteen-year-old Welsh cob mare. I bought her from a riding school where her future was uncertain due to her aggression toward the other horses. We moved her from there to a livery yard with a good reputation.

A couple of years later, my husband bought a thoroughbred-cob cross called *Red*. Owning two horses meant that we needed to find a less expensive livery yard, and so we moved again. Finally it was necessary to move to a third livery yard and this is where the horses lived for many years. This yard was also a trekking centre, and we gave Red to them in 2016 after we had retired Dee. She lived to age 27 and died of natural causes in 2017. You will hear about Dee and Red in this book.

My experience of the relationship between horse and rider has many correlations to the relationship with training the mind. Excellence in riding requires many of the qualities of excellence in Mind Training.

---

9   A male horse that has been castrated. There is a Glossary of Equestrian Terms at the end of the book, p. 353.

> 'Rinpoche nodded slightly. "In Tibet I rode horses.
> Many Nyingma Lamas rode horses.
> DoKhyentsé rode and so did Düd'jom Lingpa." [...]
> "Is it important for me to ride, Rinpoche?"
> "Oh yah! You must ride! A ngakpa must ride!
> A ngakpa must be like Ling Gésar!
> We are warriors of Ling Gésar's army!
> We must ride to overcome the savage 'thom yors[10]
> who harm others – and ... you must teach your
> students to ride."'
> Ngakpa Chögyam – *Wisdom Eccentrics*, p. 272

Ngak'chang Rinpoche and Khandro Déchen often refer to horse riding in their teachings, and their experience of receiving riding instruction. They have always seen close parallels – particularly with the role of the vajra master and their riding instructor.[11] This book also includes stories of their horse riding experiences.

When looking at the spiritual path, it can be useful to compare it to a more ordinary experience—such as horse riding—and leave aside the enigmatic and mysterious atmosphere of spirituality. This can make spiritual practice more approachable. Ultimately deep spiritual understanding is beyond words, because such understanding is beyond the capacity of intellect.

This is also true of the deep relationship developed between a horse and rider. Horses are quite different creatures to human beings, yet there is a long history of a meaningful relationship with them. Horses allow people to ride them, and willingly respond to their wishes, and this cooperative interaction can be an intimate experience on every level. Once a bond and understanding is established between a particular horse and a particular rider, the experience of riding becomes subtle and pervasive.

---

10 Tib. *'thom yor* – idiot, idiotic.
11 Vajra Master – dorje löpon (rDo rJe sLob dPon; Skt. *vajra charya*). The Teacher to whom a Vajrayana practitioner makes a commitment.

The rider is in union with the movement of the horse, and the horse is sensitive to the physical presence of the rider. The aids the rider needs to provide the horse to interpret the rider's wishes, can become increasingly subtle as the relationship develops. A beginner could flail about on Red's back, kicking, jangling the reins, shouting at him to move – and he might completely ignore them. The moment an able rider put a foot in the stirrup, Red would know that the person could ride, and would be alert to them, and more willing to respond – or to be mischievous.

The horse is a large and powerful animal. A horse cannot be *forced* to cooperate with the rider, and will resent the attempt. Similarly the mind cannot be forced. This is easily discovered through trying to force thought to disappear. The horse is a herd and prey animal, and finds confidence through the rider's leadership. The horse will respect the considerate authority of the rider, and respond by giving its best. Similarly the mind can be trained through perseverance and application.

Good riders ask, and good horses respond. Good meditators ask, and the nature of mind responds. To meditate is to cooperate with the nature of the mind, and this opens the possibility of awakening.

The rider must ride the horse *as it is*. The rider must let go of preconceptions, expectations, or aspirations with regard to the qualities of the horse. These will prevent the rider from experiencing the dimension of the horse *as it is*. Similarly, the meditator must discover *as it is*—the nature of the mind *as it is*—free from preconceptions, expectations, or aspirations.

The rider must focus on the horse. In this way, the rider is *empty* in relation to the *form* of the horse. Through this relationship, the horse is able to respond fully, and achieve its potential. The meditator learns emptiness in order to clarify the relationship with form, and thereby discover the nonduality of emptiness and form. Then the mind begins to awaken.

2 – A Brief Historical Background

to the Seven Points of Mind Training
by Chekhawa Yeshé Dorje

The Seven Points of Mind Training is a text composed by Chekhawa Yeshé Dorje,[1] in the 12th century.

The slogans of Mind Training originated from Atisha,[2] and at that time existed as an oral tradition among his followers. Chekhawa pulled the threads of the teachings together into a powerful presentation in seven points. Initially he only taught it to his disciples, but then Chekhawa discovered that the local lepers were listening to his teachings outside the tent, practising what they heard, and succeeding in curing themselves through their application of Mind Training. This led to Chekhawa teaching the Seven Points openly so that everyone could benefit from the power of the practice.

By the time Chekhawa came to compose the *Seven Points of Mind Training*, Buddhism had existed in Tibet for 400 years, but its establishment as the religion of the country was not without difficulties.

Tibet emerged as a unified country in the 7th century under the rule of Tsenpo Songtsen Gampo,[3] whose divine authority was supported by the leaders of Tibet's clans. By the end of the 8th century Tibet was the greatest military power in Central Asia. Through its dominion, Tibet made contact with the cultures and religions of its nearby trading regions, such as India, Nepal, and China.

---

1   *'Chad kha ba Ye shes rDo rJe* (1101–1175).
2   *Jo bo rJe dPal lDan A ti sha* Skt. Atiśa Dīpamkar Śrījñāna (980–1054).
3   *bTsan po* – king, ruler, monarch. Tsenpo Songtsen Gampo (*Srong bTsan sGam po*) ruled 618–649.

In 756 Tsenpo Trisong Détsen[4] was enthroned, and in 762 he declared Buddhism as the official religion of Tibet. This was a means of maintaining the unity of Tibet, as well as a spiritual aspiration. Trisong Détsen invited the great Buddhist teachers Padmasambhava[5] and Śāntaraksita[6] to establish Buddhism in Tibet. When Padmasambhava arrived at the Tibetan royal court, the assembly offered prostrations to him – except for Trisong Détsen, who, as a God-King, did not bow to anyone. Padmasambhava looked at Trisong Détsen, singeing his beard with a wave of the hand. The Tsenpo immediately understood that the power of the Buddhist teachings was greater than the power of a God-King, and also offered prostrations.

This period was the beginning of the first spread of Buddhism in Tibet. The non-celibate traditions, and the celibate monastic traditions were established as being of equal value and status. Tibet flourished spiritually and culturally, as well as politically.

Trisong Détsen's grandson, Tri Ralpachen,[7] succeeded him in 815. He invested great wealth and power in the development of Buddhism in Tibet. To demonstrate his support of the non-celibate, and the celibate monastic streams of practice, he laid out two braids of his hair on either side of him, greatly extended with ribbons. He had representatives of yogic practice sit on one braid, and of monastic practice sit on the other. There was unrest however, among the ministers and leaders of the ancient clans, who were concerned that the military strength and prominence of Tibet was being threatened by too much investment in Buddhism. This led to Ralpachen being assassinated.

---

4   *Khri srong lDe bTsan* – ruled 755–797.
5   Guru Rinpoche, the Lotus-born Lama.
6   Śāntaraksita – Tibetan name Shiwa Tso (*Shi ba Tsho*), 725–788.
7   *Khri Ral pa can* – ruled 815–836.

Ralpachen was succeeded by his brother Darma, in 836. Darma was quite a different personality from Ralpachen, enjoying hunting, drinking, and festive carousing. He had the nickname *Lang* meaning *ox* because of his strong and bull-like nature and physique, and hence he became known as *Langdarma*.[8]

To secure political power and the support of the clans, Langdarma instigated the repression of Buddhism. The wealthy monastic institutions were destroyed, and the monks killed. He also attempted to persecute and eradicate the yogic stream of Buddhism.

Sang-gyé Yeshé,[9] a great yogi, was able to terrify Langdarma however, by pointing at the sky and, through the power of mantra, manifesting a black scorpion the size of nine yaks. He then pointed at a mountain, and directed a bolt of lightning which cleft the peak in two. After this display of power, Langdarma agreed not to persecute the yogic practitioners.

Langdarma ruled for six years. He succeeded not only in halting the development of monastic Buddhism, but in almost eradicating it, before his assassination in 843. Although this was a dark age for monasticism, the non-celibate traditions flourished.

In the 10th century, Yeshé Ö [10] set out to re-establish Buddhism as the religion of Tibet. Monastic Buddhism, with its hierarchical structure and large institutions, was easier to control than the myriad small non-celibate traditions existing throughout Tibet. Atisha was invited to Tibet to help re-establish monasticism. Atisha was from Bengal, and came to Tibet in 1042. His main teacher was Sér Lingpa[11] who came from Burma.

---

8   *gLang dar ma* – ruled 836–841.
9   *Sangs rGyas Ye shes*
10 *Ye shes 'od*
11 *gSer gLing pa*, Skt. *Dharmakīrtiśrī*. *gSer* means gold, or golden, and *gLing* means place, region, or island, so Chekhawa calls him *the One from the Golden Isle*.

> '*Yeshé 'öd—who styled himself the divine monk—had a political agenda with regard to* re-establishing Buddhism *in Tibet. There was nothing to re-establish as the Nyingma lineages remained vital and unbroken. He manipulated the situation in order to unite Tibet with himself as God King – and needed the authority of Atisha to ensure his success. Yeshé 'öd hid his policies – and Atisha was persuaded that the Tantras should only be taught in the monasteries. The monasteries of course, were under the dominion of Yeshé 'öd – and thus he was free to persecute the Nyingmas and particularly the non-celibate community.*'
> Kyabjé Künzang Dorje Rinpoche – personal communication from Ngak'chang Rinpoche

Rinchen Zangpo,[12] a Tibetan scholar who had studied and practised Buddhism extensively in India, was appointed to oversee the re-translation of texts, the revival of the deserted and desolate university monastery of Samyé,[13] and the building of new temples and monasteries.

This was the beginning of the new translation schools, the Kagyu and Sakya.[14] The pre-existing Buddhist traditions became known as the *Nyingma – the old translation school.*[15] These were the traditions that had flourished since the time of Padmasambhava.

As well as the thriving non-celibate traditions, some pockets of monasticism had survived, notably in Amdo. Monks from this region were invited to central Tibet to help redevelop monastic Buddhist practice.

The followers of Atisha became known as the *Kadampa.*[16] *Ka* means Buddhist scriptures, or the words of Shakyamuni Buddha, and *dam* means advice, precept or teaching.

---

12 *Rin chen bZang po* (958–1055).
13 *bSam yas*
14 *bKa' brGyud* and *sa sKya* – the new translation schools—*Sarma (gSar ma)* schools—that arose in this period.
15 *rNying ma*
16 *bKa' gDams pa*

Lojong—Mind Training—was at heart of their practice and teachings. This took the form of simple instructions for replacing self-centred motivation with selflessness, as well as the practice of *tonglen*,[17] exchanging self with others.

Langri Thangpa[18] was a notable Kadampa practitioner and teacher, and wrote *The Eight Verses of Training the Mind*. It was this teaching that prompted Chekhawa Yeshé Dorje, the author of *The Seven Points of Mind Training*, to seek out Langri Thangpa.

He is said to have been particularly touched by two lines from Langri Thangpa's teaching:

> '*I will take defeat upon myself,*
> *And give the victory to others.*'

Chekhawa Yeshé Dorje was born in 1101. Unfortunately Langri Thangpa had already died by the time Chekhawa set out to receive further teachings on Mind Training. Instead he met one of Langri Thangpa's disciples, Sharawa Yönten Drag,[19] and remained to study with him for sixteen years. Sharawa died in 1141 and Chekhawa succeeded him as teacher at the monastery.

At first Chekhawa kept the Mind Training teachings secret, conveying them only to his disciples. But on discovering that lepers were curing themselves through the practice of tonglen, he started to teach Mind Training more publicly. This prompted him to compose the *Seven Points of Mind Training*,[20] so that the teachings could become available to everyone.

None of Atisha's teachings were recorded as written texts until some considerable time after his death, but this oral tradition was the source of Mind Training.

17 *gTong len*
18 *gLang ri Thang p*a (1054–1123).
19 *Sha ra ba Yon tan Grags* (1070–1141).
20 Lojong don dün ma (*lojong don bDun ma*).

Chekhawa died in 1175, aged 75. He spent his final years in seclusion. Chekhawa Yeshé Dorje concludes *The Seven Points of Mind Training* with this verse:

> '*The essence of the nectar-like instructions—for transforming into the path of awakening the five prevalent signs of degeneration —was passed down from the One from the Golden Isle. When karmic seeds left over from former trainings were aroused in me, I felt great interest, and so, without regard for suffering or disparagement, I sought instructions on subduing ego-clinging. Now, even in death, I will have no regrets.*'[21]

---

21 Ref: http://lotsawahouse.org/topics/lojong – translator Adam Pearcey, 2012.

3 – The Seven Points of Mind Training

1. Preliminary practice, the foundation of the teaching
   – *sNgon 'gro rTen gyi chos bsTan pa*
   This point explains the preliminary practices as the basis of all paths.

2. Awakened mind, the purpose and basis of training
   – *dNgos gZhi byang chub kyi sems sByang ba*
   This point introduces awakening as the fruit of practice and the purpose of training the mind.

3. Transforming bad circumstances into the path of awakening – *rKyen ngan byang chub kyi lam du bsGyur ba*
   This point introduces the primary methods of practice, methods of transforming the relationship with experience so that the mind can be awakened.

4. Applying essential practice and teaching to the whole of life – *tshe gCig gi nyams len dril nas bsTan pa ni*
   This point essentialises the qualities developed through the first three points which keep the practitioner firmly on the path of Mind Training and awakening throughout life and at the time of death.

5. Evaluating Mind Training – *bLo 'byongs pa'i tshad*
   This point explains how to self-evaluate progress.

6. The commitments of Mind Training
   – *bLo sByong gi dam tshig*
   This point is a pragmatic guide to remaining committed to the path of practice

7. Advice on Mind Training (completes the seven)
   – *bLo sByong gi bsLab gya dang bDun no*
   This point advises on the necessary attitude for consistent and effective practice throughout life.

First: preliminaries.

The horse and the rider must be prepared.

The first point is a single slogan:

1. First, train in the preliminaries.

If a person wishes to learn to ride, there are many things to consider before real riding can begin: how to climb into the saddle, how to put feet in stirrups, how to hold the reins, how to ask the horse to move, turn, and halt.

In any undertaking there are things to learn in order to really begin – and spiritual practice is no different in this. If the mind turns in the direction of spirituality, there has to be a way of reining in its wildness, and coaxing it in a better direction. Preliminary practices are the way to begin.

Once the basics have been grasped, riders can begin to ride. They still climb into the saddle, but know how to ease carefully onto the horse's back. They continue to put their feet in the stirrups, but know the correct length. They still take up the reins, but know the right tension for gentle contact. They now know how to ask the horse to listen to their requests of pace, direction, and halt.

> *'Preparation is essential unless one has experience of emptiness.'*
> Ngakpa Chögyam – *Roaring Silence*, p. 15

It may seem obvious that there is a need to engage in preliminary practices at the beginning, and it could be assumed that this is the only reason for this slogan being placed first in the Seven Points of Mind Training. However, Chekhawa emphasises the utmost importance of preliminaries, by not only making this the first slogan, but also by having just this single slogan within the first point.

Preliminary practices offer the means of becoming an engaged practitioner. They are not abandoned once practitioners know how to practice – rather, their value is seen even more clearly and potently.

Although they are *preliminary*, these practices are in fact embraced throughout the life of practice, not just at the beginning.

Second: awakening.

The nature of riding is examined to discover the appropriate relationship between horse and rider.

The second point of Mind Training contains nine slogans, numbers two to ten of the whole fifty-nine:

2. Consider all phenomena as dreamlike.
3. Examine fundamental unborn awareness.
4. Even the remedy self-liberates into its own natural condition.
5. Remain in the dimension of kun-zhi, the essence of the path.
6. Everything that arises in daily life is illusory.
7. Train in alternately sending and receiving; fix these two on the breath.
8. Three objects, three poisons, three roots of goodness.
9. In all activities, train with slogans.
10. Begin the sequence of sending and receiving with oneself.

This group of slogans can be considered as two sets. The first five (2 – 6) encompass *awakened* and *awakening view* – learning to recognise and understand the nature of the wild horse of the mind. The last four (7 – 10) encompass *awakened* and *awakening intent* – how to embrace the natural grace, power, and potential of the wild horse of the mind. This is like practising dressage – embracing the natural capacity of the mind and transforming it into power, beauty, and elegance. The mind is tamed and focussed, but not disempowered. It is the co-operation of horse and rider that enables the horse to achieve its athletic potential.

Third: transformation.

The rider rides.

There are six slogans in the third point:

11. When the world and life is full of malice and bad circumstances, transform it into the path of awakening.
12. Drive all blames into one.
13. Practise gratitude to everyone and everything, everywhere.
14. Meditating on the delusions as the four spheres, emptiness is unsurpassable protection.
15. Apply the four highest methods.
16. Immediately join whatever you meet with meditation.

The rider engages the qualities and faults of the horse as methods to improve riding skills. The opportunities and limitations of the equestrian arena, the horse trail, or the riding school are embraced as the perfect environment for riding.

The qualities and faults of the mind are the mount for Mind Training. The circumstances of everyday life offer opportunities to ride. Whomever and whatever are encountered, are the basis of *life as practice*. Each and every moment and circumstance are an opportunity to transform ordinary experience into awakening experience.

The rider rides. The horse is energetic or dull, attentive or distracted, willing or stubborn; the day is windy or calm, wet or dry, or sunny or overcast. The trail is scattered with wind-blown obstructions, muddy, or dappled with shadows. All are opportunities to ride. All are opportunities to deepen awareness, ability, and the relationship of horse and rider.

Fourth: the five powers.

Skill and capacity develop through riding the mind.

There are two slogans in the fourth point:

17. Apply the five perfect powers.
18. The five powers are the only crucial manner of conduct.

The five powers—Tob-nga *(sTobs lNga)*—are:

1. dad pa'i tob – *dad pa'i sTobs*
   – faith, confidence, trust, willing participation, respect, and engagement.

2. tson-dru-kyi tob – *brTson 'grus kyi sTobs*
   – perseverance, effort, energy, and application.

3. dren pa'i tob – *dran pa'i sTobs*
   – recollection, presence, alertness, paying attention, and concentration.

4. ting-dzin-gyi tob – *ting 'dzin gyi sTobs*
   – contemplation, deep concentration, attention, absorption, meditative stability, and undividedness.

5. sherab-kyi tob – *shes rab kyi sTobs*
   – discriminating awareness, wisdom, intelligence, insight, discernment, and knowledge.[1]

Riders develop confidence in their ability to be present, alert, and attentive whenever they are in the saddle of Mind Training. They apply their skills as needed, judging the demeanour of the mind, and the requirements of the riding environment, with discriminating intelligence.

---

1   As the root text does not specify the five powers, those enumerated by Kyabjé Düd'jom Rinpoche – Jig'drèl Yeshé Dorje, are prioritised in this commentary: see ref. *The Nyingma School of Tibetan Buddhism – its Fundamentals and History*, Glossary of Enumerations, p. 147. Kyabjé Düd'jom Rinpoche was the greatest Nyingma Lama of the 20th century, and Chekhawa was also a Nyingma-pa. For other versions of the five powers, see Part IV, Appendix 3, p. 323.

Fifth: evaluation.

Riding capacity and skills are evaluated.

There are four slogans in the fifth of the Seven Points of Mind Training.

19. All teachings agree at one point.

20. Embrace the primary of the two witnesses.

21. Always be joyful.

22. If you are capable even when distracted, you are well trained.

Through having applied effort and perseverance in practice, and having developed the five powers, the rider creates the capacity to self-evaluate their prowess in the saddle of Mind Training.

Sixth: commitment.

The rider becomes committed to riding the mind, and awakening.

There are sixteen slogans in the sixth point:

23. Continually train in the three general principles.
24. Be determined to practise transformation, but remain natural.
25. Refrain from talking about weak limbs.
26. Do not dwell on the opinion of others.
27. Train with the strongest afflicted emotion first.
28. Give up all expectation about the fruit of practice.
29. Abandon poisonous food.
30. With a good nature rely on the root text.
31. Do not be agitated by past grievances.
32. Do not wait in ambush.
33. Do not bring out others' secret state.
34. Do not put a dzo's load on an ox.
35. Do not hurry to reach the summit.
36. Do not pervert the meal.
37. Do not turn gods into demons.
38. Do not look for happiness in others' pain.

Committed riders hone their skills and avoid becoming complacent. They recognise any potential downfalls and obstacles and ride carefully to avoid them. The sixteen slogans in the sixth point of Mind Training describe the commitments to adopt, and the hazards to avoid whilst in the saddle of Mind Training.

Seventh: advice.

Riders take care to maintain an excellent relationship with the horse, and excellence in riding.

39. Practise all the teachings with a single intention.
40. Reverse all misfortunes with a single intention.
41. Both first and last, two things to do.
42. Whichever of the two occurs, practise patience.
43. Guard the two, even at the risk of your life.
44. Train in the three difficulties.
45. Embrace the three principal causes.
46. Practise so that the three do not deteriorate.
47. Keep the three inseparable.
48. Train without prejudice in all areas, deeply and pervasively, and once perfected, cherish everyone and everything, everywhere.
49. Always practise with whatever makes you boil.
50. Refrain from being influenced by external circumstances.
51. This time make practice the priority.
52. Refrain from falsifying and perverting.
53. Refrain from being sporadic.
54. Check how much you are gripped by training.
55. Escape duality through investigation and analysis.
56. Avoid boastful behaviour.
57. Avoid being bound by jealousy and frustration.
58. Refrain from practising just a little.
59. Do not wish for thanks.

The last point of Mind Training contains twenty-one slogans, and offers advice to committed practitioners.

These final slogans offer advice and subtle adjustments. A rider knows that if the reins are too tight, the horse may feel restricted and become stressed; too loose and the horse may feel disconnected from the rider, provoking disrespect or anxiety.

> *'Easy to understand, it is not corrupted.*
> *Easy to practice, it is entered with enthusiasm.*
> *Yet it is profound, so buddhahood is attained.'*
> Jamgon Kongtrul – The Great Path of Awakening, p. 2

When riders go out on a horse trail, the route is generally circular, in that they begin at the stable, a trail is ridden, and then horses and riders arrive back at the stable. The starting point for riding is also the destination. The purpose of the expedition is the experience of *riding*. Through engaging the practices of Mind Training, practitioners discover that it is also a circular trail – the destination is beginningless, and they have never actually been separated from it.

Mind Training is a method of *living the view* – living the methods of awakening. Just as all aspects of caring for the horse, and developing riding skills, are important to the quality of riding, the entire context of life is engaged with Mind Training. When in the saddle, experienced riders do not have to run through the manual on aids in their minds. They know where and when to apply their legs, or how to shift their balance, or whether to tighten or loosen their reins. They simply enter the dimension of riding. Riding is, as it is.

Mind Training offers a comprehensive and approachable method of living the path of awakening. The slogans continually return the practitioner to the purpose, methods, and principles of practice; to seeing the downfalls and hindrances to practice; and to recognising its benefits.

It is both profound and pragmatic, inspirational and sobering, subtle and obvious. If fully embraced, it offers a complete path and will become the cause of awakening. Through the study and practice of the Seven Points of Mind Training, it can be realised that the potential to awaken is available in each and every moment.

Part II
the slogans

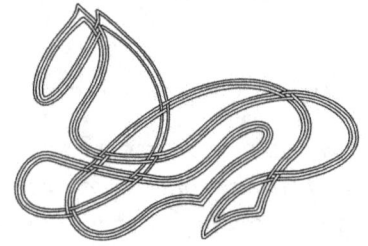

1

First, train in the preliminaries.

dang po sNgon 'gro dag la bsLab

*Preliminary practices transform
potential travellers into actual travellers.
To ride the path of Mind Training,
both rider and horse must be prepared.*

When I first started riding, at about age 10, I would turn up at the riding stables and be given a horse, already wearing its tack, to lead out to the arena. All I had to do to prepare for riding, was to wear appropriate clothing, arrive on time, and have money to pay for the lesson. As I became better known by the riding establishment, I became more involved in other aspects of preparing to ride. I would go earlier than my appointment, groom the pony I would be riding, and help put on its tack.

> *'I cannot imagine why people would not wish to groom and tack-up the horses on which they were to have their lessons – but some people seemed content to miss that part of the experience. For Rinpoche and myself, it was a vital part of getting the best from our lessons.'*
> Khandro Déchen – personal communication

Eventually, at that first establishment in my life as a horse rider, I started to visit the stables at other times when I was not booked in to ride, and help out with the ponies. I would be involved with all the ponies' care and preparation, and sometimes would lead a ride, in charge of taking out other riders.

When I eventually owned my own horse, the extra aspect that became evident that I had not experienced before, was taking full responsibility for the horse. This included regularly worming the horse, balancing feed with regard to the horse's needs at different times of year, organising care for hooves. It involved being aware of the general health of the horse and knowing when to call in the vet. Also I needed a greater knowledge about tack – what to choose for the comfort of the horse, but also to enable safe riding.

> *'Moments of realisation arise from having prepared the ground.'*
> Ngakpa 'ö-Dzin – Apprentice retreat, July 2018

Riders who never become involved in all aspects of care and preparation, will not develop the deepest bond with their horses.

When riders are involved in all aspects of the life and care of their horses, intimate relationships develop. This intimacy offers the potential for harmonious riding and the achievement of the greatest capacity of horses and riders.

The purpose of preparation in the context of Buddhist preliminary practice, performs the same function. These practices give a beginner a means of beginning. They enable deeper involvement once some experience in practice has been gained.

They eventually enable practice to be fully embraced as a method of awakening. Horse riders may retire from riding, but Buddhist practitioners never retire from riding Mind Training. The relationship with practice continues to deepen and strengthen. This creates commitment and capacity, and eventually awakening.

From the perspective of Dzogchen, there are the three vehicles of Sutra, Tantra, and Dzogchen. These are the paths of renunciation, transformation, and self-liberation. Each require that a practitioner is at the starting point for the vehicle (the base), and has learned the methods of the vehicle (the path), so that a destination can be reached (the fruit). For preliminary practice the fruit may only be a vague aspiration, but the base must be recognised and the methods embraced.

> '... *the precious human life means precisely* you.'
> Shamar Rinpoche – *The Path to Awakening,* p. 42

To *walk* a path, all that is required is a functioning human body, and the desire to travel. Walking is an effective means of travelling at a steady human pace. This could be used as an analogy for the path of Sutra.

To *ride* to a destination, a traveller needs to have access to a horse. If a mount is available, then riding skills are needed. If there is access to a mount, and the capacity to ride, then a rider is able to travel. This is a faster means of transport and potentially more dangerous than walking.

The horse and the rider have to be considered. There is the possibility of being injured through falling off the horse, or hurting others through dangerous riding. Nevertheless, with a good horse, and a good rider, this is a fast and effective means of travel. This could be used as an analogy for the path of Tantra. Other ways of travelling that require engagement and skill could also be used, such as driving a car, or piloting a plane.

There is no mode of transport that can be used as an analogy for the path of Dzogchen. It is the path of spontaneous self-liberation. It is the path of instantaneous process. Perhaps the evolution of instantaneous personal teleportation might be the closest approximation to an analogy for this vehicle[1] – or knowing that on setting out, the destination has already been reached.

> *'Preparation is not something that we just do once and then forget about it. It is easy to enter into meditation and other practices, and just continue along. But along the way, we lose track of why we decided to do any of this in the first place.*
> *By starting with the preliminaries, and going back to that starting point repeatedly, we can reconnect ourselves over and over again [with] our initial inspiration.'*
> Judith Lief – *Train Your Mind: Lojong Commentary*

The method of the vehicle encompasses everything about how to travel from the base to the fruit. In Sutra, Tantra and Dzogchen the route must be revealed by someone who knows it. The traveller needs a guide to explain the route, or better still, to accompany them. There still may be difficulties encountered on the journey, such as an obstruction on the trail, or the horse may lose a shoe, tack may break, or there may be adverse weather conditions, but if the traveller perseveres, and has confidence in the horse, the guide, and the route, then the destination *will* be reached.

---

1 The capacity for spontaneous personal teleportation—*jaunting*—is explored as an evolution of human beings in *The Stars My Destination*, a science fiction novel by Alfred Bester, Signet, 1957.

The base of Sutra is the experience of dissatisfaction. In order to experience dissatisfaction, there needs to be some experience of satisfaction. There needs to be experience of success in life – some success in creating *form* in life that is functional. Success might include: being able to hold down a job and be self-sufficient; being able to develop and sustain healthy relationships; being able to experience an ordinary level of happiness without needing to resort to drugs, excessive alcohol, or other addictive supports.

If despite having the capacity to be relatively successful in life, dissatisfaction is nonetheless experienced, this can be taken as the point of departure for a spiritual journey.

> *'Consider that the time of death is uncertain;*
> *it may arrive all of a sudden.'*
> Könchok Yenlak – *A Concise Lojong Manual*, p. 5

The base of Tantra is the experience of *emptiness*. This may occur through a dramatic life circumstance, such as the loss of a loved one, a car crash, serious ill health, or the loss of livelihood or home. Emptiness can also be experienced in relationship with an inspiring teacher – becoming empty through the wish to be like that teacher and have their qualities.

The people surrounding a teacher may also be inspiring, seeming to be free of the oscillation of expectation and disappointment. They are vivid, robust, and merry, and energetically engaged with whatever is happening in their lives. They do not seem to experience life as if being tossed around on a frenzied bucking horse, desperately hanging on. They ride and enjoy the bucks, and also calm the horse.

From the starting point of emptiness, the relationship with form can be transformed, and the path of Tantra commenced.

The base of Dzogchen is nonduality – the experience of the nonduality of emptiness and form.

This realisation can arise spontaneously or through direct introduction from a teacher. In Tantra and Dzogchen a teacher is essential to convey the methods of preliminary practice. The methods of practice given to the student will be personal and depend on the teacher, as in the examples below taken from *Roaring Silence*.[2]

> ' *"Sit from dawn to dusk and have no thoughts.*
> *You may use any method you wish to banish thoughts*
> *from your mind."* [...]
> *"Tomorrow go back to the cave and sit from dawn to dusk again –*
> *but this time have nothing but thought without interruption.*
> *Think of anything at all, all day long – but allow no gaps*
> *to occur between thoughts."* '
> Ngakpa Chögyam and Khandro Déchen – *Roaring Silence*, pp. 40 & 41

In Sutra the experience of dissatisfaction is described as 'experientially common'. Everyone is able to find themselves at this base – though not everyone will choose spiritual practice as the means to overcome the experience of dissatisfaction. If spiritual practice is chosen, then a teacher will be required here as well.

Becoming a rider started with preparing myself to ride. Then I became involved with preparing the horse for riding. Finally I was able to develop a deep and meaningful relationship with particular horses, and experience the nature of riding. Preliminary practices immerse the practitioner in practice. They are not just *that which precedes the main body of practice* or *the taster before the main meal* – they are actual engagement with the vehicle itself, and thereby are themselves of the nature of the path of awakening.

---

2   This style of instruction is traditional. It would have been the usual approach of cave-dwelling meditation masters to their disciples.

2

Consider all phenomena as dreamlike.

chos rNams rMi lam lTa bur bSam

All experiences that occur whilst in the saddle of Mind Training, are the dreamlike ornaments of riding.

Rider and horse move through the landscape. It may be an open and expansive hillside, or an enclosed woodland glade. There is the sensation of sun or wind, or cooling shadow. There are the noises of creaking tack and creaking trees, the regular rhythm of hooves. The rider may notice the smell of horse and leather, wild honeysuckle or garlic. There may be the taste of salty sweat. All sensations are experienced within the dimension of riding. The rider may recognise the horse's attention being drawn to a sound, a sight, or a sensation. These experiences are present, but they are not the focus. They arise and they subside like dreams. The focus is riding. The experience of harmony with horse and landscape is pervasive. The rider is empty in relation to the experience of riding, but still present and responsive to the phenomena that arise in the moment.

Many experiences can occur whilst riding. Horses naturally seem to stumble occasionally – this has been common to every horse I have ever ridden. Horses can send a ripple through their body to rid themselves of the irritation of a biting insect. They shake their heads and chew on the bit. Horses have eyes on the side of their heads so their range of vision is approximately 350°. As a prey animal, this gives them the best possible chance of noticing a predator. It is useful for a rider to remember this and understand that the horse is seeing things that a human cannot see. The instinct for prey animals is to pay alert attention to anything that is seen, ready to take flight and escape if necessary. The rider has to be the reassuring presence of leadership that enables the horse to relax and let go of the fear and the need to take flight. The rider has to be the herd leader for the horse. Alert attention to something seen can cause the horse to shy, change pace, spin, or react in all manner of sudden and unexpected ways. These experiences are the ornaments of riding.

Dee and I used to meet many people walking dogs on the horse trails. She would generally assume that a dog could be ignored, but would still be wary of where it was in relation to her.

A dog is a potential predator for a horse. *Dog as predator* is a perception. *Dog innocently sharing the path* is an alternative perception. Each is dreamlike as it appears, because interaction with the dog has not been engaged. The skilful rider notices the dog and is prepared for a fearful reaction from the horse, or for the need to protect the horse if the dog is aggressive, or for nothing at all to happen. The rider makes no assumptions. To anticipate any reaction of dog or horse would be to give substance to the dreamlike potential of the moment.

The rider neither joins the horse in its fearfulness, nor rejects the possibility that the dog could be an animal to be feared, nor ignores the dog assuming that it will just walk past. All are dreamlike appearances until something actually happens, and then what actually happens is ridden.

> '... *while we dream, it seems that there are objects, sounds, and so forth, which are exactly the same as they are while we are awake. We see hills, forests, houses, people, and so forth, during our dreams, but these phenomena are not as they seem. They appear to us, but they are not solid even though we can hit them, fall off them, and so on. Is everything we see in our dreams there? No. When we dream of a house or mountain, there is no real house or mountain in the room. In other words, while not existing, these phenomena still appear.*'
> Thrangu Rinpoche – *The Seven Points of Mind Training*

The dreamlike nature of *dream*-phenomena are easily understood. Dream phenomena are tangible and real to the dreaming mind, but when the dreamer wakes up, the phenomena of the dreams dissolve. It is not expected that dream phenomena will continue into the waking state.

The dreamlike nature of mind-phenomena in the waking state is not so easily recognised. The experience of the waking state is that it is reality, and phenomena are tangibly real. Yet waking phenomena also dissolve during the experience of sleep and dreaming. It is not expected that waking activity impacts on dream activity.

> *'Nothing ever happens.*
> *But because nothing happens, everything happens.'*
> Chögyam Trungpa Rinpoche – *Training the Mind*, p. 29

Phenomena manifest in particular forms, shapes, and colours; at particular times; in particular places; and are experienced by particular minds. Then phenomena change, move, or cease, and perceivers' experience changes, moves or ceases. This is the dreamlike nature of phenomena.

To ride phenomena as they arise—like dreams, changing, moving, and ceasing—is to awaken. To attempt to fix phenomena in particular forms beyond the moment of their arising, is to lose the experience of riding, and therefore the potential of awakening.

> *'But what is it that creates this illusion?*
> *It is the mind, and it does so when it takes as real*
> *that which is illusory and non-existent.'*
> Dilgo Khyentse Rinpoche – *Enlightened Courage*, p. 23

3

Examine fundamental unborn awareness.

ma sKyes rig pa'i gShis la dPyad

Primordial awareness is unborn and beginningless.
It is self-arisen and non-constructed.
Perfect riding self-arises in the moment.

My first experience of riding a fight or flight reaction was early in my life as a horse rider. I had been given *Midnight* – a larger gelding than I was used to riding. At that time I had just started to go out on trail rides with a group, mostly at a walk, with an occasional trot. Something spooked Midnight, and he bolted. I remember him cantering—possibly edging into a gallop—beyond the end of the trail and onto the road. He then calmed down of his own accord, slowed to a walk, and finally stopped. He started to graze the verge as if nothing had happened.

Not long after, the rest of the ride caught up with us. I had dismounted by then, and was sitting on the ground by Midnight crying. I was put on a different pony and rode back to the yard without incident. It wasn't until much later that it registered with me: I had ridden the bolt. It was the first time I had cantered, but I had not fallen off. I chose to dismount when Midnight stopped, but I was not thrown. I was shocked by the incident, but whilst Midnight was out of my control, I had simply ridden.

It could be said that this was my first real experience of *riding* because it occurred naturally, through the natural capacity to ride. Any possibility of engaging intellectual analysis or a concept about how to ride, dissolved into the need to stay on Midnight's back as the safest option.

> *'And when you see that [the mind] does not exist as any* thing, *you should stay in that experience without an attempt to label or define it.'*
> Dilgo Khyentse Rinpoche – Enlightened Courage, p. 24

Fundamental unborn awareness is like natural riding. It is available to discover, but is obscured by intellect and concept. Meditation enables its discovery by cutting through intellect and concept. Meditation places the mind in the reality of the present moment, just as Midnight's bolt enabled me to place my reality in riding in the moment.

Fundamental unborn awareness is *rigpa*.³ It is awakening, and the goal and the fruit of Buddhist practice. Rigpa is the experience of nonduality – the nonduality of form and emptiness.

The form qualities of emptiness are that emptiness is unchanging. The emptiness qualities of form are that form continually changes and moves. In this way emptiness and form are nondual in being inseparable. The experience of unborn awareness—the awareness of nonduality—is hidden by the process of concretising and focussing on form and ignoring emptiness.

'I'd not tied my lead-rope well and had to dismount to attend to the trailing rope. I told the others to ride on – I'd catch up.
That was my second mistake.
The third mistake was to ask for a trot.
Malachi trotted three or four strides and broke into a canter. We turned a right-angle bend in the trail – and I avoided falling by clinging to the pommel and ramming my feet forward.
Having rounded the bend, Malachi panicked on not seeing our company ahead of him. He broke into a gallop.
I clung to the pommel hoping he'd slow when he saw the other horses. Then the metal gate hove into view – and I knew that injury or death lay ahead.
Oh well ... no point in panicking: if he jumps, he jumps.
At the last moment he swung round a tree at the side of the gate and came gently to a walk behind the other horses.
"You're quite some rider!" Bill commented. I burst out laughing.
"No – I'm quite some survivor."
Panicking is never a good choice on a horse; or anywhere else.'
Ngak'chang Rinpoche recalling Malachi bolting when Rinpoche had only just started to learn to trot – personal communication

To discover unborn awareness—*rigpa*—the present moment must be embraced *exactly as it is*. It cannot be embraced as *how it might be* or *how it was*.

3   *Rigpa*

When the moment has been exactly as it is, then the moment dies. It dissolves into emptiness and the next moment arises. That is also embraced *exactly as it is*. Continuing in this way is awakening. Recognising that *exactly as it is*, is the only reality, is the experience of rigpa. The entire path of Mind Training indicates how to ride the experience of *as it is*.

> *'Analyse every moment: how does it exist?*
> *Where in the moment are the forms you see, the sounds you hear,*
> *the smells you smell, the tastes you taste,*
> *the sensations you feel?'*
> Shamar Rinpoche – The Path to Awakening, p. 77

Meditation is the primary and most essential method to examine the nature of mind and to learn to dwell in the present moment exactly as it is. This slogan is an instruction to engage in such practices. The intellect cannot discover rigpa.

Meditation practices of direct examination, rather than intellectual analysis, enable practitioners to look at the mind directly, and let go of involvement with the phenomena of conceptual mind.[4] This examination facilitates the discovery of fundamental unborn awareness. Examining the mind is an essential practice, and is the basis from which all training becomes possible.

> *'This contemplation of looking for the mind, trying to find if it has*
> *any reality or not, is a very important practice to do over and over*
> *again until we are convinced that the nature of mind is emptiness.'*
> Thrangu Rinpoche – The Seven Points of Mind Training

---

4 In the Aro gTér Lineage these practices are the four naljors—naljor zhi (*rNal 'byor bZhi*), of Dzogchen sem-de (*sems sDe*), the series of Mind: See *Shock Amazement*, by Khandro Déchen and Ngakpa Chögyam, Aro Books worldwide, 2018.

The horse responds to a thought or an imperceptible movement of leg. The rider asks skilfully and respectfully, and the horse responds accurately and willingly. This harmonious relationship is matchless. It is joyful, timeless, and beyond concept. It cannot be forced, only discovered.

Skills and experience can be developed over time, but the *moment* of discovering presence in the dimension of the total harmony of rider, horse, and riding, is spontaneous.

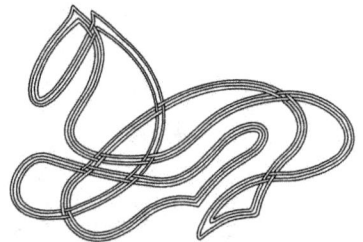

4

Even the remedy self-liberates into its own natural condition.

gNyen po nyid kyang rang sar grol

When riding is experienced as the perfect harmony of horse and rider, equestrian methods dissolve into the natural experience of riding.

The methods I was taught for English horse riding are different from those I learned for Western horse riding.[5]

With the English method, the horse moves into the pressure of the leg. With the Western method, the horse moves away from the pressure of the leg.

In English riding style, the reins are kept under tension to maintain contact with the bit in the mouth of the horse at all times. The reins hang loose in Western riding style.

In English equestrianism, to turn left, pressure is applied to the bit through the rein on the left side, and vice versa to turn right. The reins are joined at the centre with a buckle. In Western equestrianism, the reins are longer and separate. To turn left the reins are pulled across the neck of the horse to the left, in effect putting pressure on the right side of the horse's neck, and vice versa to turn right.

In English equestrianism, the reins are held one in each hand, and a whip may be carried as well as holding the rein. In Western riding, the long reins are held in one hand. The other hand holds the hanging length of reins to use as a whip – which is applied to the boot rather than the horse.

To slow the pace or stop the horse in English-style riding, pressure is applied to both reins. In Western riding, the reins are lifted vertically.

These methods are congruous within English-style or Western-style – yet they appear to contradict one another. Riding aids are method. The fruit is the same on an appropriately schooled horse: riding. The horse understands the requests of the rider, and the rider understands how to ask the horse. The method is a language. The same horse can learn both languages and adapt to the rider.

---

5   Horses can be taught to respond to any method of command. The description of the differences between English and Western riding is based on my personal experience and training, and is by no means definitive.

My very first lessons as a horse rider were with a lady of Romani descent. She taught me to ride bareback in a round pen. The primary instruction was to *lean back*, and relax into the movement of the horse. At a trot, I would be instructed to almost lie on the horse.

Then, later on riding with tack, the primary instruction was to *grip with the knees*. When I had lessons many years later in my late 40s/early 50s, *gripping with the knees* was out of fashion and I was instructed to *wrap the legs* and be loose at the knees.

> '… *once the true nature of phenomena is understood, the perceiving mind that analyses will dissolve by itself.*'
> Shamar Rinpoche – *The Path to Awakening*, p. 84

The only *truth* of equestrianism is that human beings can ride horses – a relationship can be established. Different methods of training the horse and the rider all point to the same result: equestrianism. The methods of equestrianism dissolve into the experience of riding.

The only *truth* in Buddhism is the nonduality of emptiness and form. Different methods of training the mind all point to the same result: awakening. The methods of Mind Training dissolve into the experience of awakening.

> '*Self and other*' *is the Sutrayana method vis-à-vis understanding nonduality.* Subject and object *is the Outer Tantric method vis-à-vis nonduality.* Existence and non-existence *is the Inner Tantric method vis-à-vis nonduality.* Nonduality *is the Dzogchen method vis-à-vis nonduality.*'
> Ngak'chang Rinpoche – private communication

Buddhism is not a religion of truth – it is a religion of method. The methods used will vary according to the vehicle and the teacher. The methods of one vehicle may appear to contradict the methods of another vehicle, but the congruity within the view of the vehicle is primary.

To consider a method *wrong* or a teacher's presentation *wrong* is a misunderstanding. Practitioners may find that a presentation differs to what they know from one tradition. This will be because it is being offered from the perspective of a different vehicle. The teaching will be congruent within the principle and function of that vehicle.

The rider does not need to correct the horse if there is nothing to correct. If awareness is riding the mind, the methods of Mind Training dissolve into the experience of riding.

5

Remain in the dimension of kun-zhi, the essence of the path.

lam gyi ngo bo kun gZhi'i ngang la bZhag

*When the dimension of natural riding arises,
recognise it without doubt, remain in that dimension,
and continue riding.*

It is possible to experience a oneness with the horse at any pace and in any activity. The rider becomes intimately aware of the horse – the flicker of ears, the movement of body, the decisions the horse is making about moving through the environment. The rider is also aware of the environment – noticing potential obstacles to avoid, such as the muddy puddle that may be deeper than it looks, the litter in the undergrowth that may surprise the horse, the dog walker ahead on the trail. The rider is also present in the experience of riding – the relaxation of muscles, contact with the horse, the position in the saddle to balance the horse, presence with everything arising in the dimension of riding. When all aspects of inner and outer attention are present for horse and rider, riding will be harmonious. It will be vivid and effortless, it will be alert and relaxed, it will be energetic and composed.

> *'Resting in alaya is the actual practice of ultimate Bodhicitta ... [which] is purely the realisation that phenomena cannot be regarded as solid, but at the same time they are self-luminous.'*
> Chögyam Trungpa Rinpoche – *Training the Mind*, p. 41

Kun-zhi means *all-ground*, or *ground-of-all*.[6] It is beginningless awakened mind. This is the ground of consciousness from which perception, sensation, and ideation arise. When perception, sensation, and ideation arise within the dimension of presence in kun-zhi, the mind is awakened. Recognise this without doubt, remain there, and continue.

An inexperienced rider may apply an aid incorrectly or use the wrong one. The rider may not know the horse well, so that the horse finds it difficult to interpret the rider's requests. Gradually over time, skill, relationship, and capacity increase and develop. Then riding really begins. The experienced equestrian remains firmly seated in the saddle, applying aids and letting go as needed. Riding becomes the effortless clarity and union of horse and rider.

---

6   *Kun gZhi*, Skt. *alaya*.

Inexperienced practitioners may use the methods of Mind Training incorrectly, or forget the pertinent method in the moment. There is a lack of familiarity with the nature of mind, and dullness and distraction prevent clarity. Eventually the practitioner knows the mind, and is fluent with the methods of Mind Training. Then kun-zhi can be discovered, and it is realised that it has always been present. The experienced practitioner remains firmly seated in the saddle of Mind Training, skilfully applying and letting go of meditation methods as needed. Then direct, clear, and natural perception, sensation and ideation can arise and dissolve as continual joyful appreciation within the dimension of kun-zhi.

> *'The possibility of resting in alaya is always present, and when it seeps into everyday experience, even in the form of a little pause or gap, it lightens the energy ...'*
> Judith Lief – *Train Your Mind: Lojong Commentary*

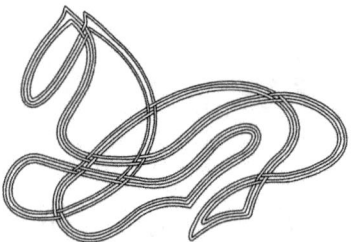

6

Everything that arises in daily life is illusory.

thun mTshams sGyu ma'i sKyes bur bya

*All phenomena are experienced as the
fleeting phantoms of form that arise, abide, and dissolve
within the dimension of riding.*

The riding school where I met Dee, and where I had lessons, was a council-owned school based in a park in a city. It had little land for grazing or for riding. Riding in the park had to follow a prescribed route and be led by a qualified instructor. Mostly, lessons happened in a huge indoor arena, or in a smaller outdoor round pen. Riding in a field or in the park was a rare occurrence.

When I first started having lessons at this establishment I was rather nervous of riding indoors. It was something I had never experienced before, and it didn't feel safe. I felt hemmed in and restricted by the limitations of the arena walls. In contrast, those who had learned to ride at this riding school had the opposite experience. They felt safe in the confines of the arena, and too exposed and vulnerable outdoors.

The safety of riding outdoors was an illusion. The danger of the indoor arena was an illusion. For others in the group, the safety of the indoor arena, and the danger of riding outdoors were illusions. Neither reference point of safety or danger was self-existent. Neither could be regarded as true, as each was dependent on the riders' perception.

> *'All phenomena being illusory must not be misunderstood as phenomena not actually existing. The Buddhist view pertains to the illusory nature of our projections onto phenomena. We see things as desirable and undesirable, attractive and unattractive, etcetera. This is the dimension of illusion.'*
> Ngak'chang Rinpoche – in conversation

This slogan looks at the illusory nature of phenomena in terms of its lack of an inherent existence and definition. It examines the relationship with ordinary everyday experience. Phenomena appear to the mind like clouds, and then change, and move, and dissipate. There is no fixed identity of cloud, or permanent abiding form, shape, colour, or texture. Any attempt to apply identity, or permanence of form, shape, colour, or texture is an illusion.

When an illusion is created by a magician to entertain an audience, the magician knows that the illusion is not real, but that the audience may believe it really exists.

> 'For the audience, there is a tiger. [...] But the magician sees the tiger as a product of the ropes, mirrors, wood, etc, that he or she has used to create the illusion. The magician will still see the tiger, but the difference between the magician's experience of the tiger, and the audience's experience of the tiger is that the magician will not, even for one moment, believe the tiger really exists.'
> Shamar Rinpoche – *The Path to Awakening*, p. 87

If the rider believes that a horse is being ridden, when in fact it is a pig – this may create problems. The pig will not understand the rider's instructions. The pig has different qualities to a horse and will not be able to encompass horse capabilities. The rider may not understand why onlookers are reacting with amusement or ridicule. The wrong view of the mount leads to an illusory experience of horse riding. However if the rider has the capacity to embrace *riding*, without reference to the mount as a horse or pig, it may be possible to achieve something. Through direct interaction with the animal as it is experienced, riding may be possible.

> '...we allow the experience of the meditation session to continue into the post-meditation. We carry out all ordinary daily activities in the knowledge that whatever appears—ourselves and others, the environment and beings—is just like an illusion and has no true reality.'
> Thogme Zangpo – *Commentary on the Seven Points of Mind Training*

Until awakening is embraced it is not possible to accurately and directly determine the nature of phenomena.
Regarding all phenomena as illusory allows the mind to be open and receptive. It prevents grasping and concretising. It is awakening view.

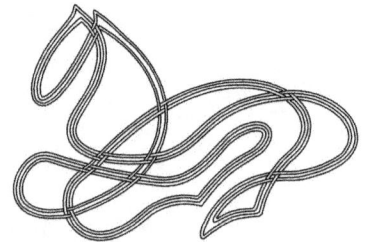

7

Train in alternately sending and receiving; fix these two on the breath.

gTong len gNyis po sPel mar sByangs

de gNyis rLung la bsKyon par bya

Riding the out-breath is compassionate response.
Riding the in-breath is compassionate receptivity.
Continually ride the breath.

Many riding instructors emphasise the importance of the breathing when riding. One riding instructor used to have us sing as we cantered in the arena. She believed that this regulated the breathing and enabled us to relax into the saddle.

The tension or relaxation of mind and body are totally connected with the breath. Horses are extremely sensitive creatures and able to notice the quality of a rider's breathing. When tense, breathing becomes shallower and faster – this will concern the horse. When relaxed, breathing becomes deeper and slower – this will reassure and relax the horse. Similarly, horses will breathe faster and snort when nervous or excited. Their nostrils will expand to enable faster breathing, taking in more oxygen, to be ready to flee, or to bound into an enjoyable gallop.

Tonglen is a meditation practice that is connected to the breath. It is said to have been a secret practice of Atisha, practised only with his disciples. It begins with visualising a person, group, or situation where help is needed. On the in-breath all pain and dissatisfaction is received and absorbed. On the out-breath limitless benefit and help is given. This is a practice of developing awakening intent – the wish to benefit others.

> *'Sending and taking are interdependent. The more negativity we take in with a sense of openness and compassion, the more goodness there is to breathe out...*
> *It doesn't matter whether it works or not: if it works, you breathe that out; if it does not work, you breathe that in.'*
> Chögyam Trungpa Rinpoche – *Training the Mind*, p. 47

The breath is a natural rhythm of being a human being – to be alive is to breathe. To use a fundamental requirement of life as a means of awakening is skilful practice. Tonglen engages this natural rhythm. Breathing in is receiving. Breathing out is giving.

Breathing in is receiving whatever circumstances offer without prejudice or filter. Breathing out is the opportunity for a natural response based in awareness of whatever the circumstances require.

Breathing in, practitioners allow whatever is perceived to define them in that moment – they are empty in relation to what is received. Breathing out, practitioners enable an appropriate response to arise free of self-support and self-protection – they are empty in relation to what is needed. Breathing in is receptive concavity in response to the convexity of other. Breathing out is appropriate convexity in response to the concavity of other.

> *'There is a very close relationship between our mind and our inner energy winds. When the practice of taking and giving is mounted upon the breath, it is connected with our inner winds and so it helps to control them and thereby control the mind.'*
> Geshe Kelsang Gyatso – *Universal Compassion*, p. 46

Tonglen is a powerful practice. When practised in a meditation room, sitting comfortably on a meditation cushion, perhaps following a guided presentation in the company of other meditators, this practice can create a warm glow of inner contentment. Helping others is a joyful experience. To truly be the practice of awakening-mind, however, the selfless and expansive intent has to extend beyond the meditation room, and into daily life.

At first the method of taking and giving has to be remembered and applied. Over time it becomes *impaled* on the breath – completely and continually present. The nonduality of awakened intent and awakened activity become the natural rhythm of breathing.

> *'Enlightenment will be ours when we are able to care for others as much as we now care for ourselves, and ignore ourselves to the same extent that we now ignore others.'*
> Dilgo Khyentse Rinpoche – *Enlightened Courage*, p. 29

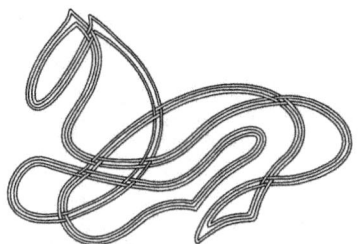

8

Three objects, three poisons, three roots of goodness.

yul gSum dug gSum dGe rTsa gSum

The horse may be responsive and supple;
it may be unresponsive and belligerent;
it may be dull and disengaged.
The skilful rider embraces all three as opportunities
to improve equestrianism.

Dee was deemed a bad horse by those instructors at the riding school who focussed on her inconvenient behaviour. They focussed on her aggression toward other horses, and the strength of her personality. They experienced aversion to Dee as a riding school horse. However some of the instructors greatly valued Dee's love of jumping, her courage, skill, and intelligence. Some valued her strong personality, and regarded her as a good horse. They also were aware of the aggression and that Dee's behaviour had to be carefully managed in group lessons, but they allowed their appreciation of her qualities to override their awareness of her difficult behaviour.

Those who focussed on her bad points tended to treat Dee rather roughly and impatiently. I'm sure she was aware of their aversion. This made her even less cooperative. Those who focussed on her good points treated her more gently and appreciatively, and she responded to this. Kindness and appreciation enabled Dee to be a better horse. Kindness and appreciation were the roots of goodness, and gave her an opportunity to be a good horse.

> *'Buddhism is a statement of our intrinsic goodness; and the possibility of discovering that intrinsic goodness. [...] When I use the word goodness, I am not using it in the sense of nicey-nicey goodness, or piety, or sanctity, or holiness –* goodness *here relates to complete value. This goodness is the goodness of freshly baked bread; the goodness of seeing a field of sunflowers; the goodness of birth and death; the goodness of being present. There is a basic goodness, a basic sanity with which we can connect. We have that – we simply need to allow ourselves the non-referential space to find it.'*
> Ngak'chang Rinpoche – interview 1993, aroencyclopaedia.org

This slogan describes the process of classifying whatever is perceived by the mind. From that classification three habitual responses arise. These responses are described as *poisons* because they arise from classification, rather than from direct experience.

Through Mind Training it is possible to discover direct, clear perception, and thereby transform the three poisons into the roots of goodness.

All phenomena are perceived in relation to personal identity. They are classified as good, bad, or neutral; or as friend, enemy, or stranger; or as supportive, threatening, or irrelevant. These are the three objects.

> *'On the basis of the three types of object—pleasant, unpleasant and neutral—we experience the three emotions of attachment, aversion and dull indifference.'*
> Thogme Zangpo – Commentary on the Seven Points of Mind Training

Classification leads to response. The good, friendly, or supportive gives rise to attraction. The bad, antagonistic, or threatening are met with aversion. The neutral, unfamiliar, or irrelevant are greeted with indifference. These three responses are described as *poisons* in this slogan. They *poison* direct perception because they filter perception through classification.

This looks like that. That was good, so this will probably be good. There is a response of attraction to the object.

This looks like that. That was bad, so this will probably be bad. There is a response of aversion to the object.

This looks like nothing in particular. I don't care about this, so it will probably be irrelevant. There is a response of indifference to the object.

> *'Three objects: labelling our world.*
> *Three poisons: fixed reactions to our own labels.*
> *Three virtuous seeds: taking responsibility for our own reactions –*
> *we first need to see this pattern at work.'*
> Judith Lief – Train Your Mind: Lojong Commentary

These three poisons—attraction, aversion, and indifference—are the three root misconceptions.[7]

---

7   Tib. nyon mong-pa dug sum (*nyon mongs pa dug gSum*); Skt. *Klesha*.

The continual pattern of perceiving an object, classifying it, and responding with one of the root misconceptions drives the wheel of cyclic existence.[8] The three poisons include the entire range of possible response.

Attraction encompasses a slight preference, to the extreme of obsessive, compulsive, uncontrollable desire. Aversion encompasses the mildest irritation, to the extreme of total rage, violent hatred, and vicious, murderous intent. Indifference is *ignor-ance* in that the object of perception is ignored. It is active ignorance rather than simply not knowing through lack of information. Indifference ranges from not caring enough to notice someone or something, to the extreme of blatantly ignoring someone's need despite having the opportunity and capacity to help.

> *'Even aversion is a form of grasping: if you reflect on it you will realise that aversion to something implies grasping at something else.'*
> Shamar Rinpoche – *The Path to Awakening*, p. 95

These three basic responses of attraction, aversion, and indifference are so habitual that they are not noticed. In fact they may be regarded as *ordinary* or *normal* human behaviour. This mistaken view of *normality* gives rise to views such as: *'Anyone would be angry if that happened,'* or *'I have a right to be angry,'* or *'There must be something wrong with you because everyone likes that.'*

The imputed *normality* of classifying objects of desire as real personal needs, gives rise to the justification of greed, selfishness, neediness, obsession, narcissism, territorialism, theft, adultery, sexual harassment, stalking, and rape.

The imputed *normality* of classifying objects of aversion as real personal threats, gives rise to the justification of incivility, churlishness, aggression, abuse, vandalism, discrimination, racism, hate-crimes, murder, war, and genocide.

---

8   Khorwa (*'khor ba*); Skt. *Samsara*.

The imputed *normality* of classifying objects as irrelevant, gives rise to the justification of nonchalance, insensitivity, carelessness, apathy, coldness, lack of sympathy, failure to take responsibility, and ignoring the needs of others.

To transform the three poisons into the three roots of goodness, it is necessary to let go of personal identification and classification. Whatever is perceived must be recognised as a new unique experience in the present moment. It must be free of self-referentiality – free from the continual habit of referencing phenomena in terms of its capacity to support, threaten, or be relevant to personal identity.

This view allows the possibility for the object to be perceived directly and with clarity, rather than through the filter of past experience and future projection. The distorted view of the objects dissolves into emptiness.

Direct and clear perception creates an open space in which response can also be open and clear. The poisonous quality of response dissolves into emptiness.

Letting go of the self-referential view of objects, and the habitual poisonous response, there can be appreciation, humour, and interest in everyone and everything, everywhere. The roots of goodness become the basis for the growth of awakening.

> *'But if your anger is not directed toward something, the object of aggression falls apart. It is impossible to have an object of anger, because the anger belongs to you rather than to its object.'*
> Chögyam Trungpa Rinpoche – *Training the Mind*, p. 67

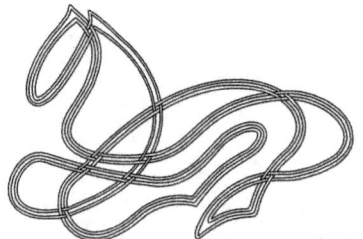

9

In all activities, train with slogans.

sPyod lam kun tu tshig gis sByangs

The engaged practitioner is always riding, and embraces each and every situation as an opportunity to train the mind.

I was grooming Dee one day, when two fully tacked, but riderless horses trotted onto the yard. The horses were happy to be secured in a stable. Then several of us started down the track to see what had happened to their riders. We met two young women looking a little dusty and slightly embarrassed. They had been for a pleasant ride through the nearby woodland. Arriving at the long track back to the yard, they had relaxed as they were so nearly home. They had dropped their feet out of the stirrups, and let go of the reins.

Suddenly a stray sheep had run out of the hedgerow, across the track, startling the horses. Both young women found themselves on the ground, and the horses—knowing they were nearly home—headed off down the track without them. The young women were good riders and would not normally have been unseated by a spooking horse, but they had allowed their attention to wander too much and were no longer really engaged in riding, so the sudden change in the horses unseated them.

> *'You cannot fall asleep at the wheel when you are driving on this big highway. It takes quite a lot of effort!'*
> Chögyam Trungpa Rinpoche – *Training the Mind*, p. 68

The key point of this slogan is *in all activities*. This stresses that spiritual practice is not something that only happens on a cushion in a quiet room. This is taking practice out into the world – the ugly and beautiful, noisy and quiet, chaotic and ordered, stressful and relaxing, distressing and joyful, exciting and dull, fearful and hopeful, threatening and gentle, challenging and easy, hateful and loving, uncontrollable reality of life.

When life circumstances are painful and not as desired, Mind Training enables practice to be maintained with good humour. When life is pleasurable and happy, Mind Training enables practice to be expansive and of benefit to everyone and everything, everywhere.

In Mind Training, even if the rider's feet are dangling, and the reins are hanging loose, the skilful practitioner continues to be a rider, and does not lose presence and awareness of mind, and of the environment.

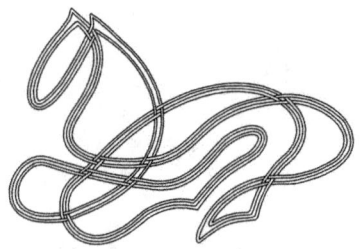

10

Begin the sequence of sending and receiving with oneself.

len pa'i go rim rang nas brTsams

Breathing in is acceptance.
Breathing out is self-healing.
Riders transform pain into inspiration in
order to ride excellently.

If tension arises while riding, it can unsettle the horse. The tension may be completely disconnected from what is happening on the ride, but nevertheless the horse will pick up on it and wonder why its rider is anxious. For the horse to be relaxed and calm, the rider must be relaxed and calm. Therefore the rider should always pay attention to their own state first.

A common phrase in Buddhism is that practice is engaged *for the benefit of all sentient beings*. Practitioners must remember that they themselves are included in *all sentient beings*. Tonglen is not a sacrificial practice. Wanting to free others of pain and be of benefit to them, does not require ignoring personal needs. Practitioners take care of themselves, recognising that their health and welfare makes them more useful to others. An everyday example of the wisdom of this approach is mentioned before flying in every aircraft safety presentation: *secure your own mask before helping others*.

If pain is being experienced, practice tonglen. Buddhism does not ask practitioners to carry a burden of pain if that pain can be relieved. There is no sense in which *real* practitioners have to suffer for their practice. Buddhism teaches original beginningless awakening, not original sin.

There can be a tendency in the West for self-deprecation and self-loathing. This is a characteristic that is not found in all cultures. Geshe Damchö Yonten was once asked about loving oneself and replied that it was not a good thing to love oneself – that one must love others. One of his Western students explained to him that in the West sometimes people really do not like themselves. Geshe Damchö looked surprised and said that it was important to like yourself, else how could you like others.[9]

---

9   I was present for this conversation. Geshé Damchö Yonten (1930–2017) was the Spiritual Director of Lam Rim Chö Ling, Wales, UK.

> *'Self-loathing is ridiculously complicated – because one would have to ask how the loather feels. Does the loather feel worthy in comparison with the loathed?*
> *If you loath yourself: who is it, who is loathing whom?*
> *This is a situation which requires two selves – one who is loathed and the other who is loathing that self.*
> *This is clearly untenable.'*
> Ngak'chang Rinpoche – in conversation

There are two approaches to practising tonglen to relieve actual present pain. The first is focussing on the pain being experienced, and dissolving it on the in-breath, and sending soothing energy to the point of pain on the out-breath. The second approach is to imagine that the pain being experienced is the pain that anyone anywhere is experiencing in that moment. Through practising tonglen with this view, it can alleviate the personal pain, but also embrace the expansive view of helping others.

> *'The practice of taking and giving is extremely helpful in all cases of degenerative disease. This is one of the reasons why Geshe Chekhawa was able to help lepers cure themselves.'*
> Geshe Kelsang Gyatso – *Universal Compassion*, p. 48

Another way that practitioners can practise tonglen for themselves, is the consideration of the pain that has existed in the past, and the pain that will exist in the future.
Ill health, loss, and unhappiness will arise throughout life. Old age, sickness, and death are the reality of being human. There is also the certainty of harm done to others in the past and the possibility of harm in the future. These can also be visualised as the focus of tonglen practice.

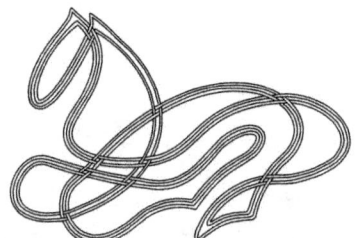

11

When the world and life is full of malice and bad circumstances, transform it into the path of awakening.

sNod bcud sDig pas gang bo'i tshe

rKyen ngan byang chub lam du bsGyur

When riding is hell — use it as an opportunity to awaken.

Every horse rider will have experienced being thrown. It is an inevitable aspect of riding. Falling off can be the result of a fearful horse or its bad behaviour. It can be the result of poor riding or bad luck. It is never appropriate to blame or punish the horse. Excellent riders learn something useful every time they hit the dirt – something that will improve their riding, or help develop the relationship with the horse, or possibly just to be patient.

> *'Life is pain, highness.*
> *Anyone who says differently is selling something.'*
> William Goldman – *The Princess Bride*

Bad circumstances offer particularly juicy objects and experiences for transformation. If an object or experience is labelled *bad*, there is energy there – there is an acuteness of dissatisfaction that is tangible and can be embraced as practice.

I had a series of incidents with Red that caused me to suffer injuries. The first was when his saddle slipped while I was mounting him, so that I landed back down on the mounting block heavily and awkwardly. I tore the ligaments in my knee. This was not Red's fault. It also was not my fault in this instance as I had not put on his saddle, but blame is irrelevant when coming to terms with the reality of a situation. The injury had to be dealt with, and the long recovery time cheerfully accepted.

Another time I was taking part in a fun ride. This was the first time of riding Red at such an event and I had not realised that he would become so over-excited. He was a big and strong horse, and I was having difficulty holding him. A friend of mine was riding a mare to whom Red was very attached. He wanted to stay by the mare, and raced after them as they approached a jump. I did not want to take the jump as it was quite high, but had no choice. Both horses ended up taking the jump at the same time, side by side. Red sailed over it beautifully but unfortunately there was an overhanging branch my side of the jump which I had to lean away from.

Consequently I came off over his left shoulder. I hit the ground hard and suffered a concussion. I could have blamed Red for this, but Red was just being Red.

These occurrences were opportunities to be patient with the situation as it was. In the first scenario, there was no point in regretting not checking the saddle myself, or in recriminating with the person who had tacked Red. In the second incident I could have lamented my bad luck at the overhanging branch or blamed my friend for her enthusiastic approach to the jump and not noticing my reluctance. To blame someone else would not have changed either situation, and may have created bad feeling.

> *'The wonderful quality of Vajrayana is the way in which it approaches every aspect of human existence as being fundamentally workable. Whatever the situation happens to be, it can be transformed through the practice of Vajrayana.'*
> Ngak'chang Rinpoche – interview 1997, aroencyclopaedia.org

In the unusual circumstance of malice actually being personally directed, practitioners recognise the confusion and delusion behind such behaviour. Harmful actions are not perpetrated by happy people nor create happiness. Bad actions are harmful all round. If harm can be responded to with kindness, this offers the possibility of a change of view. But if harm is responded to with reciprocal harm, things just get worse and worse.

It is important to have a sense of humour. A sense of humour benefits every bad circumstance and encourages a joyful mind. This is a transformative approach to bad circumstances. Things will either be resolved or not resolved. Grouching about it will not change anything. Patiently accommodating resolution, or lack of resolution, makes contentment a possibility. It is important to embrace the view that life circumstances are *empty of intent* from their side.

> 'Lisa: *'Perhaps there is no moral to this story.'*
> Homer: *'Exactly. It's just a bunch of stuff that happened."*
> The Simpsons, Blood Feud, Season 2, episode 22, 1991

When the situation is dealt with, the incident may become an amusing story for entertaining friends. The possibility of humour encourages awakening.

> '*It is from within that the trouble comes. It is due to our fixation on I, that we think: "I am so unhappy, I can't get anything to eat, I have no clothes, lots of people are against me and I don't have any friends." It is thoughts like these that keep us so busy—and all so uselessly!*'
> Dilgo Khyentse Rinpoche – Enlightened Courage, p. 41

Practitioners take responsibility for their own emotional responses. They realise that emotions, such as anger, harm themselves as well as the person towards whom the anger is aimed, because it creates an unskilful pattern. The difficult circumstances that arise in life are rarely deliberately personal from their own side. Red did not take the jump with the intention of harming me. He would have assumed that I could stay on his back. He would have assumed that I enjoyed his enthusiasm to take the jump with him.

12

Drive all blames into one.

le lan thams cad gCig la bDa'

*When lying on the ground, looking up at the horse,
the realised rider takes the blame for being thrown.*

When I am in the saddle, I have the identity of a rider. When I am in the stable grooming the horse, I have the identity of a groom. When I am lying in the dirt watching the horse disappearing down the trail, I have the identity of a pedestrian.

The identity of rider dissolves into emptiness when I dismount. The identity of groom dissolves into emptiness when I leave the stable. The identity of pedestrian dissolves into emptiness when I find my horse grazing, and get back in the saddle. Identity arises, abides, and dissolves – as is the same with all phenomena. Any impression of continuation is illusory.

I am the rider, the groom, or the pedestrian, and each identity has unique qualities and attributes. Any sense of some-*thing* moving *without changing* between these identities is illusory. A soul or self cannot be found through analysis. The body may appear to be the same, but it continually changes, and has more in common with the flow of a river than with the static quality of a rock. It is in constant change and flux. No-*thing* abides unchanging and permanent in the human body.

If not existing in the body, perhaps it may be felt that identity is therefore intangible, dwelling in energy or mind. Analysis, however, also cannot reveal anything that exists permanently and unchanging in the emotions or thoughts. Nothing remains *exactly* the same from one moment to the next. Through analysis the mind is discovered to be fundamentally empty.

The delusion that identity is a *something,* that exists independently, continually, and without changing, creates the need to protect and support it. If I arrive at the yard wanting to groom my horse and someone else is already doing it – then my groom identity may feel threatened. If I cling to that identity I may consider the other groom out of order and be aggressive – *how dare she groom my horse when I wanted to do it.*

Groom identity has to either be asserted or allowed to dissolve into emptiness. If the latter is embraced, then rider identity can be grateful that the horse is already prepared for tacking, and be appreciative.

> *'A popular phrase says, "Don't lay your trip on me." Interestingly, trips are laid on us, but not by anybody. We decide to take on those trips ourselves, and then we become resentful and angry.'*
> Chögyam Trungpa Rinpoche – *Training the Mind*, p. 77

The illusion of a self-existent identity is isolating and selfish – *I am in pain, which is much more important than your pain.* The illusion of a self-existent identity prevents enjoyment and appreciation – *you are happy, but I cannot appreciate it, because it is not my happiness.*

Pain is pain – the identity associated with pain is irrelevant. Practitioners wish to alleviate pain.

Happiness is happiness – the identity associated with happiness is irrelevant. Practitioners enjoy and appreciate happiness, and wish to increase it.

> *'All the trouble that we have had to endure until now has been caused by something that has never existed!'*
> Dilgo Khyentse Rinpoche – *Enlightened Courage*, p. 45

If I notice that a colleague at the yard has a beautiful saddle, in the moment of appreciation *I own that saddle.* Through seeing the saddle and through identification with its beautiful qualities, it is owned by that identity in that moment. Happiness can arise about the existence of the saddle. Happiness can arise at appreciation of the saddle. Material ownership and identity do not need to enter the mix. If identity feels impoverished through not materially owning such a beautiful saddle, stealing the saddle will not increase happiness. Stealing will in fact destroy the purity and clarity of the happiness that arose through open appreciation in the moment.

> *'"My Mother, she taught me how to read;*
> *My Mother, she taught me how to read;*
> *If I don't read my mind be lost – ain't nobody's fault but mine."*
> *There is always humour in Blues concerning misfortune.*
> *Taking the blame is a powerful statement in this song – rather*
> *than a statement of pathetic failure.'*
> Ngak'chang Rinpoche, quoting Blind Willie Johnson
> – in conversation

In terms of activity in daily life, the practitioner adopts the stance: *I am to blame – ain't nobody's fault but mine*. Taking responsibility for the fundamental mistake of believing in an inherent identity, means being willing to take the blame for *everything*.

This includes being willing to take responsibility for everyday occurrences even if no blame is actually due. This is because ultimately the root blame is the mistaken belief in identity – whether that is a personal mistaken belief in an inherent identity or someone else's mistaken belief in identity. All unkind, angry, and hurtful responses and actions ultimately arise from the belief in an existent identity that must be supported and protected.

Practitioners can take on the blame for everything by understanding that they are the cause of others' delusion. *I own something that you like but cannot afford to own – therefore I am to blame for your unhappiness*. This attitude makes it easy to give the item away – if that is appropriate. Let it go to the person who appreciates it.

I see that you are angry – I am to blame for being the object that created that response. This attitude prevents a protective response. It is possible to apologise and try to create a happier state of mind for the angry person. The focus on the unhappiness behind anger is the concern – rather than identification with a threat at being the object of anger. There is a wish for an end to unhappiness – whether it is personal unhappiness or someone else's.

To take the blame for everything is to understand the root cause of all pain and unhappiness as the belief in an inherently existent identity. Practitioners take responsibility for this mistaken view. To be able to embrace the view of taking on the blame for *anything* and *everything* is the most extraordinarily powerful practice of awakening.

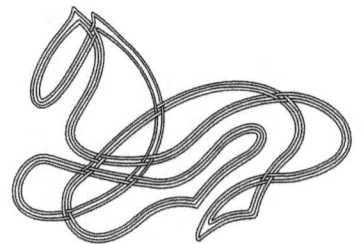

13

Practise gratitude to everyone and everything, everywhere.

kun la bKa' drin che bar bsGom

Be grateful to the bad horse that teaches how to stay in the saddle. Be grateful to the good horse that is patient with mistakes.

Dee was a challenging horse because of her history. She was totally unsuited to the institutionalised setting of a riding school, and she also had an old, unrecognised injury to her back. Not long after I owned her and had taken her away from the riding school environment, I found out about the injury by taking her to an equine hospital for an x-ray scan.

She was a dominant mare, and could be aggressive. She would not ride out on her own despite consistent encouragement over several years. She would rear, spin, and halt suddenly. During groundwork schooling she would also rear on occasion, and resisted working on the left rein when lunging.[10] Despite all this we developed a deep bond. She always came to call immediately she heard my voice. She was not given to displays of affection, but if she was unwell she would lean into me and put her head against me, glad that I was with her. Despite her aggression toward other horses, she was completely safe and gentle to groom, and look after. I learned so much from Dee. I learned when her behaviour was about me or about her. I learned to work within her limitations and at the same time challenge my own.

Some would classify her as *a bad horse,* but she was my greatest equine teacher. I am grateful for everything I learned from her.

> *'We should be thankful to all beings,*
> *for enlightenment depends on them …'*
> Dilgo Khyentse Rinpoche – Enlightened Courage, p. 47

Red was a steady horse, calm and reliable – what is often described as *bombproof* in equine circles. He had a sense of humour and could be mischievous, but he was also responsive and would not put the rider in danger. He had the capacity to be a slow and safe horse for a beginner, and an energetic and interesting ride for the experienced.

---

10 Lunging – working with a horse on a long rein from the ground.

I remember once being passed in a narrow lane by a large and noisy tractor. I knew Red would be fine with it, and just rode past. The tractor driver had been looking concerned, and complimented me on my composed horse.

Red could be classified as *a good horse*. I am most grateful to him for the many safe and enjoyable rides we shared, and for the confidence I was able to develop through his reliability.

> *'... [when sentient beings] behave in a self-centred way we can cultivate patience, kindness and generosity; and when they behave in a virtuous way we can cultivate sympathetic joy and make the wish to become as selfless as they.'*
> Shamar Rinpoche – The Path to Awakening, p. 106

Challenging and supporting circumstances each offer opportunities for practice. Practitioners awaken to the practice of transformation through relationship with others. Without interaction with other beings and the circumstances of life, there would be nothing with which to engage for training the mind. Practitioners do not stifle bad circumstances, but embrace them with appreciation as an opportunity to practice. Practitioners also embrace good circumstances, with appreciation and gratitude.

> *'If everything were lovey-dovey and jellyfishlike, there would be nothing to work with. Everything would be completely blank. Because of all these textures around us, we are enriched.'*
> Chögyam Trungpa Rinpoche – Training the Mind, p. 89

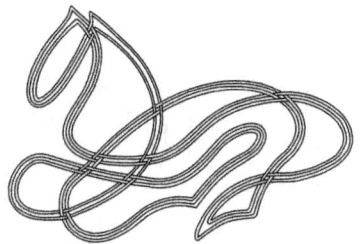

14

Meditating on the delusions as the four spheres, emptiness is unsurpassable protection.

'khrul sNong sku bZhir sGom pa yi

sTong nyid srung ba bLa na med

Harmony with the horse requires the unity of presence, attention, and physical connection. Emptiness enables the rider to enter the dimension of the unity of all three.

Riding requires engagement at the level of mind, energy, and body. It is important to be present in the experience of riding – with the mind free of distraction. This is the sphere of emptiness. It is important to be energetically aware of the horse and its response to the environment. This is the sphere of energy. It is important to be aware of the physical contact of human body and horse moving together. This is the sphere of form. When these three aspects are unified, the rider is engaged and present, and riding is harmonious. This the fourth sphere.

When I tried to take Dee out on her own, she would be fine for a while, and then suddenly refuse to move forward. She would start to back up or rear when I asked her to continue. This behaviour occurred every time. From the perspective of the spheres of being, there was the situation, and there was my relationship with the situation.

If I became irritated with Dee, this would be to take her behaviour personally. *She* was deliberately spoiling *my* ride. I could regard her as being stubborn, difficult, wilful, lazy – or a combination of all of these. This would be to focus on the form of the situation, and specifically on how the form of the situation was different from how I wanted it to be. Wanting the situation to be different would not address how the situation actually was. Irritation would not be an effective method of addressing the situation, as it arose from an imagined or projected reality. This response would be to lack emptiness.

If I was patient with Dee, this would allow emptiness to be there. I would feel concern for Dee – that I could never understand what the problem was for her and help her overcome it. She was not a lazy horse, so there was some anxiety that prevented her moving forward. With patience and sympathy for Dee, I could be empty in relation to my concern for her. I could let go of my hopes for the ride, and focus on her. I could patiently try ways of giving her the confidence to move forward, but my attempts had to be free of expectation.

In Buddhism, reality is examined through these three spheres of being [11] in order to discover their inseparability as the fourth sphere. The sphere of emptiness is pregnant with the possibility of form arising. The sphere of energy is the tension between being and not-being, emptiness and form. Intangible form manifests from emptiness – thought, emotion, attentiveness, intention, sensory perception. These are empty, yet experienced. The sphere of form is the dimension of tangible appearance – physicality, activity, sensory experience.

> *'…external phenomena of samsara are like phenomena in a dream: they do not exist and the realisation of this absence of true existence is the dharmakaya. While phenomena do not exist ultimately, on a relative level, due to mere dependent origination, they arise like appearances in a dream and this is the nirmanakaya. These two qualities of being non-existent and yet perceived or experienced are an indivisible unity which is the sambhogakaya. The unity of all three kayas or dimensions is the svabhavikakaya.'*
> Thrangu Rinpoche – *The Seven Points of Mind Training*

The three spheres—or dimensions—of being are inseparable – in the same way that the height, width, and depth of a three-dimensional object are inseparable. To experience the inseparability of the dimensions of being is to awaken. Inseparability is the nonduality of form and emptiness – the unity of the two spheres of form and the single sphere of emptiness. The two spheres of form are intangible appearance and tangible manifestation.

To deny inseparability, to deny nonduality, is to be deluded. The attempt to split form and emptiness is delusion, through denying emptiness and attempting to manipulate form.

---

11 The spheres of being *(sKu,* Skt. *kaya)* are emptiness – chö-ku *(chos sKu,* Skt. *dharmakaya),* energy – long-ku *(longs sKu,* Skt. *sambhogakaya),* and form – trülku *(sPrul sKu,* Skt. *nirmanakaya).*

The inseparability of the three spheres is expressed as a fourth sphere – the sphere of indivisibility.[12] It is impossible—of course—to force the three spheres to be disunited – and yet that is what is being attempted continually by all beings. Awakening is ceasing to engage in this process.

> '*Chö-ku is the sphere of unconditioned potentiality – the dimension of emptiness. Long-ku is the sphere of intangible appearance – the dimension of energy (the infinite display of light and sound). Trül-ku is the sphere of realised manifestation – the dimension of physicality.*'
> Khandro Déchen and Ngakpa Chögyam – *Shock Amazement*, p. 53

Emptiness is the key, because emptiness is the sphere which is denied. Form is easily recognised and there is experience with manipulating form, but there is a disconnection and lack of experience of the sphere of emptiness. This disconnection can be overcome through meditation practices that introduce the experience of emptiness, either through analysis or examination. Emptiness can also be discovered through both happy and sad life experiences. The sphere of emptiness can become available through devoted relationship with a teacher.

> '*…you begin to realise that the essence of your mind is empty, that the nature of your mind is light and clear, and that the expression or manifestation of your mind is active.*'
> Chögyam Trungpa Rinpoche – *Training the Mind*, p. 99

Emptiness is protection from delusion, because it corrects the relationship with form. It reunites that which delusion attempts to split. Emptiness makes it possible to awaken to the realisation of the nonduality of emptiness and form. Then the indivisibility of emptiness, energy, and form can be realised.

---

12 The essence or union of the three is ngo-wo-ku or dorje-ku (*ngo bo nyid sKu, rDo rJe sKu*, Skt. *svabhavikakaya*).

15

Apply the four highest methods.

sByor ba bZhi lDan thabs kyi mChog

Ride well.
Do not ride carelessly or unkindly.
Welcome difficulties as opportunities.
Appreciatively ride through whatever is occurring.

These four highest methods fall into two pairs:

- Ride well (1) and avoid bad riding (2).
- Ride whatever is occurring as an opportunity (3), and embrace that opportunity as a way to improve the skills of riding (4).

Ride well – be present and attentive, physically communicating well with the horse; notice the horse's ears, the tension or relaxation in its body; be aware of the environment; ride what is actually happening in the moment; be mentally, emotionally, and physically relaxed. This is skilful activity and to be cultivated.

Avoid bad riding – do not beat the horse; do not blame the horse when things go wrong; do not project expectations onto the horse; do not confuse the horse with incorrect aids; do not daydream; do not tense up at the unexpected; do not be disgruntled, disappointed, or depressed by occurrences on the trail. This is unskilful activity and to be avoided.

Welcome difficulties as opportunities and embrace them. A log has fallen across the trail – what a wonderful opportunity to jump. A piece of leather snaps on the bridle so contact with the horse's mouth is lost – this is an opportunity for a skilled rider to bring other riding aids to the fore to halt the horse. The weather is windy which is making the horse frisky – a great opportunity for an extended period of trotting, or even a gallop. The horse jumps sideways to avoid the kick of the horse in front – a great opportunity for the rider to check security in the saddle. Whatever difficulties are met on the trail, they are all opportunities to build and enhance the relationship between horse and rider, and engage the skill of the rider. Meet such difficulties with open enthusiasm – they are opportunities to ride.

Skilful activity moves in the direction of awakening. Unskilful activity moves in the direction of delusion.

> *'It means that we actually have to commit ourselves rather
> than just having somebody sprinkling water on us,
> trying to make us feel good and happy.'*
> Chögyam Trungpa Rinpoche – Training the Mind, p. 120

In Buddhism, the cultivation of skilful activity is often presented as *the accumulation of merit*. Accumulation in this context refers to increasing the frequency of skilful awakening activity. It is not accumulation in the sense of putting pennies in a piggy bank. Increasing the frequency and recognition of awakening activity creates an impetus. Skilful action must at first be engaged through effort, determination, and application of the methods of Mind Training. Eventually it becomes a way of being. This is accumulating merit. This is awakening.

Similarly, the accumulation of unskilful action—such as anger, greediness, jealousy—that increases neurotic patterning is not materialistic. It is accumulated by continual indulgence and the frequency of occurrence. Being angry increases the likelihood of anger arising again. The accumulation of unskilful patterning can spontaneously dissolve into emptiness through awareness and goodness.

> *'Without any reason we are suddenly terrified.*
> *Without any reason we are so angry and uptight.*
> *Without any reason we are so lustful.*
> *Without any reason we are suddenly so proud.'*
> Chögyam Trungpa Rinpoche – Training the Mind, p. 116

Awakening is possible in each and every present moment. Awakening cuts through any sense of needing to *work through* patterning. In the moment of discovering rigpa, patterning disappears. Patterning may re-emerge in the next moment, but that is also an opportunity to transform and awaken.

In the moment patterning occurs again, rigpa is lost. There is, however, always the opportunity to awaken in the next moment – to appreciatively embrace whatever opportunity is encountered whilst riding the mind.

Opportunities to practise transformation can suddenly arise, such as an unexpected disturbance to the mind. Unexpected occurrences can evoke surprise, amazement, shock, fear, apprehension, wonder, disbelief, laughter – all of which offer the possibility of alert presence in the moment. Such opportunities should not be wasted.

The second pair of the four highest practices, wills each situation to be exactly as it is. This is the battlecry of the awakened-mind warrior. This is the battlecry of freedom of Doje Tröllö:[13]

> '*Whatever happens, may it happen!*
> *Whichever way it goes, may it go that way!*
> *There is no purpose!*
> Whatever happens, may it happen! *deals with what is just about to happen or what happens next.*
> Whichever way it goes, may it go that way! *deals with the future. when the outcome cannot yet be seen.*
> There is no purpose! *relates to the fact that there is no overarching purpose – as in* the will of God *or* God is working his purpose out.
> There is no purpose! *does not mean* there is no need for there to be a purpose. *It means that there is no* One Purpose.
> *In terms of compassion there are infinite purposes – because compassion is form and form is multiplicity.*'
> Ngak'chang Rinpoche – apprentice retreat, Wales, 2016

Whatever arises is welcomed exactly as it is. Whatever direction the situation takes is heroically embraced. There is no need for there to be a purpose, so there is no room to wriggle out of responsibility through justification, whingeing, blaming others, and so forth. The awakened-mind warrior's battlecry is: '*Bring it on!*'

> '*If you have the slightest temptation to step out of the dharmic world, the protectors will herd you back*—hurl *you back—to that world.*'
> Chögyam Trungpa Rinpoche – *Training the Mind*, p. 122

13   *rDo rJe gro lod*

16

Immediately join whatever you meet with meditation.

'phral la gang thug bsGom du sByar

*Ride the circumstances of life, joining whatever
is encountered with meditation.
Ride, rather than allowing life circumstances
to be in charge of the whip and spurs.*

Horse riding demands attentive presence. Horses are unpredictable animals and may shy or stumble on the trail. There is also always the possibility of a horse bolting, prancing, rearing, or bucking – though these may occur only occasionally. Riders must embrace being prepared for any eventuality, and capable of riding it. The skilful rider is always joined—immersed, grounded, engaged—with the experience of riding.

This slogan expresses an heroic stance. It is the view of never taking a vacation from being responsible and working to benefit others. It is the view that whatever delusions and afflicted emotions arise they will be joined with practice. The opportunity to be present and kind is embraced in every circumstance.

> '*A practitioner with experience of samten is a rider rather than one who is ridden. [...] The rider displays a co-operative movement in relation to the movement of circumstances – and the nature of that cooperation is Dharma.*'
> Khandro Déchen – *The Ten Paramitas*, aroencyclopaedia.org

Meditation is not used in this slogan in the sense of a formal meditation session, sitting on a cushion. It is the application of meditation as *presence of awareness in the moment*. It is remembering Mind Training in every moment. It is paying attention to what is actually going on and embracing that as the path of practice.

> '*In the everyday world, a practitioner with experience of samten*'[14] *prioritises practice over their compulsive patterning. This does not mean that the person is not afflicted by conflictive emotions – but simply is not ridden by them.*'
> Khandro Déchen – *The Ten Paramitas*, aroencyclopaedia.org

---

14 Samten (*bSam gTan;* Skt. *dhyana paramita*) – concentration or meditative stability.

Meditative stability enables practitioners to take responsibility for themselves at all times and in all situations. This enables them to also take on responsibility for others. Being able to join whatever is encountered in life with meditative awareness is to be fully engaged with awakening. Practice has reached a point of stability and *life as practice* is fully embraced. There is certainty about the methods of Mind Training, and confidence in an ability to apply them accurately and effectively.

> *'In this slogan, the word* join *has the feeling of putting together butter and bread.'*
> Chögyam Trungpa Rinpoche – *Training the Mind*, p. 126

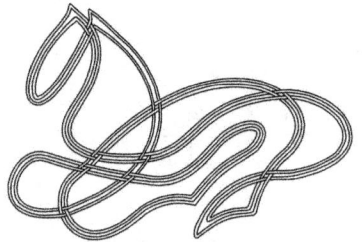

17

Apply the five perfect powers.

sTobs lNga dag dang sByar bar

Ride confidently – so the horse has a leader.
Ride actively – so the horse is supported.
Ride with presence – so the horse is relaxed.
Ride with attention – so the horse and environment are embraced.
Ride with awareness – so the dimension of riding is engaged.

Once, on a cold winter morning, Red used his teeth to take off the woollen hat that I was wearing. He did it rather inaccurately and slightly bit my scalp, which was a painful experience. I was grooming him. I knew what I was doing and was making a good job of it, but I was not really *present*. I was not paying attention to *him* as a being with personality. I was concentrating on the job of grooming his coat, but was disconnected from communication with Red as the being embodying the coat I was brushing. Red knew this and brought me back to the present and attention to him, with his usual sense of humour. Rubbing my head, it took me a moment to appreciate his humour, and to be able to thank him for the teaching!

> *'We are extremely dishonest about realisation. We want it – but not now. We need a few more minutes in bed. We need to vent our spleens. We need to retreat into the form of boredom at tonight's dinner plan. All this, rather than sit in the discomfort of non-conceptuality. What we really want is to get as close as possible to realisation ... and then sit back and admire the accomplishment.'*
> Khandro Déchen – The Ten Paramitas, aroencyclopaedia.org

If there is mutual confidence and trust between the horse and the rider, this must not become the cause of complacency – riding must be energetically active, the horse and the rider must pay attention, and they must be intelligently aware of what is going on around them.
If the horse and rider are energetically engaged in any equestrian activity, they must still be paying attention. Attention must not become tight and highly strung, but be tempered by intelligent discernment. Alert presence is not being uptight – in fact it encourages humour and spontaneity. Being overly serious and tight would indicate a misinterpretation or distorted understanding of alert presence.

Engaged practitioners have confidence. They have respect for the methods of Mind Training, and willingly participate in practice with faith and trust. This is the first power.

Engaged practitioners energetically apply the methods of Mind Training. They apply effort and perseverance. This is the second power.

Engaged practitioners are alert and present. They pay attention to the needs of the moment and remember the methods of Mind Training, applying them appropriately. This is the third power.

Engaged practitioners apply meditative attention to Mind Training, with contemplation, deep concentration, and undividedness. This is the fourth power.

Engaged practitioners apply intelligent discernment, with discriminating awareness, knowledge, wisdom, and insight, to every situation. This is the fifth power.

The words *confidence*, *energetic application*, *alert presence*, *meditative attention*, and *intelligent discernment* will be used to refer to these five powers in this commentary.

> '*The energy of tsöndrü,*[15] *ensures that we do not miss the swell of opportunities as they arise in the ocean of our life circumstances.*
> Khandro Déchen – *The Ten Paramitas*, aroencyclopaedia.org

The five powers develop through engaging with Mind Training. They are the natural capacity of the awakening mind.

---

15 Tsöndrü (*brTson 'grus*; Skt. *virya paramita*) – diligence, energy, delighted involvement.

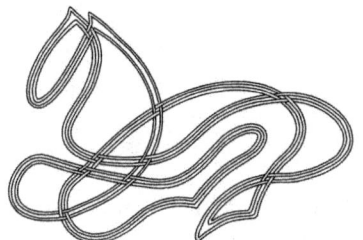

18

The five powers are the only crucial manner of conduct.

sTobs lNga nyid yin sPyod lam gCes

Confidence, energetic application, alertness, meditative attention, and intelligent discernment are all crucial for good riding.

One evening I greeted an acquaintance from the livery yard and noticed that she had a cut on her forehead. I asked her what had happened. My livery colleague laughed and told me that she had been knocked off her horse by the overhanging branch on the Wenallt trail. All the riders knew about this branch, and the need to duck down onto the horse's neck to go under it. Her horse had been quietly plodding down the trail, but because she was looking at her mobile phone, she did not notice that they had arrived at the low-hanging branch. Consequently she'd been knocked to the ground over her horse's rump.

The rider was confident and trusted the horse, but there was a lack of energetic engagement with riding, a lack of presence and attention. The low branch was not discerned, instead it was forgotten and overlooked.

Riders must always be alert and present with the activity of riding, and paying attention. If all five powers are applied there is the potential for good riding. If it is Mind Training that is being ridden, there is the potential for awakening.

> '... there is no choice regarding the development of shérab [16] – flashes of insight simply begin to occur. You find out – you understand who you are. You discover the stylistic patterns by which your perception is conditioned. You discover the texture and fabric of your concept consciousness, your projections, and your relationship with your world.*
> Khandro Déchen – *The Ten Paramitas,* aroencyclopaedia.org

This slogan stresses that the engagement with the five powers is crucial at all times, and is the only manner in which practitioners should conduct themselves. These powers—or strengths—are the foundation of awakening intent and activity.

Practitioners do not indulge doubt in the teacher or the methods of practice. They are not lazy or slovenly in their approach to practice or with life circumstances.

---

16 Shérab (*shes rab*; Skt. *prajna paramita*) – knowledge, insight.

Practitioners do not take the easier and less demanding option that may disadvantage others. They are never satisfied with *good enough* or fail to fully engage with any activity. The riders of Mind Training never *switch off*, but always embrace responsibility for their own conduct, and the responsibility to help others.

The five powers apply to all areas of life, including sleeping and dreaming. When falling asleep, the psycho-physical elements dissolve into emptiness and the dream body is born. The dreamer has dream personality and dream life circumstances. If the five powers are engaged, openness and kindness can be practised. If they are not applied, dream activity may be deluded and move toward patterning and self-protection – just as in waking life. Responsibility remains for any activity that is engaged while dreaming, and the consequences of patterning remain the same as in waking activity. Murderous *intent* in a dream carried through into *activity* in the dream will carry the same consequence of patterning as with waking intent and activity. Holding the five powers protects the mind.

The process of falling into sleep is similar to falling into death. The psycho-physical elements dissolve in the same way – but in death the dissolution is complete and connection to the physical body is lost. The elements manifest, not as a dream body, but as a bardo body.[17] The bardo body experiences dreamlike phenomena until this also dissolves into emptiness, and the elements re-emerge to manifest as physicality in a new body. Just as in waking life and in dreaming, the five powers offer protection during bardo experience.

There is a similarity between the experience of falling asleep, dreaming, and waking up, and the process of dying, bardo, and rebirth. It is extremely valuable, therefore, to gain experience of maintaining awareness through the process of falling asleep, dreaming, and waking.

---

17 Bardo (*bar do*) – the intermediate state between death and rebirth.

This is excellent preparation for dying. Practitioners can also become accustomed to dying through simply observing the death of each moment, the death of an event or activity, the death of a thought.

> *'We learn how to live by learning how to die*
> *and we learn how to die by learning how to live.*
> *Each informs the other.'*
> Judith Lief – *Train Your Mind: Lojong Commentary*

Kyabjé Chhi'med Rig'dzin Rinpoche was an extraordinary example of the capacity to continue to be a powerful and inspiring presence right up to the time of his death. This was despite the health issues of his failing body which were evident to all those around him. I was fortunate to be able to attend teachings with him just weeks before he died. A frail old Lama struggled onto the teaching throne, but an extraordinarily powerful being delivered the teachings. He displayed complete relaxation with his physical condition.

> *'I have realised that power has got very little to do with* power to – *but rather,* power not to. *It is not a question of super-normal abilities. It's a question of being prepared to die in the next moment – to be totally insignificant. The power to be unafraid of looking like an idiot. The power not to care about what people think or say. It is not a question of being physically, intellectually, or emotionally strong – but of being open to annihilation. Everything has to* matter—*and* not matter—*at the same time.'*
> Ngakpa Chögyam – *Wisdom Eccentrics*, p. 242

Once there is power and firmness in the saddle of Mind Training, there need be no fear that awakening will cease. The five powers will not be lost in sickness or in health, in good times or in bad times, in the exuberance of youth, the failing physical capacity of old age, or even at death. Confidence and trust in Mind Training, alertness, meditative attention, and intelligent discernment, enable awakening to be a potent possibility in every moment.

19

All teachings agree at one point.

chos kun dGongs pa gCig tu 'dus

*All the methods of Mind Training
lead to excellence in riding.*

Whether a person learns to ride Western style or English; specialises in dressage or show jumping; wants to practise endurance riding or just go for a quiet hack;[18] likes to take the horse out in a martingale, a crupper, and a double bridle, or bareback in a hackamore[19] – they all involve being able to be on the horse's back and ride. Mind Training is the same in that it offers a range of approaches to the single practice of awakening the mind.

There is only one *truth* about horse riding: that horses can be ridden. Human beings can develop a relationship with a horse where it allows the human to be on its back, and it cooperates with the requests of the rider.

There is only one *truth* in Buddhism: the nonduality of emptiness and form. Practitioners can discover emptiness through Mind Training and change their relationship with form, so that the mind awakens into the experience of nonduality.

This nonduality of emptiness and form is expressed in the Heart Sutra:

> 'Chenrézigs—absorbed in the contemplation of unconventional wisdom—perceived duality as empty. On seeing this directly, he turned to Shariputra saying:
> *"Form is emptiness, and emptiness is form."*
> Then—in order to clarify—he continued:
> *"Form is not different from emptiness – emptiness not different from form. That which appears as emptiness is form – and that which appears as form is emptiness.*
> *You will not find emptiness apart from form – nor form apart from emptiness.*
> *The psychology of duality, sensation, sense connections, thought, and consciousness – these are also emptiness and form.*

---

18 In equestrianism, non-competitive riding on trails is called hacking.
19 These are various forms of horse tack – please see the Glossary of Equestrian Terms, pg. 353.

> *"So Shariputra – you can only characterise form in terms of*
> *emptiness – and emptiness in terms of form.*
> *The phenomena of reality are neither existent nor non-existent.*
> *They are neither pure nor impure.*
> *They neither increase nor decrease.*
> *Psychological attributes are neither existent, nor non-existent.*
> *The perceptions of eyes, ears, nose, tongue, body, and*
> *mind – are both reality and illusion.*
> *Likewise form, sound, colour, taste, touch, and objects.*
> *Likewise the dimension of vision and awareness.*
> *There is neither understanding, nor absence of understanding.*
> *There is no suffering, old age, or death – nor do they end.*
> *There is neither merit, nor accumulation of merit.*
> *There is no annihilation, no path, and no wisdom.*
> *There is neither realisation nor non-realisation.*
> *There is neither attainment nor absence of attainment."* [20]

The nonduality of form and emptiness is true of all phenomena – everyone, and everything, everywhere. The nonduality of personal identity, however, is the most difficult to realise. The realisation of the nonduality of identity is of primary importance, because it is from this primary delusion that all self-centredness and unkindness arises. The belief that identity is form and never changes, never dissolves, but always abides, gives rise to the self-centred support and protection of identity, and the belief that it is more important than the needs of other beings.

> *'The harm-doer highlights how we are without an*
> *antidote and how we fail to notice the onset of the*
> *mental afflictions, so they are like an emanation*
> *of the teacher or Buddha.'*
> Thogme Zangpo – *Commentary on the Seven Points of Mind Training*

---

20 Extract from the Heart Sutra, Tib. *sNying mDo* (Skt. *Prajnaparamita Hridaya Sutra*) – see full text in Part IV, Appendix 2, p. 311.

The whole range of negative emotional responses can be recognised as arising from supporting and protecting personal identity:

>   greediness and territorialism – *this is mine, not yours, I want it;*
>   fear and aggression – *you look as though you might hurt me, I will attack first to protect myself;*
>   isolation – *this is my pain, and therefore much more important than your pain;*
>   jealousy and paranoia – *you seem to be doing better than me, I must trample on you to get ahead;*
>   ignorance – *I am in pain, so it is unreasonable to expect me to have any interest in you.*

Recognising this is to begin to awaken.

20

Embrace the primary of the two witnesses.

dPang po gNyis kyi gTso bo bZung

Riders of Mind Training assess competence through the demeanour of the mind, and their capacity to remain in the saddle in all circumstances.

The longest period of time in my life in which I received formal instruction in horse riding, was between 2002 and 2005. I was getting back in the saddle after a long period of riding only very occasionally. This was before owning a horse of my own.

The riding school where I took weekly instruction had a tier system of five grades. The two higher grades were for people who wanted to seriously advance in equestrianism, in dressage, show jumping, or as a riding instructor. Everyone started at Grade I and had to prove readiness to move up to the next grade.

Grade III had a particular lesson for adults that I wanted to join. This was because of the time of the lesson and the group of people attending it, and also because I had noticed that the instructors bothered to learn the students' names. In Grade II lessons, I could feel a bit like the equestrian equivalent of a handmaid,[21] being addressed as '*On-Boysey*' or '*On-Buck*' or '*On-Sammy*'. I struggled to convince the instructors at Grade II, that I could move up to Grade III. They did not communicate the basis of their reluctance. Eventually they decided that they would *take a risk* and allow me to join the Grade III group. I got along just fine in the lessons. They did not overstretch my capabilities or ask anything of me beyond the riding of my early years.

My experience at another riding establishment during that same period of recommencing riding regularly, was in sharp contrast. We visited the coastal equestrian centre now and then to enjoy a beach ride. The first time we rode there, the owner of the establishment, who was leading the ride, turned round in the saddle to say to me, '*You've ridden all your life, haven't you?*'

---

21 Reference to *The Handmaid's Tale* by Margaret Atwood. The handmaids are given names that refer to their being owned by the male head of the household – such as Offred means *of-Fred*, and Ofglen means *of-Glen*.

He regarded me as a most competent rider, and would put me on his best and most forward-going horses. Once he put me on a horse he described as *built for speed*. On that ride we galloped across the long stretch of flat sand at the beach, and then continued a fast canter along the trail between the dunes. I must have maintained balance position for about 20 minutes or more – certainly the longest continuous period I would have ever have been in the saddle on a horse maintaining such a pace. It was a most exhilarating and satisfying experience.

> *'The principal witness, therefore, is an unembarrassed look at one's own mind. To examine oneself thoroughly with an honest mind and have no cause to feel ashamed is a sign of having trained the mind.'*
> Thogme Zangpo – *Commentary on the Seven Points of Mind Training*

It is difficult to make sense of these opposing views of my competence as a rider. In the end I had to judge my capabilities for myself. I knew that I had the skill to stay in the saddle and ride through most eventualities. I had the capacity to develop a workable relationship with a horse. My riding may have lacked classical elegance, and I always struggled with leg-wrapping rather than gripping-with-the-knees – but I was a competent rider.

> *'It is easy to become so used to looking for the approval of others that we lose confidence in our own self-knowledge. But according to this slogan, we must learn to trust what we know and not rely so heavily on others.'*
> Judith Lief – *Train Your Mind: Lojong Commentary*

Not long after the beach ride, but at the riding school in the Grade III class, we had a lesson on the balance position. Unusually we were outdoors, in one of the fields. We were asked to go in pairs, and canter around the perimeter of the field maintaining balance position. As was often the case, the horses were a little excited being outside, as most of their working lives were spent in the arena. It was also spring, after a winter when the horses would have been stabled for long periods.

I was riding Dee. She took off at quite a pace, overtaking my companion. I decided to let her stretch her legs and gave her her head rather than collecting her, and maintained balance position until we came to a halt back with the rest of the class members. It was probably about a three-minute canter.

As I came to a halt the instructor, looking rather surprised, made the comment *'That was actually rather good.'* I patted Dee on the neck, and smiled to myself, remembering the beach ride.

> *'I think the stress in this slogan is being honest with yourself.'*
> Ngakpa 'ö-Dzin – apprentice retreat, 2018

Practitioners know whether they are engaged in Mind Training or not; whether they are becoming more open and kind, or more deluded; whether they have sufficient experience of emptiness to catch the moment a hurtful remark rises to the lips or whether it is out before they know it. The mind that is present, attentive, and engaged is the primary witness of progress in Mind Training.

21

Always be joyful.

yid bDe 'ba' zhig rGyun du bsTan

Riding naturally becomes joyful when the horse and rider are well trained. Rest in this joyful mind.

There were many joyful riding experiences, and riding was always enjoyable – even when soaked to the skin by a sudden shower, or so cold that fingers and toes were numb. One particular experience stands out as particularly joyful and this was when I trusted Dee and trusted my riding. I was taking part in a fun ride. This included an hour of hacking and then a cross country course. Dee loved to jump and had competed in cross country as a young horse with a previous owner.[22]

We came to a part of the course where a stream could be jumped. The bank was high on the approach with a low landing point on the other side of the shallow stream.
It made for a long jump to clear the stream, with the necessity of jumping from high ground to low ground.
I had never jumped anything like that before, and I was not keen.

It was perfectly possible to go down beside the high bank and splash through the stream, and many horses and riders were taking this route. Twice I asked Dee to go beside the high bank to cross the stream, but she really wanted to jump it. I knew from experience that she was completely trustworthy. If she believed she could jump it, then she could. I took her round again and let her go for it. I held on to the pommel of the saddle and tried to relax, trusting Dee and trusting my ability to stay on. We sailed across, clearing the stream by a metre. She cantered on to the next jump with ears pricked, completely in her element. I was able to enter the dimension of her enjoyment, and found the whole course a most joyful experience. None of the regular riders had seen Dee and I taking part in this sort of activity before, and were most complimentary about our capabilities. I happily assured them that it was all down to Dee.

---

[22] I was most fortunate to have this previous owner contact me through seeing my blog about the horses: http://ceffylau.blogspot.com. She sent me a wonderful photograph of a six-year-old Dee taking a jump in a competition. She was also able to let me know a little more about Dee's history.

Joy naturally arises from trusting beginningless awakened mind. Joy naturally arises from letting go of self-centred protectiveness and having a more expansive view. Awakening is joyful.

> *'We do not have any logic that acknowledges, understands, or presents a concept like original sin. From our point of view, you are not basically condemned. Your naughtiness is not necessarily regarded as your problem – although it is witnessed, obviously. You are not fundamentally condemned; your temporary naughtinesses are regarded as coming from temporary problems only.'*
> Chögyam Trungpa Rinpoche – *Training the Mind*, p. 157

The mind does not need to be unseated from riding joy when mistakes are made or difficulties occur. If there is great sadness, it arises in the moment and does not need to disturb the background potential of contentment. When sadness dissolves, then joy is present again. When it is noticed that mistakes have been made or a neurotic and harmful pattern has been indulged, this should not disturb basic happiness. Regret the mistake—certainly—but be joyful in the capacity to *notice*.

> *'According to this slogan, we should not practice the dharma with gritted teeth, but with delight. We should appreciate our good fortune in having found a teaching that not only talks about uprooting suffering and its cause, but also shows us how to do so. We should have a little humor.'*
> Judith Lief – *Train Your Mind: Lojong Commentary*

There is pain and sadness in the world – this cannot be ignored. Awareness of pain and sadness, however, does not need to be a barrier to joy. Grief, for example, is not a linear experience. There is not a period of continual sadness which ceases at a certain point and doesn't return. Moments of happiness arise within even the immediate period around the loss of a loved one.

There may be relief that their suffering is over. There may be moving moments sitting with the body of the deceased and talking to them, where sadness and joy intermingle in memories and saying goodbye. Funeral gatherings can be extremely joyful occasions with everyone sharing stories about the person who has died, remembering them happily, with laughter and joy. The joy at such occasions is natural and does not deny the depth of the sadness.

Over time the immediacy of sadness recedes, but can re-arise unexpectedly and suddenly in the moment. I find certain odours and sounds particularly evoke memories of family members who have died. The jingling of coins in someone's pocket, and the smell of pipe tobacco, vividly remind me of my father. Sometimes I still find myself thinking: *I must remember to tell mum about that.* Joy and sadness each arise – joy at the memory, and sadness at the loss. Then the moment passes. There is no purpose in holding on to it.

If strong emotions, such as grief, are clung to, because of their vividness, there is the danger of adopting grief as a reference point, as an identity. Then joy cannot arise. The definition of *grieving* has to be allowed to naturally dissolve of its own accord, as and when it will. Similarly in the moments that sadness is suddenly potently present, it need not be suppressed or ignored. Let it be. Embrace the experience of sadness, but let it dissolve when it will.

> '... *practising Mind Training, great happiness will develop in your mind. When you experience this result you should neither be overly excited, nor worry if the happiness goes away. [...] maintain a clear and stable mind, a state of equanimity, and gradually you will be sustained continuously by a joyful mind.*'
> Shamar Rinpoche – *The Path to Awakening*, p. 133

Life circumstances and the behaviour of others are not always enjoyable, but there is still always something that can be found to appreciate in any circumstance.

Battlecry of Freedom

> '*When you're chewing on life's gristle*
> *Don't grumble, give a whistle*
> *And this'll help things turn out for the best.*
> *And always look on the bright side of life.*
> *Always look on the light side of life.*'
> Monty Python – *Always Look on the Bright Side of Life*

If other people are unkind or unpleasant – be joyful at the opportunity to practise patience. Be joyful at opportunities to help others.

Caring about the welfare of others is important, and wishing to be of benefit to others is awakened intent. This is not a burden, however, and does not demand sombre seriousness. If people are suffering ill health or emotional pain, help offered with a joyful mind will be of the most benefit. Joining in with their misery will hinder the capacity to be able to help and will not be helpful to those suffering.

The message of this slogan is simple. Awakening view and awakening intent create joy. Continue to practise and always be joyful.

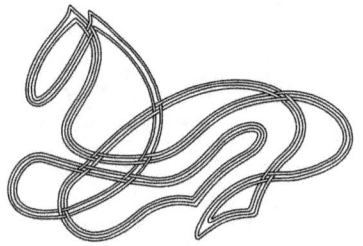

22

If you are capable even when distracted, you are well trained.

yengs kyang thub na 'byongs pa yin

*If you stay in the saddle of Mind Training
even when the mind shies through distraction,
you are a skilful rider.*

Horses are skittish animals. They are easily frightened by something suddenly perceived. This may be a piece of glass catching the light, the rustle of a plastic bag in a tree, a sudden bright colour in the undergrowth, the movement of a squirrel perceived in peripheral vision, a twig falling onto their rump from the canopy of trees, or a distant sound. Their response could be to unexpectedly shy, spin, or bolt, or to stop, alert and tense. A skilled and relaxed rider will simply accommodate the sudden and unexpected reactions of the horse even if they are distracted.

> *'... essentially, if you can notice the moment of distraction – this is the mainstay of practice.'*
> Ngak'chang Rinpoche – in conversation

One spring at the riding school, we were riding around the park. Dee was rather lively and was unhappy about being asked to stay in her usual place at the end of the line. The instructor suggested bringing her up to follow the lead horse until she was more settled. This went fine for a while and I was enjoying the light shimmering on the river, the new leaf buds on the trees almost ready to open, the cold air on my face, and the pleasure of riding out of the arena. Suddenly I had no idea what was going on. It was as if Dee had erupted like a volcano beneath me. My hat was knocked over my eyes and my glasses distorted and pushed uncomfortably into my cheek. I lost one stirrup and lurched onto the front of the saddle. Dee had pranced backwards and kicked out at the horse behind us with both rear legs several times. The incident was over as suddenly as it began. *'Well sat,'* said the instructor.

> *'... if you are a good rider, your mind might be wandering, but you will not fall off your horse.'*
> Chögyam Trungpa Rinpoche – *Training the Mind*, p. 163

Life can suddenly erupt like a volcano – or a skittish horse. It can be busy and challenging, with many distractions. Attempting to control the content of life is itself a distraction – life is as it is. All the circumstances of life are available as the means to transform the mind.

Emotions can suddenly erupt like a volcano. They can be powerful and overwhelming. If Mind Training comes to mind in such moments of distraction, this is a clear indication that practice has been embraced and is being effective. As experience of emptiness develops through meditation practice, gradually the patterning of the mind becomes increasingly transparent, and neurotic patterning can be caught earlier and earlier.

> *'... the moment a distraction arises, it brings us right back. The instant we notice we have lost our attention, we have regained it. So for a well-trained mind, when sudden distractions arise, they do not interrupt your practice, but reinforce it.'*
> Judith Lief – *Train Your Mind: Lojong Commentary*

Practitioners ride the mind – skilfully relaxing into their confidence in Mind Training. In this way the skittish circumstances of life, and the distracting energy of emotion, do not cause the mind to shy, and practitioners do not lose their seat. They remain in the saddle. They simply continue riding into awakening.

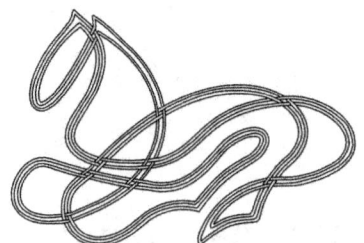

23

Continually train in the three general principles.

sPyi don gSum la rTag tu bsLab

Ride the mind excellently — with honourable reliability, dignified composure, and impartial patience.

Dressage could be said to be the embodiment of the three general principles: honour, dignity, and impartiality. The rider asks with the most subtle and imperceptible instructions. Everything looks effortless, as if horse and rider are a single unit gliding across the arena. The beauty of the performance is the result of hard work and relies on the development of a relationship built upon honour. Trust between horse and rider is essential. Each relies upon the other.

In dressage, the horse is in control of the full range of its potential. The collected trot is composed, the working trot relaxed, and the extended trot energetic. All movements are executed perfectly. The horse is beautifully turned out with plaited mane, quarter marks, and exquisitely polished tack. The rider is elegant and dignified in long boots with spurs, white breeches, white shirt and stock, a black topcoat with tails, white gloves, and a top hat.

The rider wishes to perform well and asks this of the horse, but treats the horse fairly. If the horse is unsettled or unwell, upset by the noise of the arena, stiff from the journey to the stadium, or otherwise below par, the rider will retire gracefully from the test if necessary. If a mistake is made through inaccurate riding, the rider takes responsibility and does not blame the horse.

An aspect of honour, is the capacity to keep a promise. Being able to follow through on intention is the integrity of being a practitioner. It is important for practitioners to see for themselves that they can keep promises, and are reliable. This develops confidence and certainty.

It is sensible to start with small vows – such as keeping to a daily meditation practice commitment. Once experience is gained in keeping little vows, larger or more formal vows can be embraced – such as the commitment of refuge, precept vows, or the vows of ordination.

> *'The first aspect of the dPa'wo's honour is to be worthy of admiration. [...] The dPa'wo is evidently honourable with respect to the manner in which he makes decisions – especially those which affect others. He does not seek escape routes at the expense of others – nor does he default on promises, even if they are made in ignorance of criteria, which would have predicated against a promise being given.'*[23]
> Ngakpa Chögyam and Khandro Déchen
> – *Entering the Heart of the Sun and Moon*, p.179

Honour is also essential in daily life. Keeping promises made to friends and family, in the workplace, even in personal health and fitness regimes, are just as valuable.

> *'The third aspect of the dPa'wo's honour is to be genuine, credible, and reliable. Having the self-respect of knowing that he can live by his word and knowing that he has done so over a period of time is a strong foundation.'*
> Ngakpa Chögyam and Khandro Déchen
> – *Entering the Heart of the Sun and Moon*, p. 179

The dignity of practitioners riding the mind, is very like a dressage performance – there is no outward show of effort, and achievement self-arises through engagement with method. The horse is asked, and performs intricate movements that display the natural strength, flexibility, and beauty of the horse. The practitioner trains the mind to discover its natural power, flexibility, and clarity.

> *'The eighth aspect of the dPa'wo's honour is the grace which accompanies acknowledged reputation. [...] The dPa'wo has illustrious grace because he is not swayed by concepts of status or prestige. He owns his own situation without pride or self-abnegation.'*
> Ngakpa Chögyam and Khandro Déchen
> – *Entering the Heart of the Sun and Moon*, p. 180

---

[23] The activity of the pawo—*dPa bo*, the male aspect—does not express gender bias. In Tantra, men are externally form and women are internally form. It is the *form* of conduct that is being discussed here, which is equally relevant to female practitioners.

Committed practitioners are grounded in emptiness.
They are empty in relation to teacher and method.
They understand that awakening is dependent on everyone and everything. They hold the natural dignity of empty appreciation.

Practitioners wholeheartedly embrace the reality that life is not fair, and do not rail against harsh life circumstances. They respond impartially when they are the object of good or bad fortune. They are impartial in their wish to help the victims of ill luck. They are impartial in their enthusiasm to celebrate with the recipients of good luck. Awakening heroes do not choose to be kind to some and ignore others, but respond appropriately wherever a need is perceived. They are receptive to the needs of others, breathing in pain and breathing out benefit, and offering practical help where possible. There is no partiality or ulterior motive in being patient, or in acts of kindness. This is the path of awakening.

24

Be determined to practise transformation, but remain natural.

'dun pa bsGyur ba rang sor bZhag

Ride the path of transformation with determination — as you are.

As a teenager, I used to ride with a girl from school occasionally. Her parents bought for her the most beautiful horse. He was a strawberry roan, with a dappled coat, and a long white mane and tail. His comportment was pleasing with a well-rounded neck, and well-tucked haunches. He looked lovely. My friend was a good rider and had good posture in the saddle. My friend looked marvellous. It seemed certain that they would achieve great things together.

Unfortunately it turned out that the horse had little personality and lacked intelligence. He could not respond if anything demanding was asked of him beyond basic manoeuvres at walk, trot, and canter. He was not courageous or enthusiastic. My friend had great potential and wanted to improve her riding and start competing. But the horse was bought for his looks, and that was all he could give. He was perfect for showing off and attracting appreciative looks and comments, but for the potential development of my friend's riding skill he had little to offer. His capability was very limited. It would have been better for her development as a rider to have been bought a less showy, and more capable horse.

> *'Mind Training should be engaged in discreetly.*
> *It should not be done with external show, in a way*
> *that attracts attention and creates a reputation…'*
> Dilgo Khyentse Rinpoche – Enlightened Courage, p. 72

To practise Mind Training is to be most fortunate. The methods are beyond culture, time, and societal norms. The background, education, and social standing of a practitioner is irrelevant to practice. Anyone possessing basic human capabilities and intelligence can embrace it. There is no particular advantage, for example, in being born as a European, Asian, American, African – everyone can engage in Mind Training. The natural qualities of each and every person are both the source of delusion and the source of awakening.

Practitioners can recognise that *how they are* as deluded beings experiencing afflicted emotions, is not completely disconnected to *how they will be* as awakened beings. Delusion is the fuel to run the engine of transformation.

Awakened-mind is the fundamental condition of all beings, and therefore it is natural. It does not require the adoption of an *artificial Buddhist personality.* To do so would be to adopt a referential outer form of practice that is disconnected to inner transformative experience of practice. An exhibitionist display of the outer form of practice could in fact indicate a lack of inner transformation and awakening.

Examples of adopting an artificial Buddhist personality could be: wearing a particular type of clothing that is considered *more spiritual;* adopting the preferences of the teacher even though the practitioner does not share that style of appreciation; or a native English speaker copying the broken English of an Asian teacher. It could be argued that such behaviour is respectful, affectionate, and appreciative, but it is not natural.

> '*What we try to encourage is appreciation.*
> *True appreciation is, of course, natural elegance. [...]*
> *From the point of view of Dzogchen, the beauty of genuine decorum lies in the non-manipulativeness of its natural etiquette and unpretentious elegance.*
> *We should all therefore aspire to appreciate what is beautiful in each other ...*'
> Ngakpa Chögyam and Khandro Déchen
> – Emailing the Lamas from Afar, p. 196

The adoption of such outer forms can become the cause of unkindness. I have seen older students scolding a new visitor to a Buddhist centre for placing a practice book on the floor, or for stepping over Dharma books. Treating practice books and Dharma books with respect is a useful method of transforming view.

Scolding new visitors who could not possibly know this method, is rude and unkind. It is lacking in any wish to help the newcomer feel at home, but rather tries to impress them with knowledge and assumed status.

I have witnessed other questionable behaviour in Buddhist centres such as *insider conversations* with excessive technical terminology; indicating a special inner circle of practitioners; whispering rather than talking at a normal volume; being overly serious. Such behaviour can be most off-putting for newcomers, and may even prevent them following up, and learning more about Buddhist practice. It creates an atmosphere that discourages open enquiry. Newcomers become afraid of asking something that might be deemed foolish or too simple.

> *'The slogans altogether have an odd way of combining radical challenges with the suggestion just to relax.*
> *... get over yourself and just relax!'*
> Judith Lief – Train Your Mind: Lojong Commentary

The transformative practices of Mind Training demand full-blooded engagement with every aspect of personality, and the vivid and good-humoured exploration of preferences. Any and every type of endeavour can be engaged as a means of embracing Mind Training: horse riding, cooking, scientific research, and all the arts. This is the approach of the *drubthob chenpo*,[24] the mahasiddha. Whatever style of mind, style of energy, or style of physicality a practitioner displays, they are all ornaments of awakening. They are individual indications of how to practise transformation. They are the natural style of the individual in this life and are there to be embraced and appreciated. Awakened being is totally connected to confused being. Awakening arises from delusion. Practitioners practice as they are.

---

24 *Grub thob chen po*

25

Refrain from talking about weak limbs.

yan lag nyams pa brJod mi bya

*Talk of shortcomings undermines relationships
and adulterates the capacity to ride the mind.*

Working with Dee to overcome her difficulties was a long and slow process. At first there were many *weak limbs,* or shortcomings, to overcome. When I first had her she was difficult to tack. She was head-shy, and would try to avoid having her bridle put on. She would put her head up high, stretching her neck so that I couldn't reach her head. She would also snap at me as I tightened the girth.

I overcame the bridling problem by making a point of asking her to put her head into the bridle. I held it open and low. I never forced anything. Initially I would sometimes have to wait quite a while for her to drop her head, but after a while she always just dipped her head into it. We also followed this process in the field with the head-collar.

With the girth, she quickly realised that I was not going to inconsiderately hitch the girth up roughly and over-tight, or carelessly pinch her skin. She became peaceful and receptive to having a saddle put on. My successes with Dee were always achieved through kindness and patience.

Whatever her shortcomings, I did not give up on Dee, and I did not allow them to get in the way of our developing a relationship of trust and respect.

It is not helpful—on the path of awakening—to dwell on weak limbs, or to regard such shortcomings as huge obstacles. Practitioners may be acutely aware of their own shortcomings. They may notice mistakes and missed opportunities to train the mind, but this does not matter if the commitment to practise remains firm. The important thing is to recognise when a mistake has been made, regret it, and sort out any repercussions if that is possible. Then it can be let go, with the intention to do better next time. There is always a next time. There is always another opportunity to practise transformation.

It is excellent to notice mistakes, but dwelling on them creates a depressive atmosphere lacking energy. It prevents joy and appreciation. It prevents inspiration.

Dwelling on the mistake does not change the situation, and only traps the mind in the past, rather than paying attention to the present. Regret it, and move on.

It is also not inspiring to be with someone who dwells on personal shortcomings. It can be difficult for the listener to know how to respond in a way that is helpful. This is something that Ngakpa 'ö-Dzin and I were asked about one time by one of our apprentices,[25] and our reply appeared in our book *Illusory Advice*.

> *'Apprentice: [...] I wonder how to react when they are talking about their failures or running down their qualities. I find this quite difficult, because it's not inspiring for them or for me either, when I just listen or when I contradict.*
> *Teachers: [...] Perhaps if they say negative things about themselves, their ordinary friends continually deny this and assure them that they are fine. Perhaps they find this comforting and allow a pattern to be created of expressing self-deprecation in order to again be comforted. Sangha members are the annoying friends who help each other to be real in the world and live their lives as practitioners. They do not offer comforting platitudes ...'*
> Ngakma Nor'dzin and Ngakpa 'ö-Dzin – *Illusory Advice*, p. 136

---

25 In the Aro gTér Lineage, students are called 'apprentices'. Apprentices (gé-trug – *dGe phrug*) are 'apprentice tantrikas' i.e. those in training to become tantrikas – ordained members of the gö kar chang lo'i dé (*gos dKar lCang lo'i sDe*). Once ordained, some train in order to become teachers who may then accept their own apprentices. Apprenticeship encompasses the potential for gaining expertise. The community of practitioners is called *sangha* (Skt.) (Tib. gendün – *dGe 'dun*).

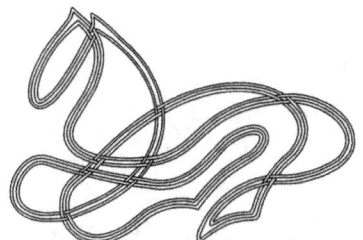

26

Do not dwell on the opinion of others.

gZhan phyogs gang yang mi bSam mo

*Opinions about capacity to ride are empty and subjective.
Do not dwell on them.*

One time in the Grade III class at the riding school, we had a teacher who was there for just a couple of weeks while another instructor was away. We had a lesson on leg aids in the small outdoor round pen. I had been given Mary to ride – a huge mare who was stubborn, unresponsive, and disinterested. She really was not a suitable mount for a Grade III lesson. We were being asked to make complicated schooling movements, circling and crossing the pen using leg aids. It was impossible on Mary.

The instructor—who had never met me before—was rude and confrontative about my inability to ride the manoeuvres. She thought it unbelievable that someone in a Grade III class could not complete the schooling pattern. I told the instructor that I was perfectly capable of riding the test, and would do so easily if I was riding a decent horse. I suggested that she let me attempt it on the lovely little gelding being ridden by a trainee instructor. The new instructor scoffed, but agreed to let me mount the other horse. I got on him and immediately perfectly rode the schooling pattern. The trainee instructor nobly clambered up onto Mary's back and tried to ride the schooling pattern, but was also completely unable to get Mary to do anything. I noticed that nobody was ever given Mary to ride in our Grade III class from then on.

This incident is a good example of the importance of not taking someone else's opinion too seriously.

> *'It should be sufficient to say, "Form is emptiness, and emptiness is form – they are nondual." [...] That is actually all there is; one needs no other instruction... What is emptiness and form? [...] What is it in terms of hope/fear, praise/blame, meeting/parting, gain/loss? These polarities are the jig-ten chö-gyèd, the eight worldly dharmas, and are expressions of emptiness and form. Everything within Dharma is an expression of emptiness and form and how they are nondual.'*
> Ngak'chang Rinpoche – *Compassion & The Nine Yanas, Part II – Bodhicitta,*
> aroencyclopaedia.org

Praise and blame are two of the *jig-ten chö-gyèd* – the eight worldly dharmas.[26] The jig-ten chö-gyèd teach steadiness – to not be overly influenced by the highs and lows of life and opinion. The opinion of others may be enjoyable or it may be upsetting, but it should make no difference to practitioners of Mind Training – they just continue to practise. Everyone's opinions are subjective and ultimately empty. It is the responsibility of a practitioner to take care of their own practice, and to learn to rely upon it.

---

26 *'jigs rTen chos brGyad*. The sets of eight vary from teacher to teacher. According to the Aro gTér Lineage: hope and fear, praise and blame, gain and loss, meeting and parting. According to *The Nyingma School of Tibetan Buddhism – Its Fundamentals and History*, by Dudjom Rinpoche Jigdrel Yeshe Dorje, Wisdom Publications, 1991, Glossary of Enumerations, p. 162: profit and loss, pleasure and pain, fame and defamation, praise and blame. At Lam Rim Chö Ling I was taught: fame and shame, pleasure and pain, loss and gain, praise and blame.

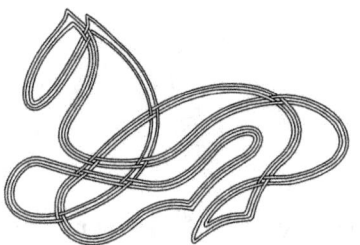

27

Train with the strongest afflicted emotion first.

nyon mongs gang che sNgon la sByangs

*When training to ride the mind,
work on the greatest difficulty first.*

It would be hard to say what was the strongest and most important difficulty to work with when I purchased Dee. At first I continued to livery her at the riding school. She still worked for them a little and I was able to ride her at other times, including in the Grade III lessons. This became increasingly dissatisfying because the riding school was still in charge of her care and Dee was still subject to their routines. I decided to move her.

This evoked a surprising reaction: they told me I couldn't take her away from the riding school. They said she was too dangerous and needed the restrictions of her institutionalised existence. I legally owned her, however, and they had no choice but to allow it. I hired a man with a horse box and turned up at the riding school at 07:00 to get her ready. Hardly anyone was about when I led her from the stable and straight into the horsebox – no difficulty there. It felt very much like breaking her out of prison.

There followed a long period of getting to know each other, and her getting used to more freedom and less work. The strongest problem that came up then was realising that she was in pain, and eventually discovering that she had a spinal injury. This had to be addressed first.

I would say that the riding school were both correct and incorrect in their assessment of Dee as a dangerous horse. She was powerful, determined, aggressive to other horses, and had a strong personality. She was also highly intelligent, willing, sure-footed, and respectful if treated with kindness, clear parameters, and consistency. I valued Dee for what she was, and wanted to work with all her attributes. Even Dee's aggression to other horses was understandable within the context of her view of herself as herd leader. She was not aggressive to me or to other people who handled her. Eventually, even this aggression proved valuable when she became herd leader at the trekking centre.

> *'The first thing to do is determine which disturbing
> emotion we have the most trouble with.
> Once we recognize that, then we need to work on it
> because it is our special weak point.'*
> Thrangu Rinpoche – *The Seven Points of Mind Training*

The first livery stable was good and we made a lot of progress, but Dee was still spending long hours in a stable and was still turned out on her own, in solitary confinement in a small field. I decided to move her again.

I looked around the area and found a small and very basic livery yard right on the horse trail. I explained to the owner about Dee's aggression and that she would need to be in a field on her own. Her response was: *'That's ridiculous. She's a horse – a herd animal. She'll go out with the others. They'll sort it out.'*

And the horses did sort it out. They had plenty of space to be together or to avoid each other as they wished, and no horse was injured. Dee was suddenly living in a herd of ten horses. The aggressive behaviour to other horses was dominance not malice, and as long as the other horses respected her place in the herd, there were no problems. She settled for second mare in that herd. This was the turning point for Dee. She became more content and relaxed, more responsive to ride, peaceful to handle and groom, and many behaviour problems gradually dropped away. We had Red by then and they were always close to each other in the field. Her life of institutionalised isolation turned out to have been her greatest affliction.

> *'In general there are 84,000 afflictions, which can be subsumed
> into 212 causes. They can be further subsumed into the
> six root and twenty derivative afflictions.
> These, too, can be further subsumed into the five
> or three poisons, and when subsumed further still,
> they are reduced to a single affliction, namely self-grasping alone.'*
> Thupten Jinpa – *Essential Mind Training*

Practitioners of Mind Training must recognise the patterns that arise again and again, and those which are difficult to face and transform. Is it irritation that continually arises? Is it jealousy and an inability to appreciate? Is it a feeling of impoverishment that prevents a generous attitude?

It can be painful to look directly at afflictions and honestly acknowledge them, but this is essential for Mind Training. Transform what is seen, and look accurately and deeply. Mind Training is wonderfully pragmatic. It addresses the reality of how things actually are. There is no room to hide from this reality, but also no need to fear it. The greatest affliction is also the greatest opportunity.

28

Give up all expectation about the fruit of practice.

'bras bur re ba thams cad sPangs

*Yearning to arrive at the destination
will detract from enjoyment of the ride.
Just ride.*

I fell in love with Dee. I was aware of her problems and the riding school's opinion of her, but somehow I knew she was a good horse. It would have been wiser to have bought a quieter horse with less personality that I could easily manage, but Dee was the horse I met and felt a bond with.

Despite the warnings from the riding school, and despite the evidence of my own experience with her, I had a rosy view of my future with Dee. We would overcome everything and ride together in harmony, out on the trail day after day, like I had experienced with Whiskey all those years ago.

The reality of owning Dee was somewhat in contrast to my projected experience. It quickly became clear that we would not be hacking out alone over the long days of summer. Dee would not even walk the entire length of the track from the yard to the road on her own, let alone ride the Wenallt trail. If I had held tightly to my hopes of riding out with Dee, my experience of owning her would have been wholly unsatisfactory. In letting go of this goal, or holding it lightly—ever as a possibility—I was able to enjoy achieving other goals. In this way my relationship and experiences with Dee were satisfactory and enjoyable.

> *'If meditation practice is goal-driven, or if results become an object of attachment, the practice itself will be spoiled. [...] For meditation to be effective, it must not be undertaken with worries about whether one is qualified, will experience results, or if the practice is worthwhile. Similarly one must not have expectations about realisation, results, and experiences. For meditation to be effective, the mind placed in meditation must be uncontrived.'*
> Shamar Rinpoche – The Path to Awakening, p. 87

What is the fruit of Mind Training? How can this be known if the fruit is not yet tasted? Many words and phrases that express the fruit of practice may be known by practitioners: enlightenment, realisation, awakening, buddhahood, nonduality, oneness, peace, fulfilment....

There are likely to also be quite a few words in other languages: bodhi, bodhicitta, rigpa, changchub sem, kun-zhi, and so on.[27] Yet even if these words are deeply understood through study, the fruit of practice cannot be known until it is tasted. Once tasted, any conceptual understanding simply drops away.

Meditation practice leads to meditational experience. A meditational experience is called a *nyam*.[28] Nyams can be pleasant, unpleasant, or simply peculiar. They can be connected to any of the senses – experiences of sensation, sight, hearing, taste, smell, or ideation. Nyams occur through the settling of the psycho-physical elements during meditation.

> 'Nyam *means* meditational manifestation, *or* meditational experience; *so it is not the nondual state – it is an experience. There are all kinds of nyams that arise in terms of practice. The general advice on nyams is to let go of them; you do not become a seeker of nyams. This is true in Sutra; it is true in Tantra.'*
> Ngak'chang Rinpoche – The Four Naljors and the Four Ting-ngé'dzin, aroencyclopaedia.org

A nyam that regularly occurred for me in my early years of meditation was one of physical sensation. When meditating with eyes closed, the sensation would arise that my body was leaning at a strange angle from the perpendicular. I would open my eyes briefly to check my posture, and find that I was still sitting perfectly upright.

Nyams are ignored in sutric and tantric practice, but recognised as a sign of progress.[29] Nyams arise through meditation, so a nyam indicates meditation is being practised.

---

27 Bodhi (Skt.) – Tib. changchub (*byang chub*); bodhicitta (Skt.) – Tib. changchub sem (*byang chub sems*); rigpa (*rig pa*) (Tib.) – Skt. *vidya;* kun-zhi (*kun gZhi*) (Tib.) – Skt. *alaya.*
28 *Nyams*
29 In Dzogchen, nyams are not always ignored. There are particular nyams that are engaged as method.

There is an ancient Zen saying: '*If you meet the Buddha on the road, kill him.*'[30] This warns the practitioner not to be distracted by amazing visions or insightful experiences, but to simply continue on the path.

Awakened mind is beginningless and indestructible, but for deluded mind, moments of awakening are fragile and easily lost through grabbing. If the nyam is a vision of the Buddha, it is killed – that is, it is allowed to dissolve.

To engage with a nyam is to indulge distraction. If practitioners allow themselves to be continually distracted in this way or particularly fascinated by a nyam experience, they may become *seekers of nyams*. This is guaranteed to prevent such a nyam occurring ever again. The nyam arose through engagement with meditation practice, not through seeking the nyam.

Riding in the modern world usually has little to do with travelling to a destination. In the past when horses were more specifically used as a mode of transport, the destination would have been the reason for riding. Nowadays, however, the purpose of setting out down the horse trail is to enjoy the experience of *riding*. Riders may have goals they wish to achieve, such as winning rosettes in competitions, being part of an Olympic equestrian team, jumping higher fences, succeeding at dressage – but day-to-day riding will be the main experience and still be valued.

Mind Training can be embraced in the same spirit. *Training the mind* is the purpose of setting out on the path of awakening. Trust Mind Training and fully embrace the experience of riding the mind. It will create harmonious riding, unity of horse and rider, and take you over the highest obstacles – soaring into awakening.

---

30 Attributed to the Zen Master Linji Yixuan, 9th century.

29

Abandon poisonous food.

dug can gyi zas sPangs

When riding the mind is harmonious, joyful, and effective – don't spoil it.

Tack is used to enable the rider to control the horse. The more difficult the horse is to control, the more stringent tack tends to become. Even the gentlest bit in a horse's mouth can be painful if the rider has insensitive or unkind hands on the reins. There is a considerable variety of tack available to help keep a horse under control, but tack should not be used as a substitute for understanding the horse and developing an intimate working relationship. Tack can actually increase alienation between horse and rider and poison the relationship.

Dee would fight the bit when I first owned her, even though it was a gentle bit. She could not keep her head quiet. She would raise her head and open her mouth. I put her in a drop noseband and this solved the mouth opening, but she was still not happy. I tried a martingale to keep her head lower.[31] After her spinal injury was diagnosed I was told by the vet to rest her from riding for three months, but to continue to exercise her. This meant that I did a great deal of groundwork with her in the manège.[32] I also researched natural horsemanship methods and used a lot of those sorts of exercises.

When it was time to ride Dee again, the unhappy head was back. I decided to take a radical direction that I had read about in natural horsemanship: rather than adding corrective tack, reduce the amount of tack to a minimum. I bought a cross-under bitless bridle that uses gentle pressure to the nose, jaw, cheek, and poll to maintain contact with the horse.

---

31 A drop noseband has an extra band of leather that fits under the chin of the horse below the bit to encourage the horse to accept the bit. A martingale hangs from the reins and is attached round the horse's neck and to the girth. Its function is to encourage the horse to lower its head.
32 A rectangular schooling arena marked with points on the perimeter to assist with orientating schooling manoeuvres. It is often written as 'menage'.

With no metal bit in her mouth, there was nothing to fight against. Dee was like a different horse. Her head dropped and was quiet. She responded to the reins and carried herself better. She was much happier. I rode her in this lightweight and simple bridle for the rest of our riding days together.

I believe that Dee was a good horse, but had been spoiled —poisoned—by the life circumstances imposed upon her. By unravelling as many of the poisonous aspects of her life circumstances as possible, I tried to allow Dee to be the good horse that she wanted to be.

> 'There is a saying: "Wholesome deeds performed with selfish aims are just like poisoned food."'
> Dilgo Khyentse Rinpoche – *Enlightened Courage*, p. 74

Food is nutritious. It is what sustains life. It is inadvisable to eat spoiled food – it creates illness. It would be foolish to poison good food – that would be self-harming. Mind Training is spiritual nutrition. It can be poisoned by too much application, too little application, or wrong motivation.

If the mind is dull and lacking in focus, pay attention. Apply methods to lift and brighten the mind, to bring clarity and presence to the meditation session. If the mind is distracted and lacking in focus, pay attention. Apply methods to settle the mind and let go of distraction, so that the mind can be calm and clear. If the mind is relaxed and focussed, let it be. Do not squeeze and create tension, but remain alert and present.

It is important to establish a daily practice habit, but this must not just become something that is fulfilled and ticked off on a list of things to do. Each and every meditation session is an opportunity to awaken and must be embraced with energetic application. Failing to apply effort poisons the potential of practice – and turns an opportunity to awaken into a routine.

> *'"If I sit properly, with the greatest discipline and exertion,
> then I will become the best meditator of all"*
> *— that is a poisonous attitude.'*
> Chögyam Trungpa Rinpoche – *Training the Mind*, p. 178

Examine the motivation for committing to Mind Training. Is it for praise? Is it for fame? Is it for gain? Is it for profit? Does the practitioner think it is impressive to be a person with a daily meditation practice? Does the practitioner use the capacity gained through practice to manipulate others, or to feel superior to others?

> *'You can use these slogans to build up your ego. For instance, you refrain from talking about others' defects or maligning them but only so people will praise you.'*
> Pema Chödrön – *Always Maintain A Joyful Mind*, p. 39

Awakened is the natural state of being. The methods of Mind Training cooperate with beginningless awakening to strip off the delusion and patterning that prevent it sparkling through. All beings are beginninglessly awakened, but through the inability to see this are *actively* distorting it into delusion. Beings are not the *victims* of cyclic existence, but the *perpetrators*. To stop distorting, is to start awakening.

30

With a good nature rely on the root text.

gZhung bZang po ma bsTen

*Rely on the methods of Mind Training
with confidence and relaxation.
Then ride with a happy mind.*

Grade III was where the riding school introduced jumping. Perhaps this was the reason for their reluctance to have me move up to Grade III. I struggled with leg wrapping, having always ridden gripping with the knees. Perhaps they did not feel I was sufficiently secure in the saddle for jumping.

Nevertheless I was allowed into Grade III and jumping lessons began. None of the group were particularly keen on jumping. We were all mature adults and actually enjoyed riding schooling patterns, working in pairs or as a group, and dressage exercises much more than jumping. The schedule however, described Grade III as the level where jumping was introduced, and so jumping lessons were a frequent occurrence.

I quickly realised that riding Dee was a great advantage. A lot of the school horses were also not keen on jumping. Three scenarios would unfold in every lesson: the horse would swerve out just before the jump; the horse would stop just in front of the jump; the horse would almost stop in front of the jump, then decide at the last minute to jump it and do a big bunny hop. All of these scenarios were difficult to ride and we all ended up on the ground on many occasions. Most of the school horses had to be pushed on, trying to keep them in canter and engaged right up to the jump. There was a much better chance that they would take it if the approach was good. Those riders who were nervous and reluctant to jump, would tend to not push on enough which only made a refusal, halt, or bunny hop more likely.

Not so with Dee. She came alive in jumping lessons. Point her at a jump and she would keep up a good speed on the approach, and sail over the jump perfectly. Sometimes there would be an excited buck or two after landing, but these were no problem to ride. The first time I was given her to ride, the instructor warned me at the beginning: '*You must realise that as soon as you turn that corner in the arena, Dee is going to take the jump.*'

With Dee I was lucky. All I had to do was to let go of nervousness, have confidence in my seat in the saddle, and trust Dee. To *avoid* going over the jump would have taken quite a lot of work on my part as a rider. To take it, all I had to do was relax, check my riding position, and have confidence in Dee's expertise. I had to get out of the way of Dee's capability, and avoid hindering her ability and desire to take the jump.

> '*Watching this* push and pull – *toward and away from the rules which we have applied to ourselves, is a primary practice of living the view. It induces an energetic sensation with which we must sit until it dissolves – this, is the acute claustrophobia of being a practitioner.*'
> Khandro Déchen – *The Ten Paramitas*, aroencyclopaedia.org

Dee was the root text – the certain method of achieving the jump. I had to rely on her and cheerfully let go of nervousness. This slogan encourages the same trust in the root text of Mind Training. Confidently engage in the methods of Mind Training, with cheerful patience.

Practitioners just need to trust the methods and apply them. If the methods are being applied there will be progress and practitioners can feel content. Ceasing to engage in the neurotic patterning that prevents awakening, is the responsibility of riders. Trusting in the capacity to awaken is the responsibility of riders. Relaxing into awakening is the result.

Mind is beginninglessly awakened—it knows how to take the jump—so relax, and let it awaken. Point the mind at awakening. Trust mind and method. Then relax, and awaken.

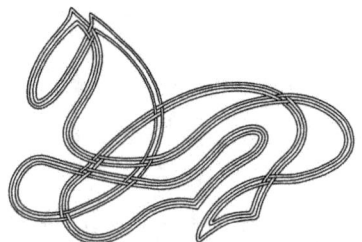

31

Do not be agitated by past grievances.

shag ngan ma rGod

Let the past be the past.
Ride into the potential of the next jump,
and forget the dropped pole behind you.

There was a horse at the livery yard where Dee and Red were stabled who was notoriously hard to catch. It was not surprising, because the owner had created the situation. The owner would start out with the expectation that the horse was going to be difficult to catch, because of previous experience. This caused this person to have an aggressive outlook from the start, calling the horse belligerently and approaching it confrontatively. The horse would spin away, putting more distance between them.

The owner would become increasingly frustrated with the horse, as it could take an hour or more to bring it in from the field. When the horse eventually allowed itself to be caught, usually through the temptation of a bucket of pony nuts, the owner would then berate the horse. The owner would shout at the horse, red in the face, and even slap the horse on the neck. This person did not let go of the time spent chasing and cajoling, but held onto it as a grievance, even though the horse was now in a halter on the yard.

Why would the horse want to come to such a welcome? If the owner had let go of the grievance, and rewarded the horse's arrival with gentle words and soft caresses, it is likely that the situation would have gradually improved.

> '... *give up altogether your long history of antagonism.*'
> Chögyam Trungpa Rinpoche – *Training the Mind*, p. 180

This slogan is straightforward – let go of the past. Each present moment is a new opportunity. Do not let past grievances distort the relationship with whomever or whatever is in the present moment. The past is the past. Leave it there. Awakening—when it arises—will be in the present moment.

32

Do not wait in ambush.

'phrang ma sGugs

*Do not look for an opportunity to vent
subjective view, or gain revenge.
Ride the present moment.*

The jumps were not high or wide in Grade III lessons. They were well within the capabilities of all the horses. To ride over them was not much different to riding a canter. The distance between jumps and their placement were expertly paced out by the instructors. There was often a ground pole in front of the jump as an indication for the horse where to take off. The novice riders had responsibility for the pace at which they approached the jump, and a correct position in the saddle. Everything else was down to the horse.

Everything was set up so that the horses could clear the jump, and, riding Dee, I did not even have to push her on. She would just go for it. If I had insisted on trying to control Dee in some way—correct her pace, her stride length, or when she turned to face jump—it would have gone horribly wrong. It was *her* skill and expertise that made jumping safe and enjoyable, not mine. To insist that *I* was the rider and should therefore take charge in some way, would have been to ambush her – to hinder the flow of her capability.

> *'... in Tibetan culture, children are encouraged from a young age to remember the wrong done them as a form of self-protection. Tibetans who can remember every harm suffered are praised for being strong.'*
> Shamar Rinpoche – The Path to Awakening, p. 159

Holding on to past wrongs, and looking for an opportunity to ensure that wrong-doers get their comeuppance, is an attitude that fixes the mind in the past, and distorts the present moment. Practitioners should avoid this mind-state. The perception of a wrong having been committed is subjective, and it cannot be assumed that the motivation of the perpetrator is accurately understood. It is best to avoid taking anything that happens in life personally, and to let go of the self-protective justification that might lead to waiting in ambush.

There are other ways to pounce, and fail to dwell in the present moment. Conversation is a good example.

It flows and moves and changes. The listener is empty in relation to the talker. Then the roles change, and turns are taken in being listener or talker. The listener is emptiness and the talker is form. This is the creativity and enjoyment of conversation. The flow is as important as the content.

In a group setting there may be a point to make, but the other talkers are so engaged that the moment passes. If a person insists on holding onto their point, and forces it into the conversation even when the topic has moved on, this is waiting in ambush. It is an inability to be empty in relationship to the flow. It is being attached to controlling the conversation, and waiting in ambush to make a point. It is a need to dominate. It is aggressive, based in a fear of losing identity in the movement of the conversation.

Another way of ambushing a conversation is to make it *all about me*. When several people are talking round a topic, one person continually dominates. This person has the most interesting and important anecdote to tell every time, or is in charge of all the facts, or happens to have the expert experience that is most relevant. Everyone else is forced into the role of listener.

Being deliberately provocative and trying to start an argument is another form of waiting in ambush. In modern day social media, this takes the form of trolling.

> *'In Internet slang, a troll is a person who starts quarrels or upsets people on the Internet to distract and sow discord by posting inflammatory and digressive, extraneous, or off-topic messages in an online community (such as a newsgroup, forum, chat room, or blog) with the intent of provoking readers into displaying emotional responses and normalising tangential discussion, whether for the troll's amusement or a specific gain.'*
> Wikipedia – *troll*

Waiting in ambush—in any context—is unskilful. It moves in the direction of delusion, rather than in the direction of awakening.

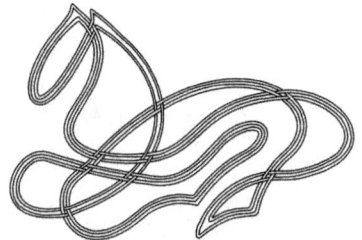

33

Do not bring out others' secret state.

gNad la mi dBab

*Skilful riders focus on their own skills,
and refrain from revealing or commenting
on the shortcomings of others.*

In the early days of owning Dee, she was still living at the riding school. This meant that she could be in her stable for up to 18 hours a day, depending on the time of year. I would often take her onto the yard to groom, so that she had a break from being in the stable.

I was always fully aware of the potential for Dee to act aggressively toward another horse. I would avoid visiting during their busiest hours, would take Dee to a quiet area of the yard, away from the main thoroughfare to the arenas, and always tied her lead rope securely. When one particular instructor was on duty and I took Dee onto the yard, she would loudly call out, '*Dee on yard!*' as a warning to everyone. I found this upsetting. No other instructor did this or seemed to feel it was necessary. It was like announcing the instructor's perception of Dee's *secret state* to the world – or announcing disapproval of my *secret state* of confidence in taking Dee onto the yard. It felt unkind.

> '*This slogan also means not to humiliate people.*'
> Chögyam Trungpa Rinpoche – *Training the Mind*, p. 183

The *secret states* of other people are that which they wish to keep secret – it is their sore spot, the heart of their feelings, or their vulnerable place. It is not kind to reveal that which someone chooses to keep secret. It is unkind both from the insensitivity of revelation, and from the arrogance of assuming the right to reveal.

This slogan is connected to gossip. Indulging in gossip can be a means of feeling more secure through shared opinions. Practitioners of Mind Training take responsibility for their own states of mind, and regard the mind-states of others as none of their business. They know that even if they believe that they have clearly seen to the heart of situations, this does not give them the right to offer that insight to others.

> *'When we look into a mirror, we see a dirty face because our own face is dirty. In the same way, the defects of others are nothing but our impure way of seeing them.'*
> Dilgo Khyentse Rinpoche – *Enlightened Courage*, p. 73

The recognition of a *secret state* also does not convey the right to disparage. Negative criticism is never pleasant to receive, so a practitioner must be totally sure of having the authority to offer such criticism before causing another discomfort in this way. Such authority has to be given by the other person, not assumed by the critic. Ordinary life circumstances may mean that it is necessary to criticise – as a teacher, an employer, or a parent, for example. Even then, great care needs to be taken in commenting on anyone's vulnerable inner state.

> *'One problem that arises when discussing compassion is the notion of* wrathful compassion *which people often seem to confuse with the idea of sometimes having to be cruel to be kind. [...]*
> *To manifest wrathful compassion one has to be able to guarantee a positive outcome. If this is not possible then one has to restrict oneself to kindliness.'*
> Ngakpa Chögyam – *Rays of the Sun*, p. 63

In the context of Mind Training, to have the authority to criticise another, would be to have been placed in the role of Lama. The Lama is *given* authority by the student. The Lama is then able to make direct comments with the intention of benefitting the student. The role of Lama cannot be assumed without an appropriate Vajrayana relationship with the student.

To assume the authority of a Lama outside the Lama/student relationship, would be inappropriate and arrogant. Practitioners of Mind Training need to be confident in their capacity and rely on their insight – but should not be careless or distort this into arrogance.

'The rôle of the vajra master is quite astonishing from the point of view of the student. In the context of riding lessons, Ngak'chang Rinpoche and I decided to treat Melissa Troupe as our vajra master. Although we made no mention of the idea to her, the sense of our seriousness—and willingness to be pushed beyond normal limits—became apparent to her.'
Khandro Déchen – personal communication

*'It is clear to me that without Melissa Troupe – I would never have done more than trot rather badly. Having said that: it was partly her tuition – and partly: my decision to do whatever she suggested.
If she suggested raising the height of the jump,
I agreed without hesitation. It's not that I never fell—under her tuition—but every time I fell I knew quite precisely that it was my fault. I never had to drive all blames into one – because there was no doubt that I was the one to blame.
It was often quite comical – and there was a great deal of laughter in our lessons.'*
Ngak'chang Rinpoche – personal communication

The intention of the awakening hero is to be of benefit to everyone and everything, everywhere. This should be remembered at all times. Err on the side of caution and keeping quiet, rather than risking hurting someone through applying the sting of the whip.

34

Do not put a dzo's load on an ox. [33]

mDzo khal gLang la mi 'byo

Do not put a beginner on a feisty thoroughbred.
Do not expect a pony to do the work of a draught horse.

[33] The dzo is a cross between a yak and a cow, and is stronger than an ox. The practitioner is the dzo – with the capacity and training to carry a load far greater than the non-practitioner, the ox.

When attending a horse riding establishment, the size of the rider will be a consideration in choosing the mount. Large adults will be given large horses. Small children will be given small ponies. This is commonsense. From the perspective of the riders, however, the result is not always so logical. Ponies can be particularly energetic and naughty. Large horses can be particularly quiet and docile. Inexperienced children may find themselves on the back of lively ponies that do not always behave. Experienced adults may find themselves on the back of horses that are a little too dull for their liking.

Riding Mind Training is like being in the saddle of the largest, strongest, and most noble draught horse, which also possesses the vitality and mischievous personality of a pony. There is the full scope of possibility and potential for excellent riding—awakening—with no hindrances. This capacity comes with responsibility. This mount is not a novice ride, but an experienced and committed practitioner of Mind Training is not a novice rider.

With an absolute beginner, the riding instructor is responsible for the choice of mount and the safety of the rider. No riding skills are known by the beginner, so the rider has no responsibility. The beginner is likely to be put on a quiet mount and told to let the reins hang loose. There may be a neck rope for the beginner to hold, or a pommel strap on the saddle. A lead rein may be attached to the bridle and the horse led for the first lessons. The beginner is allowed to become accustomed to being on the horse without any expectation of actually controlling the horse at all. All that can be asked of an absolute beginner is kindness to the horse, and courage.

> *'If there were no you to initiate situations,*
> *there would not be any problems at all. But since you exist,*
> *therefore there are also problems.*
> *We do not want to transfer that load.'*
> Chögyam Trungpa Rinpoche – *Training the Mind*, p. 184

Practitioners automatically have a greater degree of responsibility in any situation by virtue of *being* practitioners. They are not beginners, being led around the arena, but are established in the practice of riding the mind.

Experienced practitioners understand their great good fortune in having been taught how to control their mind. They fully embrace the responsibility that comes with this: to be in control of the wild horse of the mind at all times. Non-practitioners have not had this good fortune. They have not been given the methods of Mind Training. Recognising this, practitioners expect absolutely nothing of non-practitioners. They acknowledge that non-practitioners may inadvertently harm them, but take responsibility for that as well. This responsibility is present at all times, whatever the practitioners are experiencing in their life circumstances – good or bad.

Practitioners ride their magnificent steeds into awakening, as much as possible carrying the load for everyone they encounter.

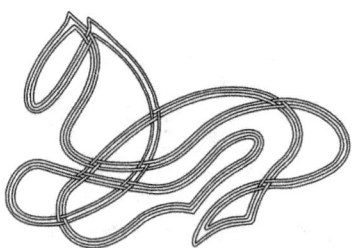

35

Do not hurry to reach the summit.

mGyogs kyi rTse mi brTod

There is no need to rush.
Ride the mind at a steady pace,
and the destination will be reached.

We moved Dee and Red to the second livery yard in 2008. This was situated on one of the local trail rides, so it was perfect for exploring the area on horseback. I joined the owner of the yard on rides over the first few weeks to learn the horse routes. This was an interesting experience. She would never trot where she could canter, and would never walk where she could trot. We covered good distances. Although this was most useful for learning the routes, I did not become familiar with the trails' ambiance. This I discovered later when riding alone or with Ngakpa 'ö-Dzin.

The ancient presence of the Ganol [34] could not be savoured at a fast trot. The extraordinarily knobbly tree on the Wenallt trail could not be noticed at a canter. The bluebells, the wild garlic, the views, the sounds and smells of the woodland could only be embraced at a walk. All these aspects of riding were as important to me as the pleasure of a good canter.

> *'But if our practice is regarded purely as a race, we have a problem. The whole thing has become a game rather than actual practice, and there is no seed of benevolence and gentleness in the practitioner.'*
> Chögyam Trungpa Rinpoche – *Training the Mind*, p. 185

Mind Training is a way of living, not just a means to an end. Travelling the path of practice *is* the fruit—or will become the fruit—without the need to worry about whether anything is being achieved quickly enough. As long as the mind is being trained, there will be progress. There will be awakening.

> *'Practice is a marathon, not a sprint.'*
> Ngakpa 'ö-Dzin – apprentice retreat, 2001

The path to awakening is a marathon not because awakening is a gradual process *of itself*, but because increasing the *frequency* of awakened experience is gradual.

---

34 *Fforestganol* – often called *the Ganol*. *Fforest* is the Welsh for *forest*, and *ganol* means *middle*. It is an area of wild woodland situated between *Coed y Wenallt* and *Fforest Fawr*. *Coed* means *wood*, *wenallt* means *white wooded slope*, and *fawr* is Welsh for *large* or *great*.

Awakening is achieved by tensioning the rein, but still allowing freedom of movement. If the tension is too tight or too loose the mind is not able to recognise pressure on the rein as an instruction.

Learning to judge the balance between tightness and looseness takes time. It has to be discovered in the empty dimension of riding the mind. It is an intimate and integrated experience.

> *'Impatience is a means of seeking to control the momentum and direction at which circumstances unfold.'*
> Khandro Déchen – *The Ten Paramitas,* aroencyclopaedia.org

Awakening will occur at the time it occurs. It will be whatever it is. It will arise from whatever situation it arises. The responsibility of the practitioner is simply to practise.

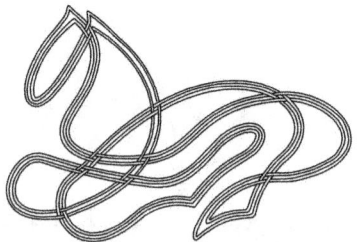

36

Do not pervert the meal.

ITo log mi bya

*Having attained accomplishment in riding the mind,
ensure that the skills are used well.*

The rider has learned how to ride. The dressage performance is perfect. People heap accolades on the rider, but the heart of the performance has been lost – it has become routine.

The incredibly high jump is taken to show off skill rather than for the pleasure of riding it. The horse is developed physically to have the power and strength to accomplish that single feat.

The horse is schooled every day, but only to consolidate its performance. The horse is too precious to take out on the trail, just for the joy of riding. The rider has lost touch with the simple pleasures of being in the saddle.

> *'Question: Is it possible then, merely to go through the motions of practice and be untouched by what you're doing?*
> *Ngak'chang Rinpoche: Certainly. That is a highly significant problem for anyone following any religion. A person can seem to be doing everything* by the book *and yet get nowhere at all. Some people can become abundantly knowledgeable concerning the teachings, and engage in considerable practice – but it doesn't necessarily mean anything.'*
> Ngak'chang Rinpoche – interview 1994, aroencyclopaedia.org

This slogan uses a meal as an analogy for the capacity created through Mind Training. The ingredients of Mind Training have been skilfully combined and a meal has been created that is nourishing. The purpose of creating a meal is to eat it – to be fed; to savour the combination of tastes, textures, and colours. A meal is even better if it is enjoyed and shared with others.

However, if the purpose of the meal is not embraced, then it is perverted. It becomes a showcase meal, a meal to win accolades and impress others with the subtlety of flavours, balance of nutrients, and beauty of presentation. A judge may take a taste and gush about the fabulous explosion of tastes. The meal is praised, and talked about, and photographed. It is gazed upon with wonder and left to go cold. Then finally, it is thrown away.

The cook may continue to develop the skills of combining ingredients and perfecting the meal, but it has simply become a demonstration of skill. It is no longer being created for feeding anyone – for the benefit, appreciation and enjoyment of eating. It is not shared and enjoyed.

This type of approach creates a twist and perverts the qualities and capacity that have been developed through Mind Training. The purpose of practice is to awaken and to be of benefit to others. This is crucial.

> *'Acting with a twist is a form of spiritual materialism.*
> *It is always having the ulterior motive of*
> *working for your own benefit.'*
> Chögyam Trungpa Rinpoche – *Training the Mind*, p. 186

Practitioners may not recognise it, but they do have power. Dedication to practice creates a presence, a dignity, and a demeanour that is communicated to others. It is important to be straightforward and remember naturalness, and ordinariness. Practitioners must not become disconnected from the warm heart of awakening intent.

37

Do not turn gods into demons.

lHa bDud du mi dBab

Do not turn riding skills into impositions.
Ride in harmonious response to the qualities
of horse and environment in the moment.

Dee was certainly a horse with qualities that could be misunderstood. She could be demonised. She was a dominant mare and asserted her authority in the herd. She would punish the disrespect of other horses. When in the field with Dee and the other horses, it was always important to be careful. Dee might discipline a horse that came too close, and it was essential to make sure that you were not in the way.

I was so lucky to find the trekking centre where she lived for most of the years I owned her. They believed in letting the horses live as natural a life as possible. There were thirty or more horses in the herd at its peak, and Dee was the lead mare. She was very close to the lead gelding, Falcon. Falcon was quite old and sometimes had to be kept in. If he was not out with the herd, Red was the substitute head gelding.

As lead mare, Dee was certainly in charge of discipline. This was the aggressive behaviour for which she was famous at the riding school and which made her such an inconvenience in that setting. In the natural conditions in which the horses were able to live at the trekking centre, however, other aspects of this aggression came to the fore. Dee would protect the old, the young, and the sick horses. She would make sure that they had their share of the hay in the winter. I found it moving to witness my aggressive mare sharing her food with a young or a sick horse. One time a little rescue Shetland pony even stood underneath her to feed. He clearly did not consider himself in any danger from Dee.

Dee was a horse, being a horse; a dominant mare being a dominant mare. The qualities that enabled her to be the dominant mare were also valuable to the rider: courage, intelligence, agility, confidence. She was a confident and courageous jumper, for example, and always knew where to stand and how to help when I needed to open and close a gate on horseback.

> *'We should not make painful that*
> *which is inherently joyful.'*
> Chögyam Trungpa Rinpoche – *Training the Mind*, p. 187

In Mind Training, capacity must not be misused or ignored. If a neurotic pattern is noticed arising in the mind, transformation must be embraced. Once sufficient experience of emptiness has been developed, afflicted emotional responses can be noticed more and more quickly. Then there is space to choose to stop habitual patterning or to let it run.

It is fine to feel happiness and pride at being able to recognise awareness in the moment – a moment of success when the open choice becomes available through seeing the pattern directly. That sense of pride however, must not become a reason to play with awareness as an internal game of skill, disconnected from the needs of others and insensitive to others.

> *'Those who cause pain teach you to be patient, and those who give you presents may keep you from practising the Dharma. So it depends on their effect on you if they are Gods or Demons.'*
> Machig Labdrön's [35] words to her son – wikipedia.org

If the *god*—the capacity to notice—is not used to advantage, then it is turned into a *demon* by indulging the habitual pattern. The sharp intelligence of the trained mind —the god—is perverted—turned into a demon—if it is only used to impress others with spiteful wit or sarcasm. If an opportunity to help is seen, to fail to give help because it is inconvenient or too much effort, is turning goodness into delusion.

Awakening practitioners recognise the goodness of the gods that arise in the mind and in life circumstances and harness them for the practice of Mind Training. They empower them to dissolve the deluded demons, and to awaken the mind.

---

35 *Ma gCig Lab sGron* (1055–1149).

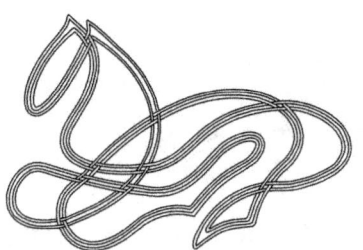

38

Do not look for happiness in others' pain.

sKyid gyi yan lag tu sDug ma tshol

Do not delight in an enjoyable ride if it has been the cause of pain or distress for the horse.

Horse riding offers many opportunities for *Thelwell moments*.[36] Riders may sail over jumps – without their mounts; riders may lose their stirrups and reins and end up wrapped around their horses' necks. I once saw a young lad slide sideways off a horse at the trot over the course of several footfalls. It was like watching a cartoon. Horses acting unpredictably, and riders being discombobulated, can give rise to amusing scenarios. Once it is ascertained that no one has been injured, there is no problem in finding such situations amusing.

It would be inappropriate for a practitioner, however, to look for such situations as a source of happiness. There were certain horses at the riding school that were notorious for stopping just in front of a jump. Buck was one of them. It would not have been an awakening attitude to watch a rider on Buck approaching a jump, wishing for him to stop at the last minute.

> *'Happiness that is built on pain is spurious and only leads to depression in the long run.'*
> Chögyam Trungpa Rinpoche – *Training the Mind*, p. 188

As Dee would not hack out on her own, I was always looking for people I could join up with for a ride. One time I joined a couple of people for a ride to Fforest Fawr. The lady who was leading the ride noticed that her mare had a loose shoe. I thought this would mean that the ride was cancelled, but to my surprise we set out anyway.

The mare would not be in pain from a loose shoe, but there is always the possibility that a loose shoe becomes a lost shoe. Then it could be a problem. Many of the tracks have pebbles and rough ground that could make a bare hoof sore when it is used to the protection of a metal shoe. Nevertheless we rode out, and we were riding for three hours altogether.

---

36 Reference to the cartoons of Norman Thelwell (1923–2004). These depict horses and ponies, and their riders, in humorous situations.

The lady's mare did not become lame, or appear to be uncomfortable, though the shoe was indeed lost. My personal feeling is that I would not have embarked on a three hour ride on a horse with a loose shoe. I would have felt too concerned for the welfare of the horse. Even though it was not my mare, and I was not responsible, it did effect my enjoyment of the ride. I could not help myself keep looking to check whether the mare still seemed to be alright.

> *'Life is not fair. We experience the results of the causes we create – but there is also the chaotic unfolding of the universe. Things happen for which no rhyme or reason can be found. If we require life to be fair in order to be happy, we are doomed to unhappiness. There will always be people who are more successful than we are; even though we work harder.*
> *... according to the Tibetan story: when the Good Luck Lady comes to live with me – I can be sure it will not be long before her sister, the Bad Luck Lady, will want to come and live with me as well. The two sisters cannot be separated.'*
> Ngak'chang Rinpoche – from a talk given at Pema 'ö-Sel Ling

Life can be experienced as unsatisfactory. Sometimes things go well and sometimes things go badly. Life is also not fair, and sometimes things go well for bad people, and badly for good people. There could be a temptation to feel satisfied when things go badly for bad people. There could be the feeling that misfortune is justified for a bad person, and they deserve it. These attitudes are not helpful to Mind Training.

Commiserate with bad luck and try to help. Recognise what is bad and breathe it in. Appreciate and celebrate good luck – whomever is experiencing it. Appreciate what is good and breathe it out. It is not necessary to own or personally experience good fortune to enjoy it. There is no need to examine justice or fairness. Awakening practitioners wish *all* beings to be happy, and to find the path of awakening. Their aspiration does not have any caveats: *all beings except*....

> *'Sometimes it is useful to reverse a Mind Training slogan and see how ridiculous that would be as an instruction.'*
> Ngakpa 'ö-Dzin – Battlecry of Freedom retreat, Munich, 2017

If this slogan were reversed it would be: *Seek happiness in others' pain*. Very few people would wish to admit that they gained happiness in that way, yet unfortunately many people do find others' pain entertaining, as demonstrated by many Reality TV shows. This attitude is detrimental to Mind Training. It opposes the intention to benefit others. The wish to help others can also be occluded through wishing life to be fair, and in wishing people to get what it is felt they deserve.

> *'Tantrikas understand that it is impossible to disconnect from killing. They understand that this is so, simply because they have human bodies. They recognise that to have a body—and to exist—is to cause death. From this knowledge they establish compassionate connections with everyone and everything, everywhere.[…] Tantrikas are aware that they cannot extricate themselves from involvement in exploitation, social injustice, oppression, and theft.'*
> Ngak'chang Rinpoche and Khandro Déchen – *the Five Owl Precepts*, aroencyclopaedia.org

Another aspect of avoiding seeking happiness in others' pain, is taking responsibility for the effect personal activity has on others. Everyone is always completely compromised. It is not possible to live in the world without cooperating with the exploitation of others, or without inadvertently hurting others. Everyone everywhere is totally dependent on everyone else. Everyone's lives are interconnected.

This is not about being politically correct. It is not about buying fairly traded products, and recycling to save the planet, donating to charities, working as a volunteer, and so forth – though such activity may be beneficial. It is about accepting the reality of being unable to live as a physically present human being without harming others.

It is about taking responsibility for harm through that acceptance, rather than abdicating responsibility because there is no intention to harm. It is about attempting to live causing as little harm as possible, and making life meaningful by being as much benefit as possible.

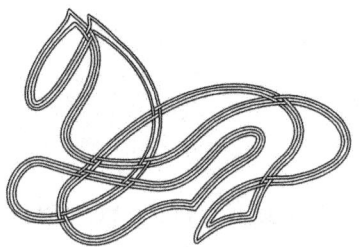

39

Practise all the teachings with a single intention.

rNal 'byor thams cad gCig gis bya

The single intention is to ride the mind in order to benefit others.

My wish in buying Dee from the riding school was to secure her a future, and to liberate her from what looked to me like a pretty miserable existence. She worked in riding lessons three hours a day, six days a week. All the working horses were stabled throughout the working day. In the summer Dee was turned out overnight in a field on her own. In the winter she would be in a stable for up to eighteen hours a day, only turned out for two or three hours in the morning.

I had always wanted to own my own horse, and had romantic fantasies about what this would be like. When, at 50, I did at last own a horse—Dee—many of the fantasies of horse ownership were shattered. The reality bore little resemblance to what I'd imagined. Some things were indeed marvellous, and some aspects were not so good.

Nevertheless I took responsibility for my decision to take on Dee, and experienced great joy and satisfaction seeing her change and start to have a good life. It was wonderful to let her live until she was old and die of natural causes. It was wonderful to see her living in a herd and no longer in solitary isolation. Many of my desires in owning a horse were not fully fulfilled in owning Dee. Nevertheless I took on the responsibility for Dee, and my primary intention of giving her a better life was, I believe, fulfilled. I am satisfied that I succeeded in that.

> *'The one intention is to have a sense of*
> *gentleness toward others and a willingness*
> *to be helpful to others – always.'*
> Chögyam Trungpa Rinpoche – *Training the Mind*, p. 189

It is always pleasurable to help others. It is the joy of the path of awakening. Awakening has the two aspects of view and intention. These can be called ultimate and relative awakening. The view is the realisation of the nonduality of emptiness and form, self and other, existence and non-existence. This is the felt recognition of the lack of inherent identity. The intention is to give priority to the needs of others and be of benefit to them.

Emphasis can be placed on view or intention, but ultimately they are the same. Judging what is kind is easier than judging what is wise. So it is always better to err on the side of kindness and benefitting others. The single intention of benefitting others is the focus.

Kindness is not always wise. Sometimes trying to be kind in supporting someone in a situation does not help that person escape it, and there could be a wiser approach. Nevertheless such kindly intent is free of blame.

Assuming the capacity for wisdom, however, can be dangerous and far from kind. It could be deemed that there is a need to *be cruel to be kind*. Practitioners may believe this is skilful wrathful activity, when in fact it is just stupidly stumbling around hurting people.

> *'The only internal damtsig is wisdom.*
> *The only external damtsig is kindness.'*[37]

The vow of the awakening hero is a little like an extraordinary joke. The awakening hero vows to remain and not attain full awakening until all other beings are awakened. Yet the fact of the vow—if it is maintained—guarantees full awakening. It guarantees full awakening because it embraces the nonduality of view and intention. To live in a manner that upholds this vow, is itself the cause of awakening.

> *'Kindness is where we start. Compassion means so much more, n a certain sense, than simply being kind. Compassion means kindness, but it also means communication – fierce, florid, and fecund communication.'*
> Ngak'chang Rinpoche and Khandro Déchen – *Kindness and Compassion,* aroencyclopaedia.org

The single intention of all the teachings, and of the practice of Mind Training, is to awaken and be of benefit to everyone and everything, everywhere.

---

[37] Damtsig *(dam tshig)* (Tib.) – means *vow, commitment.* These sentences are from the Aro gTér Lineage refuge ceremony.

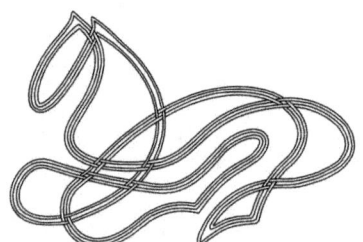

40

Reverse all misfortunes with a single intention.

log gNon thams cad gCig gis bya

Holding the single intention of benefitting others, ride this joyful motivation through every difficulty that is encountered, reversing all misfortune.

Despite Dee's courageous personality, she was always nervous when hacking. I do not know whether something bad had happened to her during the two or three years of her history before she was bought by the riding school. I was unable to find out about that part of her life. I do not know whether the time she had spent at the riding school, working in a closed arena, and spending long hours in a stable, had undermined her confidence in hacking.

Over the last couple of years of her life, going out on a trail ride at all, started to become too much for Dee. She became more anxious and more unpredictable. I was getting older too, and although I had not experienced being thrown since coming off Red over a jump, I was not keen on being on the back of an increasingly jittery and unreliable horse.

The last time I rode her in 2015 she bolted. From walking steadily behind Red, she suddenly spun round and bolted for home. This was the first time Dee had ever bolted with me. I was able to bring her to a halt, but she resolutely would not go forward, and started backing up, and then rearing. At this point I decided it was time to let go of my desire to ride, and to relieve Dee of her anxiety. I retired her and let her live her final days grazing the fields.

> *'The power of being a vow-holder, is that once one has made an aspiration or promise – one is tied to that.*
> *It is an energetic stance – and one has to act.'*
> Ngak'chang Rinpoche – personal communication

When there is the primary intention of appreciating and wishing to benefit others, it is not possible to feel disgruntled when secondary intentions are not fulfilled. The single intention of awakening—wishing to benefit others—removes the focus of every response away from identity and personal needs. By focussing on others, rather than on personal needs and desires, the causes of dissatisfaction become empty. In this way misfortune is reversed.

If there is no *me* wanting something, then wanting dissolves into emptiness.

If there is no *me* hating something, then hating dissolves into emptiness. The deluded definition of misfortune dissolves.

By wishing *you* to be happy, everything becomes available to appreciate and share without the sticky consideration of identity.

By wishing *you* to be free of pain, energy becomes available to help, liberated from the limiting considerations of identity-fixation.

The awakening intention of wishing to help others protects the mind from self-centredness and the experience of dissatisfaction.

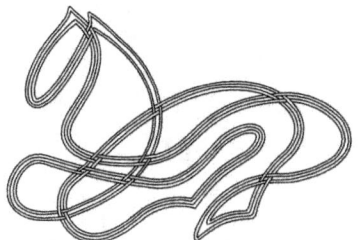

41

Both first and last, two things to do.

thog mTha' gNyis la bya ba gNyis

Start with the intention to ride excellently.
At the end of the ride, review how it went.

Every time I rode with someone I would make the arrangement to ask Dee to take the lead for a while. Usually she would do this. Occasionally she would even lead at a trot, but rarely at a canter. If she did lead at a canter it would be only for a few paces, and extremely nervously.

At a trot or walk, she could seem fairly relaxed, and then suddenly she would stop – ears pricked, body tense, and snorting. The only way to move forward again then, was to let my companion take the lead once more. Then Dee would relax and continue.

Every ride had to be taken as it was. I would set out with the intention to increase Dee's confidence in the lead. Back at the stable I would measure our success. Did Dee lead for the length of the long track through the Ganol today? Did she trot or canter as lead horse? Every ride was a new opportunity. I never gave up on the possibility of overcoming this problem, though I would never press it or insist, if Dee did not seem relaxed enough during the hack to try her in the lead. I had to prioritise Dee's comfort, and be happy with little successes in my desire to increase her confidence.

> *'If you have not committed any transgression, then rejoice, thinking, "I have indeed made my human existence meaningful."'*
> Thupten Jinpa – Essential Mind Training

Every day is a new opportunity to awaken – to embrace awakening view and intention. Start the day with the aspiration to engage Mind Training and embrace awakening view and intention. At the end of the day review how the day went.

Celebrate successes: moments of kindness and openness – a kind word to someone who looked unhappy, helping someone struggling with a task, succeeding in seeing an emotional pattern before it caught the mind.

Regret any failures: mistakes and missed opportunities
– the failure to get involved when an opportunity to help was recognised, a clever but spiteful remark that was out before it could be stopped, the irritation that wasn't caught in time.

Then let success and failure dissolve into emptiness. Do not become proud or complacent with successes. Do not go over and over any mistakes, or feel guilty. Recognise the mistake, regret it, and let it go. Then the day is over and it is time for sleep – which is also an opportunity to practise. Tomorrow is another day, and another opportunity for Mind Training.

This slogan is quite straightforward: start well and end well. Ultimately it becomes possible to have awareness at the beginning and end of each moment. Starting and ending well becomes the flow of endless moments of Mind Training. This is living life as practice. This is awakening.

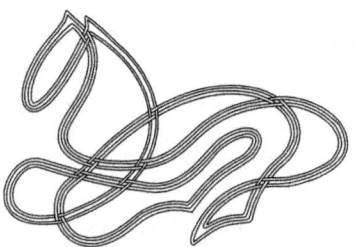

42

Whichever of the two occurs, practise patience.

gNyis po gang byung bZod par bya

Whether riding goes well or badly
— practise patience.

Red was a comedian. He liked to test how well you were attuned with him – and how well you were paying attention. I could feel his intention to do something *interesting* as it arose, and was able to circumvent most of his ideas. Riders with less experience, and a less developed relationship with Red, found it difficult to recognise when some notion had occurred to him.

Ngakpa 'ö-Dzin had little riding experience before we bought Red. He'd had a few lessons at the riding school, but most of his instruction came from a horse called Gus. In 2004 we took part in an equestrian retreat with our Buddhist teachers and sangha, on a ranch in Montana, riding all day every day. I was given a lovely mare called Black Star. Ngakpa 'ö-Dzin was at first given an old and rather slow horse, but when the wranglers recognised his natural ability and willingness to trust the horse, they switched him to riding Gus. Gus was an experienced and intelligent trail horse, and he took Ngakpa 'ö-Dzin along the trails safely at all paces. He respected Ngakpa 'ö-Dzin and allowed him to be his leader, and Ngakpa 'ö-Dzin respected Gus and allowed him to be his teacher. They developed a delightful working relationship.

Ngakpa 'ö-Dzin's limited experience was clear to Red and sometimes Red took advantage of this. In a sense this was a compliment to Ngakpa 'ö-Dzin's ability. Red was only mischievous with riders whom he felt had the confidence and capacity to deal with it. So Red would do things like walking into a hedge, or going so close to a tree that there was no room for the rider's leg, or deciding he didn't want to go left because that would mean a longer ride and he wanted to go the shorter ride, or just aimlessly deciding to wander off the trail. He never put Ngakpa 'ö-Dzin in danger, but just liked to create a little amusing situation to be dealt with, to test Ngakpa 'ö-Dzin's capacity.

All that had to happen to deal with Red's ideas, was for the rider to recognise what was happening as quickly as possible and patiently take charge.

> '*From the view of Vajrayana, patience does not mean acceptance,
> forbearance, and suffering. According to Vajrayana,
> patience involves* intelligent open-minded striving, *in which the
> situation is propelled at its optimal velocity – neither forcing it,
> nor failing in the attempt to facilitate movement.
> Both apathy and coercion are the result of referentiality
> with regard to the pace at which visible success is apparent.
> Patience looks different according to circumstances.*'
> Khandro Déchen – *The Ten Paramitas,* aroencyclopaedia.org

Life is inevitably a mixture of happiness and sadness, desirable occurrences and undesirable occurrences.
A student once expressed a reluctance to practise with happy experiences – for fear of losing the happiness, and also a reluctance to practise with unhappy experiences – for fear of concretising the unhappiness. The lack of logic in this was clear to the student, but the fear persisted.
The solution is more practice. Practise and find out through experience that Mind Training will not dilute happiness or intensify pain. Mind Training creates a joyful mind, so that happiness increases whatever is being experienced.

> '*Patience is required in terms of learning anything:
> shi-nè, horse riding, thangka painting, or marksmanship with
> a .500 Linebaugh. If you have found the right Lama,
> patience requires the implementation of their instructions.*'
> Khandro Déchen – *The Ten Paramitas,* aroencyclopaedia.org

Practitioners are patient with the good and the bad. Whatever arises is greeted with patience – the capacity to let it be as it is. Every occurrence is seen as the opportunity to awaken. The good is appreciated, but not clung to. It is not allowed to intoxicate the mind. The bad is recognised, but not rejected. It is not allowed to unseat the mind. Neither ruffles composure in the saddle of Mind Training. Each is ridden as the path of awakening.

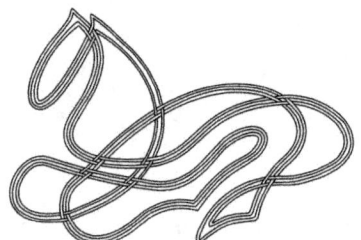

43

Guard the two, even at the risk of your life.

gNyis po srog dang bsDos nas bSrung

Guard awakening view and intention, and ride the mind for the benefit of everyone and everything, everywhere.

If there is a wish to ride, there needs to be a horse. If there is a horse, that horse must be valued and cared for. Then it is possible to ride. Once it is possible to ride, the riding environment must be appreciated. This may seem rather simplistic, but ultimately awakened view and awakened intent is simple.

To awaken, the mind must be caught and trained. In order to train the mind, the methods of training must be embraced. The mind must be valued and cared for, at all times and in all circumstances. To awaken the trained mind, the intention to benefit others must be a priority. Guard awakening view. Guard the methods of awakening, embracing all circumstances as opportunities. Guard awakening intention. Certainty in the efficacy of this approach is called refuge.[38] Refuge is the starting point for all Buddhist practitioners. It is the assertion of becoming engaged with Mind Training in order to awaken view and awaken intent. It is the most basic Buddhist vow, and is often proclaimed in a public ceremony.

The conventional meaning of refuge is somewhere to escape to avoid painful life circumstances. This might be a material place of refuge – such as a refuge for the homeless, a women's refuge, or a refugee camp. Or it might be an emotional or psychological refuge to hide from the harsh realities of life. Security might be sought in: finding better employment, a greater income, the perfect partner, the perfect horse, more possessions, better possessions, a bigger house, a smarter car, happier experiences, distraction from dissatisfaction, and engaging in activity to numb the mind of dissatisfaction such as drinking excessive alcohol, taking drugs, watching endless television, playing games, gambling, and so on.

Refuge in terms of Buddhism, does not look for security outside the reality of the present moment, and the reality of *as it is*. Security is discovered in awakening.

---

38 Kyab (*sKyab*).

When Buddhist practitioners take refuge, they assert their recognition of the possibility of awakening; they embrace the methods of awakening; and they engage with the circumstances of life as the means of entering the path of awakening.

It is an assertion that awakening, awakening intent, and awakening activity, have become the empty sources of security. It is the recognition that awakened view and awakened intent are the only source of security – the security of nonduality; the security of no longer seeking material security. It is security in the emptiness of fixed identity, and in the form of eternal identity through the continuation of momentary definition. It is security in empty receptivity, and in the form of the eternal response to the needs of others, of being the cause of their happiness and awakening.

> 'We should therefore observe these vows at all costs,
> just as we guard our eyes from thorns
> when we are walking through the woods.'
> Dilgo Khyentse Rinpoche – *Enlightened Courage*, p. 82

Refuge is a state of being that is continually renewed, rather than a state that is regarded as acquired during a refuge ceremony and then forgotten about. The certainty of holding refuge is the ground of practice. Holding that certainty as a lived reality is practised. Mind Training is rooted in this refuge

The instruction to hold this commitment *even at the risk of your life* is direct and uncompromising. To be able to experience as a felt reality, that commitment to Mind Training as more important than life itself, there has to be considerable experience of practice.

There has to be a *felt reality* that emptiness protects the mind. There has to be a *felt reality* that identity is illusory. There has to be a *felt reality* that the needs of other beings are more important than personal needs.

Mind Training must have become so much a part of the practitioner, and the purpose of Mind Training so *present*, that it is recognised as the only valuable purpose in life.

Awakened view and intent are more important than *this life* because they are not only the basis of personal happiness in this and future lives, but also the basis for the possibility of helping all other beings to find happiness in this and future lives.

If a practitioner is not currently able to wholeheartedly embrace the idea of rebirth in terms of personal experience, the word *moment* could replace the word *life* – and the message would remain the same. Awakened view and intent are more important than *this moment* because they are not only the basis of personal happiness in this and future moments, but also the basis for the possibility of helping all other beings to find happiness in this and future moments. Guard the view and intention that have the potential to awaken the present moment.

44

Train in the three difficulties.

dKa' ba gSum la bsLab par bya

Recognise the suggestion of misbehaviour.
Patiently ride the correction.
Ride with the certainty of continuing good behaviour.

Intention, response, and satisfaction create patterning in the mind. The riding scenarios below are examples of how this might function.

Example One:

1. *Intention*: The horse is perceived by the rider as badly behaved. The rider classifies the horse as *bad*. Expecting bad behaviour the rider experiences aversion and mounts the horse with the intention of riding forcefully and aggressively to preempt any bad behaviour.

2. *Response*: The rider attempts to dominate and bully the horse to behave well – even before any bad behaviour has manifested. The horse responds with fear and bad behaviour, trying to rid itself of the aggressive rider.

3. *Satisfaction*: the rider ends up on the ground with the horse careering round the pen bucking like a bronco. This confirms, to the rider's satisfaction, that the horse is bad. The rider is satisfied that overly strong and dominant riding was necessary, and the horse is a lost cause. This confirmation of intention and response is the experience of satisfaction. This may not be a happy feeling, but it is satisfaction in terms of confirming perception and response and further establishing the perceptual pattern.

The horse is perceived as bad. The reaction of aversion to badness creates a response. When expectation is fulfilled—it goes badly—there is satisfaction that perception was confirmed and response justified. This interaction creates a complete pattern.

If any of the three factors of patterning is missing, the pattern will not be complete. The pattern will not be so strongly established. This is illustrated in the second example.

Example Two:

1. *Intention*: The horse has a reputation for bad behaviour. The rider trusts their riding skills and decides to keep an open mind, approaching the horse quietly and respectfully.

2. *Response*: When the horse bucks and prances, the rider remains in the saddle. The rider asks firmly but kindly for the horse to respond. The horse realises that the rider is not attempting to dominate, and is not being aggressive, and gradually relaxes. The horse begins to respond to the rider. Horse and rider begin to enjoy harmonious communication.

3. *Satisfaction*: The rider is happy that the open approach worked, and that harmonious riding became possible.

This interaction will have created a positive pattern. It will be a root of goodness. The rider had open perception and responded directly to what was actually happening, rather than to what might have been expected to happen.

The third version of this example is not so positive in terms of the relationship between horse and rider, but is still a root of goodness because it is based in open perception and direct response:

Example Three:

1. *Intention*: The horse has a reputation for bad behaviour. The rider trusts their riding skills and decides to approach the horse quietly and respectfully.

2. *Response*: When the horse bucks and prances, the rider remains in the saddle. The rider asks firmly but kindly for the horse to respond. The horse is so used to domination and aggression, that it is not able to relax and respond to the rider. After a reasonable length of time, the rider gives up the attempt to work with the horse.

3. *Satisfaction*: The rider is happy that the horse was given the best chance to overcome habitual behaviour. The rider is satisfied at having avoided being prejudiced by the horse's reputation.

Maybe in time, after more groundwork and schooling, the horse will start to trust the open and friendly approach of the rider, and be able to relax and respond, so that harmonious riding becomes a possibility.

> *'If, for instance, an uncontrollably strong emotion comes over us, so that we feel helplessly in its power, we should nevertheless confront it and question it. Where are its weapons? Where are its muscles? Where is its great army and its political strength?'*
> Dilgo Khyentse Rinpoche – *Enlightened Courage*, p. 83

This slogan describes *karma*—*lé-kyi*—the process of conditioned perception and response.[39]

The three difficulties refer to:

- the difficulty of seeing the moment of perception,
- the difficulty of catching the habitual response,
- the difficulty of cutting the flow of habitual perception and response.

Perception continually arises. If perception is direct and clear, and the response is open and appropriate, then awakening is possible. However if perception is conditioned by attraction, aversion, and indifference, and rooted in past or projected experience, then response will be based in habitual patterning, and add to that patterning.

> *'The first difficulty is to realise the point at which you are tricked by your own emotions... The second difficulty is to dispel or exorcise our emotionalism. The third difficulty is to cut the continuity of that emotionalism.'*
> Chögyam Trungpa Rinpoche – *Training the Mind*, p. 194

---

39 Tib. lékyi (*las kyi*), Skt. *karma*. As karma is the more commonly recognised word, I will use it in this commentary rather than the Tibetan.

Karma is the ruling force of *khorwa* (*samsara* – cyclic existence). It creates the experience of dissatisfaction through habitual patterning. For a pattern to be fully created, or to strengthen an existing pattern, there need to be three factors: intention, action, and satisfaction. *Intention* arises from perception. There is the intention to respond to what is perceived. The response is *active*. Activity is then engaged in response to what is perceived. *Satisfaction* is experienced through seeing that the perception and response correlate and confirm one another. If any of these three factors is absent, then a pattern is not fully created, or an existing pattern is weakened rather than strengthened.

> '... *fortunately* the Law of Karma *can also be changed. If* the Law of Karma *could not be broken there could be no enlightenment – or enlightenment would have to be causal. The* law *of karma belongs to the world of dualism which—like ego, distracted being, or the famous* I—*is illusory. The* legal system *of karma has no jurisdiction in terms of nonduality. When we realise beginningless enlightenment, the law enforcement agencies of karma evaporate. They boil away into space – because they were our unenlightenment.*'
> Ngakpa Chögyam – *Rays of the Sun*, p. 47

Karma does not have to be undone item by item. This would be to view perception and response as materialistic and mechanical. In *every* moment there is the potential for perception to be free of conditioning. There is the potential for response to be free of conditioning. Karma simply dissolves in the moment that perception is clear and direct, and response is open and appropriate. This is awakening.

> '*Meditation is our only weapon against this repressive regime and it constitutes civil disobedience in the form of passive resistance. By allowing the development of experiential space through the practice of shi-nè—according to the four naljors—we discover our own intrinsic awareness.*'
> Ngakpa Chögyam – *Rays of the Sun*, p. 55

The response to a stimulus cannot be known until that stimulus is perceived. Perception can give rise to startlingly strong responses.

> *'When mental afflictions arise, it is difficult to notice them in the beginning, difficult to avert them in the middle and difficult to interrupt their continuity in the end.'*
> Thogme Zangpo – *Commentary on the Seven Points of Mind Training*

Emptiness protects the mind from such unknown and unpredictable stimuli by enabling conditioned perception to be noticed immediately.

Unconditioned perception is empty. The habitual response may still engage if there is a lack of experience of embracing unconditioned perception, but the pattern will not be so strong. Eventually unconditioned perception enables unconditioned response. Then karma self-liberates in the moment. The third difficulty is then addressed – that of continuing to allow unconditioned perception and unconditioned response. This cuts the strings of conditioned patterning.

> *'Of the three, the most important is to try to tame each negative emotion as soon as you notice it.'*
> Shamar Rinpoche – *The Path to Awakening*, p. 152

The discontinuous continuity of direct, clear perception, and compassionate, appropriate response, is the experience of rigpa, nonduality, awakening. Understanding the three difficulties, seeing them, and training in overcoming them, is the path of awakening.

> *'Once we've woken up a bit, we have responsibility. A practitioner is someone who can regret a thought. No one has seen the thought, heard the thought, or suffered from it – but the practitioner regrets it nevertheless.'*
> Ngakpa 'ö-Dzin – apprentice retreat, 2018

45

Embrace the three principal causes.

rGyu yi gTso bo rNams gSum bLang

Find an inspiring riding instructor; learn the techniques of riding and get to know your horse; then joyfully appreciate every aspect of riding.

One aspect of lessons I found difficult at the riding school was the continual change of instructor. We rarely had the same instructor two lessons in a row. There were three main instructors, but several others that might take the Grade III lessons fairly frequently. Although all the instructors were supposedly teaching the same methods of equestrianism, the details could vary considerably. I might continue to apply a detail I had learned from the previous week, and be told it was incorrect, and to stop doing it by that day's instructor.

There was one instructor in particular I liked and trusted. I felt I had a personal relationship with her. She would answer questions, and never made students feel foolish or of less value than others in the group. She knew all the horses individually and had a relationship with each one. She had the capacity to kindly accommodate their strengths and weaknesses in a lesson. She was always affectionate to Dee and did not seem to find her an inconvenience. She never treated Dee roughly.

We were having a jumping lesson with this instructor one afternoon, and had three trainee instructors with the usual Grade III group. Toward the end of the lesson, mostly for the benefit of the trainee instructors, we were asked to try jumping without reins. A rider's relationship with the reins can be rather illogical. Reins do not keep you on a horse. They offer no security for staying on the horse's back at all. Yet, because they are held in the hands, the reins feel like they help you stay on.

Grade III riders were used to tying a knot in the reins and dropping them on the horse's neck, in order to focus on the riding position: sitting deeply in the saddle, the position of the legs, and so forth. But to jump a fence without reins felt like a big challenge, and it was the first time this had been asked of us. The trainee riding instructors were of course expected to embrace the instruction and jump the jumps without reins. It was optional for the rest of the group and only a few of us did it.

It was probably one of the most significant lessons for me in becoming fully aware of my physical connection to the body of the horse, through letting go of the reins as imagined security. As we approached the fence at a canter, we had to drop the reins and put our arms straight out in front of us, either side of the horse's head.

Dee and I soared over several jumps and it was an extraordinary experience of trust in the instructor, trust in my body in the saddle, and trust in the horse. In this anecdote, the instructor, the method of jumping without reins, and the experience of connection with Dee were the three principal causes for this extraordinarily awakening riding experience. They were the teacher, the method, and the circumstances conducive for practice.

> *'The slogans are a hybrid teaching that span the yanas. The Sutric, Tantric, or Dzogchen emphasis depends on the lineage – and on the Lama who gives commentary.'*
> Ngak'chang Rinpoche – in conversation

In whichever of the vehicles practice is based, the teacher is important. The teacher is the source of teaching and method. It is possible to learn about Mind Training from a book and practise what is learnt. To ask questions about Mind Training, however, it will be necessary to have a physical teacher to ask. To discover the potential, depth, and subtleties of Mind Training as a method of awakening, it will become necessary to receive transmission from a qualified Lama. Then it is essential to have a personal relationship with a teacher.

Ideally the teacher is present as a continual inspiration for the student throughout their life. I am sure that my riding abilities would have advanced more quickly and deeply if I had been fortunate to have the same teacher week after week. A relationship with a teacher is the first principle source of awakening.

The second principle is the method of practice – it is the Mind Training instructions expressed in these teachings. The methods have to be practised to have any effect – practitioners must move beyond merely studying them. Only through testing Mind Training in the laboratory of practitioners' own experience can practice be tasted and found to be valuable. There is no benefit to be gained if the methods of Mind Training are not applied. Mind Training must move beyond the realm of intellectualism.

The third principle is the importance of valuing circumstances that support practice, and establishing how to embrace current life circumstances as a support to practice. Practice must not be dependent on a notion of *ideal* circumstances. Alternatively *less-than-ideal* circumstances should not be used as a reason not to practise, when it is in fact laziness, distraction, or lack of discipline that is preventing engagement in Mind Training. It is helpful to create supportive circumstances if possible, such as a quiet room in which to meditate. Being part of a community of other practitioners is also extremely supportive. Practitioners who are fortunate to have the time and opportunity to practise, must value and appreciate this as the most priceless and exceptional opportunity, and as the third principle cause of awakening.

> *'If we have these three essential factors complete we should be happy at the thought we have all that is necessary to practise the teachings. It is as though we have been equipped with a good horse for an uphill journey—the way will be without difficulty.'*
> Dilgo Khyentse Rinpoche – *Enlightened Courage*, p. 84

In order to truly make progress it is necessary to commit to a *particular* teacher, and a *particular* path of practice. To really progress, the teaching and methods of Mind Training need to be consistent and applied consistently, at all times and in all circumstances. Then these will truly become the principal causes of awakening.

46

Practise so that the three do not deteriorate.

nyams pa med pa rNams gSum bsGom

Do not let the three deteriorate: relationship with the teacher; engagement with practice; and the joyful appreciation of every aspect of riding the mind.

At times I allowed the riding instructor to overrule my rationale in a lesson. I would engage in an equestrian activity that seemed unsafe or beyond my ability, because of my confidence in the teacher. This could be riding without stirrups or riding without reins, closing my eyes to experience the rhythm of the horse, practising a demanding exercise, jumping a fence or log that seemed too big, or any number of equestrian activities.

When my instructor had the confidence in me as a rider to ask me to perform a difficult or challenging activity, it was essential to trust the teacher and embrace the activity without doubt or fear.

It is the same in Mind Training. This slogan urges practitioners to nurture the three principle causes: the teacher, the path of practice, and conducive circumstances. Having developed a relationship with a teacher, embraced the path of practice, and established the circumstances that enable practice – keep them. Nurture them so that they are continually held as the cause of awakening.

> *'... devotion ... could sound too subtle, too abstruse to understand – but the same phenomenon exists in the world of the Arts. Almost anyone can enjoy world-class music – but only a proficient musician can know the worth of a world-class musician. The greater your musical ability the more astonishing a master-musician becomes. Mozart is a composer of extremely pretty melodies – until you learn enough about music to understand his compositions. JS Bach is a composer of marvellously intricate sonic adventures – until you learn something about contrapuntal composition.'*
> Ngakpa Chögyam – Wisdom Eccentrics, p. 19

To embrace the vision of the instructor in such a way and have trust in the instructor, is called *devotion* in Buddhism.

> *'The first thing you should not let wane is devotion ... The second thing you should not let wane is a delightful attitude toward lojong, or the taming of your mind. [...] And the third thing you should not let wane is your conduct ...'*
> Chögyam Trungpa Rinpoche – Training the Mind, p. 198

The teachings and methods of Mind Training are the path to awakening. There must be a willingness to embrace them, and to let go of the domination of conditioned view and rationale. Doubts should be discussed with the teacher, but eventually Vajrayana students have to relinquish personal rationale. Personal rationale has to be relinquished on the basis of *learning-faith* – rather than *emotional-faith*. When one has confidence in the teacher—through the experience of following instructions—one can take a leap into the unknown that is logical.

Some aspects of Mind Training have more to do with the sphere of magic, than the sphere of logical reasoning. The intellect can only take understanding so far. From the perspective of the intellect, fully embracing the journey to awakening takes a leap into the unknown, and the unknowable. For this, the teacher's guidance and advice has to be entertained experientially. Then devotion arises and the relationship with the teacher is recognised as beyond price, so that the strong intention is established to never allow it to deteriorate.

> *'It is not a matter of learning how to behave well* on principle. *Behaving badly, with regard to the Lama, has to be impossible. It has to be as impossible as grinding your own body away with a meat grinder — a meat grinder which required that you turn the handle yourself. A less extreme description would be doubting that money had value – and believing that nothing could be bought with money. Once having spent money, you would know that goods can be purchased with it, there would be no doubt.'*
> Ngak'chang Rinpoche – in conversation

When the methods offered by the teacher have been embraced, experience develops in their efficacy. The student becomes devoted to the methods of practice, as well as to the teacher who offers them.

Then the methods of practice are recognised as beyond price, so that the strong intention is established to never allow them to deteriorate. Practising becomes a loved and appreciated activity, just as climbing into the saddle to set out on the trail was always looked forward to and enjoyed.

When performing a difficult or challenging equestrian activity, through devotion to the instructor, and trust in the method, the relationship with the horse is also an important factor. The horse would be the conducive circumstance in that instance. My confidence in a jumping lesson, or my willingness to work without stirrups for an hour, would depend on the horse I was given.

Most instructors were sympathetic to the need for the right horse for the task of the lesson, and knew which horses were reluctant to jump, or difficult to sit. Dee was a conducive circumstance in a jumping lesson because she would jump anything and everything. She was not the ideal mount for a lesson without stirrups, being quite bouncy at the trot and not particularly broad in the back. Nevertheless in terms of my embracing the challenge of sitting trot without stirrups and improving my posture and balance as a rider, she was still a conducive circumstance if I was willing to rise to the challenge – more so than a broader-backed and less bouncy mount.

When practising Mind Training, conducive circumstances that support practice must be valued as beyond price, so that the strong intention is established to never allow them to deteriorate.

47

Keep the three inseparable.

'bral med gSum dang lDan par bya

Keep inseparable: presence, energetic attention to riding, and physical contact with the horse.

It wasn't until I studied natural horsemanship that I appreciated the depth of relationship I had enjoyed with Whiskey, the pony I looked after as a teenager. An important beginning stage with working with a horse using natural methods, is *joining up*.[40] With this method, the horse is in an enclosed space with the trainer, ideally a round pen. First the horse is *sent away*—encouraged to go out to the perimeter of the pen—and also encouraged to be active. A long rein or whip is used for this, but no contact is made with the horse. Staying in the centre, facing the horse, and letting it circle around the pen, the trainer looks for signs of the horse accepting them as leader. These will be indications of relaxation, such as the horse lowering its head or making chewing motions with its mouth. Then the horse is allowed to stop moving. The trainer turns side on to the horse and slowly walks away. If the horse is ready to *join up*, it will move up and follow the trainer, continuing to drop its head and make chewing movements. The trainer can then make physical contact with the horse, stroking and talking to it.

Whiskey was difficult to catch, but I instinctively found a way to get him to join up with me, and then it was always easy. He trusted me and knew that I treated him well. I had confidence that he enjoyed being with me. This was the basis for us being able to join up. This psychological and emotional joining up on the ground without physical contact, was an invaluable basis for a joining up experience when riding, with physical contact on his back. Joining up was a magical communication to experience with Whiskey, and later with Dee.

Joining up with a horse that is free and loose in a pen, without tack, and chooses to come to you is communication at the levels of mind, speech, and body. These are the empty, energetic, and form spheres of being. In Mind Training it is also necessary to embrace all three aspects of being, in order to *join up* with the mind.

40 As a method used in natural horsemanship, this is usually attributed to the horse trainer Monty Roberts.

Mind embraces awakening view. It is empty alert presence that is pregnant with the possibility of form arising. The sphere of energy or speech, embraces awakening intention and communication. The sphere of form and material physicality, embraces the enactment of awakening view and intention in activity, lifestyle, and effort.

The inseparability of these three means that all activities must be congruent with view and intention. It is not congruent to engage in loving kindness meditation and feel purified and holy, but to then speak harshly to a person who accidentally treads on practice equipment. It is not appropriate to visualise the refuge tree and devotedly mumble the refuge prayer, but then later steal someone's sandals left outside the shrine room at the retreat centre.[41] It is not skilful to engage in prostrations to a being who symbolises awakening, with a mind that is distracted by a grievance and plotting revenge. Every aspect of being must be inseparable and engaged in Mind Training.

> *'His presence is always a teaching – because you cannot manipulate or appropriate the sheer power of his being. His personality display is always a teaching – because you cannot find any habit formation or pattern in how he is. His life circumstances display is always a teaching – because he always undermines the creation of contrived structures around him; even at the expense of his life and health. He is prepared to be utterly precarious in his life situation. It is astonishing.'*
> Ngak'chang Rinpoche – talking about Kyabje Chh'imèd Rig'dzin Rinpoche in an interview, 1993, aroencyclopaedia.org

Practitioners who have developed a deep relationship with a teacher can also keep body, speech, and mind inseparable through the method of taking the three displays of the Lama as the path of awakening.

These three are presence display, personality display, and life circumstances display. Embracing these is a Dzogchen practice.

---

41 This happened to Ngak'chang Rinpoche in England, in the 1970s, and he had to return to Wales barefoot.

Students are empty in relation to the presence of their Lamas. Students allow the empty personalities of their Lamas to be a teaching. The Lamas' engagement with life circumstances is embraced as inspirational.

Teachers do not necessarily manipulate their presence, personalities, or life circumstances in order that they are viewed *as a teaching* – though this would not be beyond the Lamas' capacity. It is devoted students who embrace the experience of their Lamas in this way. To experience Lamas as presence display, personality display, and life circumstances display has the potential to affect students' experience of their own presence, their own personalities, and their life circumstances in an extraordinary manner. It is to experience teachers as mirrors. It is a method of awakening.

48

Train without prejudice in all areas, deeply and pervasively, and once perfected, cherish everyone and everything, everywhere.

yul la phyogs med dag tu sByang

khyab dang gTing 'byongs kuncla gCes

Pay attention to all aspects of training the mind. Cherish the horse, riding skills, and every riding opportunity as the sources of joyful and excellent equestrianism.

Horse owners are good examples of the meaning of wholehearted devotion. I have always been impressed with the devotion they display for their horses. Even quite young girls will get up really early to see to their horses before school, and devote most of their free time at weekends and in holidays to their horses. They will fit in riding and looking after their horses around schoolwork and socialising. They love their horses and riding so much that they are able to put their horses' needs first. This is the wholehearted attitude that needs to be applied to Mind Training – devotion and love of riding the mind.

Riders recognise that the enjoyment of riding depends on their horses, and cherish them. Riders of Mind Training recognise that awakening view and intention depend on everyone and everything, everywhere, and cherish everyone and everything, everywhere.

Mind Training must be embraced in the same wholehearted manner, with all aspects of practice considered. The practices that have been given must be practised diligently and cherished as the cause of awakening. Teachings must be studied diligently and become completely familiar. It is possible to read the same book or text repeatedly and gain something new from each reading. Practice equipment should be cared for. It is inspiring to create items connected to practice, such as protective bags for instruments, a cloth for the shrine, brocade tails for drums. If practitioners are engaged in visionary practice, it is helpful to create visionary imagery, such as calligraphies, or paintings. Any and every aspect of the arts can be embraced as practice.

> *'It is not enough to verbalise the Mind Training instruction since that is not useful to anyone.'*
> Shamar Rinpoche – *The Path to Awakening*, p. 154

I did not ride often after we retired Dee and gave Red to the trekking centre. I felt that this part of my life had come to an end, but occasionally the wish to be back in the saddle arises.

In summer, 2016, I decided to ride at the trekking centre The owners knew me well and regarded me as a competent rider. I was given Bo, a fairly young mare who had a reputation for being a bit of a plodder. I had known Bo since she first came to the trekking centre, and knew that she was extremely well schooled and had been a most responsive mare. I was surprised to hear her described as a dull mount.

I was put at the back of the ride as the horse most likely to be slow. I decided to ride Bo without prejudice and see how she responded. I rode politely and openly. She did not plod. She responded to the most subtle requests. I asked and then let go, and she responded. Ceasing to ask—as a method—was as crucial as asking: a touch of the rein to change direction, and immediately let go; a press behind the girth to ask for a change of pace, and immediately let go; a slight tension on the reins to slow the pace, and then immediately let go.

The other riders in the group were amazed to see Bo behaving so energetically. We moved up the line to be behind the lead horse because Bo was so enthusiastically engaged. I believe she responded to being trusted. The process of riding became almost invisible. It was exhilarating to feel such an immediate connection to Bo, despite it being the first time riding her.

Mind Training must be trusted and approached without prejudice. It must become like a love affair. Ask the mind to awaken and it will respond. Embrace emptiness of identity, and the intention to care for others, and awakening intention will arise. Nurture Mind Training so that it is ever-present in the mind.

The joy that arises through riding Mind Training in this way and caring for every aspect of riding the mind, naturally creates the wish for others to share this joy.

Thus awakening intention becomes ever-present. Then the possibility of being an inspiring example, so that others will also wish to experience the joy of Mind Training, further deepens involvement. This inseparability from practice radiates and communicates, and benefits everyone and everything, everywhere.

49

Always practise with whatever makes you boil.

bKol ba rNams la rTag tu bsGom

Regard the difficulties that arise—those that make you boil—as the greatest opportunities to engage the skills of riding.

If the horse misbehaves and the rider becomes angry, the three ordinary methods of dealing with anger are to express it, suppress it, or dissipate it.

Expressing anger at the horse's misbehaviour might involve shouting at the horse, whipping the horse, and generally being riled up (*boiling*). This adds fuel to the fire and will not help sort out the horse's behaviour. It is more likely to escalate it. To react in this way is to take the horse's misbehaviour personally, as an attack. The rider and horse become antagonists rather than riding partners. It is not possible to build a relationship of trust and confidence if the rider is continually experiencing and expressing anger.

Suppressing the anger is like putting a cap on a volcano. It is still there, roiling and boiling under the surface, but outwardly there is calm. This control may sooth the situation in the short term, but the horse will become aware of the volcanic tension below the calm veneer, and it will endanger the relationship. Seething unexpressed anger eats away at the rider. The sensation of the anger will make the horse nervous. Boiling anger that has been suppressed, can eventually become frozen. Then the rider may withdraw affection from the horse. The rider no longer communicates openly. Care of the horse becomes a duty rather than a pleasure. This will also destroy the relationship.

Dissipation is the least destructive of the three ordinary methods of dealing with anger. To dissipate the energy of the anger, the rider might make the horse trot for an extended period of time, or take it out for an unusually long ride. Alternatively, the rider may dissipate the anger apart from the horse through vigorous mucking out, or energetically polishing tack. The anger will not harm the horse through expression or suppression, but dissipation will still hamper the development of a deep relationship with the horse, although to a lesser degree.

Mind Training enables the *transformation* of anger so that none of the three ordinary methods are applied.

Transformation engages the energy of the boiling anger, but lets go of the conceptual content. It is the self-justification of anger, and dwelling on what is viewed as the external cause of it, that fuels the boiling.

The horse has misbehaved and the rider is angry. The rider takes responsibility for the anger, rather than laying the blame for it on the horse. The rider *owns* the anger, and lets go of the concept of the horse being the cause of the anger. The clarity of owning the anger enables the rider to address the horse's misbehaviour calmly and patiently. The rider can quietly ask something of the horse: a change of pace, a schooling exercise, a halt and spring into canter, to back-up – anything to engage the horse. If the horse responds, the rider can praise the horse. Then that is the end of it and the ride continues. Bad behaviour and anger are left in the past. They do not need to be looked at again.

If the horse continues to misbehave, the rider with clarity —rather than anger—is much more able to look at the cause of the misbehaviour. By avoiding a combative response, the basis of bad behaviour can be examined. Is the horse in pain? Is the horse misunderstanding or being asked incorrectly? Is too much being expected by the rider? So often the rider is the cause of a horse's misbehaviour.

> '... there is a real risk of losing your mind training in relation to those who harbour ill-will against you even though you have caused them no harm, and those you find unpleasant even though they harbour no ill-will toward you.'
> Thupten Jinpa – *Essential Mind Training*

Anything which provokes a strong emotional reaction—which makes the practitioner *boil*—is the greatest opportunity to practise. Immediately engage Mind Training.

Boiling is an experience of hot anger. Anger is said to be the most destructive of the afflicted emotions.

The ordinary methods of dealing with hot anger—expression, suppression, and dissipation—are connected to the three root misconceptions of attraction, aversion, and indifference.

> *'The moment we notice that painful tightening and constriction, that closing down, is the time to interrupt and undermine that whole destructive process.*
> *We can catch ourselves in the act, so to speak.'*
> Judith Lief – *Train Your Mind: Lojong Commentary*

50

Refrain from being influenced by external circumstances.

rKyen gZhan dag la lTos mi bya

Enter the dimension of riding the mind, and do not be diverted by external distractions.

When riding Dee or Red, I always tried to be completely engaged. Whatever occurred during the ride, I embraced as part of the experience. I tried to avoid dwelling on worries or difficulties in life, as this would distract from the enjoyment of riding. It would also be insulting to the horses. They deserved full attention whenever I was with them.

> *'When we feel very happy, our health is good, and everything seems to be going well, we feel that we can practise, whereas when we are feeling ill and things are going poorly, we think that we cannot practise. This is relying on external conditions to determine if we will practise or not.'*
> Thrangu Rinpoche – *The Seven Points of Mind Training*

Do not let life circumstances insult—or assault—Mind Training commitment. Pay full attention, and whatever occurs in life can then be experienced within the dimension of Mind Training. Such immersion in the dimension of practice, means that the methods of transforming life circumstances do not have to be drawn from memory. They are simply immediately present and available, and spontaneously applied.

The mind can be tricky. The practitioner settles down to meditate in silence, letting go of the content of mind – and suddenly the mind is bombarded with many *important* things that need immediate attention. These distractions must not be entertained. It is important to remain with the practice intention. If something is truly important, it will come to the mind again.

Speech can be tricky. The practitioner is about to sing a well-know practice, that is always sung to begin a session – and the tune is completely lost, or the words cannot be remembered. This must be observed with amusement and spaciousness, until memory returns.

The body can be tricky. When sitting comfortably and ready to meditate, the practitioner is suddenly afflicted with all sorts of itches, tickles, sensations, and irritations that make it impossible to sit still. To be resolute in practice, these must be ignored and sat through with stillness. It is not possible to settle the mind while fidgeting.

> *'It is very simple: if your situation is right, breathe that out; if your situation is wrong, breathe that in.'*
> Chögyam Trungpa Rinpoche – *Training the Mind*, p. 200

There is no such thing as a *bad* practice session. Even if it proves impossible to settle the distracted mind, the session is valuable in itself, because practice has been attempted wholeheartedly. Nevertheless perseverance is essential and an honest examination of distractions. There must be a willingness to avoid indulging them.

Life circumstances can be tricky. The practitioner wants to enter solitary retreat, or spend more time in formal practice every day, or simply be more present in every moment. Somehow, however, life circumstances always prevent it – life is too busy, or painful, or stressful, or there is ill health, loss, or many types of worries. Such difficulties may require attention, but it is not sensible to put off practice because of them. There will always be difficulties and distractions. It is important to practise through such circumstances, and embrace them as the fuel for practice. Practice cannot be reserved for an ideal time, place, or situation – that may never appear.

Mind Training must be applied to what is actually happening. Phenomena themselves are not the problem. Dissatisfaction arises from a distorted *relationship* with phenomena. Phenomena are blamed as the cause, but it is the untrained mind that is the cause of dissatisfaction. Everything is actually perfect *as it is*. Everything is actually the perfect opportunity for practice *as it is*.

Correct the relationship with phenomena—see clearly and directly—and life circumstances become the source of awakening rather than a distraction from engaging in Mind Training.

51

This time, make practice the priority.

da res gTso bo nyams su bLangs

*This time—this life, this moment—make presence,
alertness, and excellence in riding the mind
the most important priority.*

Living life without presence and attention, is like being on the back of a panicked and bolting horse – but not being aware of the consequences. It is like being on a bucking bronco, but being oblivious to the danger of being thrown. It is like approaching a high and challenging jump without preparing physically and mentally – the rider is unlikely to stay on the horse's back. The rider must wake up and notice what is happening. Action is needed, at once.

The need to engage Mind Training at all times and in all situations is immediate and urgent. There is immediate and present danger in the deluded patterning that has been indulged forever, and is preventing awakening. Action is needed. *Now.*

> '*If our clothes were on fire we would put out the fire immediately and urgently. The fire of neurotic patterning is burning us now, but we don't feel it, so we don't recognise the urgency. We put off practice till tomorrow… or the next day… or maybe next week…*'
> Ngakpa 'ö-Dzin – apprentice retreat, 2011

This time refers to this life, and this moment. There have been countless missed opportunities to help others in the past. There have been innumerable responses arising from delusion that have harmed others in the past. Mind Training enables practitioners to be present, alert, and attentive in the present moment. *This time* the opportunity to help need not be missed. *This time* the hurtful response can be avoided. Joyfully recognise the extraordinary power of Mind Training and engage it now, this time, every time.

This time recognise that only Mind Training can effectuate real change and lead to awakening.

This time see that only practice can put an end to the continual experience of dissatisfaction for oneself and others, and lead to awakening.

This time break the pattern of delusion, and engage the practices of awakening view and awakening intention that can create the experience of satisfaction for everyone everywhere.

> '... *the best practitioners wear out their meditation cushions, not the soles of their shoes.*'
> Dilgo Khyentse Rinpoche – *Enlightened Courage*, p. 88

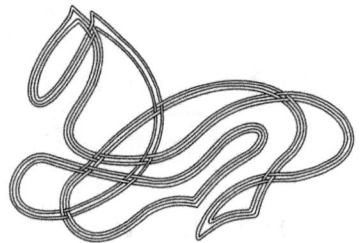

52

Refrain from falsifying and perverting.

go log mi bya

Do not limit the potential of Mind Training by riding the mind incorrectly or distorting the methods.

In *Black Beauty* there is an incident when Black Beauty knows that the bridge has been damaged by the flood water, but the carriage driver tries to urge him forward.

> '*We were going along at a good pace, but the moment my feet touched the first part of the bridge I felt sure there was something wrong.*
> *I dare not go forward, and I made a dead stop.*
> *"Go on, Beauty," said my master, and he gave me a touch with the whip, but I dare not stir; he gave me a sharp cut;*
> *I jumped, but I dare not go forward.*
> *"There's something wrong, sir," said John, and he sprang out of the dog-cart and came to my head and looked all about.*
> *He tried to lead me forward.*
> *"Come on, Beauty, what's the matter?"*
> *Of course I could not tell him, but I knew very well that the bridge was not safe.*
> *Just then the man at the toll-gate on the other side ran out of the house, tossing a torch about like one mad.*
> *"Hoy, hoy, hoy! halloo! stop!" he cried.*
> *"What's the matter?" shouted my master.*
> *"The bridge is broken in the middle, and part of it is carried away; if you come on you'll be into the river."*
> *"Thank God!" said my master.*
> *"You Beauty!" said John...*'
> Anna Sewell – *Black Beauty*, 1911 American Edition, p. 37

Black Beauty knew something was wrong and should have been trusted. The owner's experience of *Black Beauty* should have informed him that this was unusual behaviour and did not warrant the whip.

Mind Training creates the capacity to know, to have discriminating awareness. Attention must be paid to this and it must not be ignored. The trained mind can assess the situation accurately, but the mind of distraction wants to plough on across the bridge anyway. The trained mind knows that the methods of Mind Training should be trusted, but the distracted mind whips circumstances, and blames them for a lack of progress.

> '*We were off trail and approaching a ravine when we heard the sound of distant thunder. I looked up through the trees and saw a perfectly clear blue sky. I wondered how there could be thunder. Maybe it was a long way off? Suddenly the three horses stopped. The other riders were about to urge their horses forward — but I said "Let's just see what happens — maybe our horses know something." In less than a minute, over a hundred elk stampeded down the defile ahead of us — and up the other side. If they had succeeded in urging their horses forward — it could have ended horribly.*'
> Ngak'chang Rinpoche — recounting a story of riding in Montana with two apprentices.

Do not look for reasons to ignore the advice of the Lama. Do not take the easier or more convenient option, when there is an opportunity to engage in awakening. This slogan looks at deliberately ignoring or distorting the qualities that have been developed through Mind Training; or deliberately ignoring or distorting the methods.

> '*Our primary ambivalence is that we wish for realisation at the same time as wishing against it.*'
> Khandro Déchen — *The Ten Paramitas*, aroencyclopaedia.org

Practitioners want to let go of identity, but identity-fixation wants to remain and watch itself disappear. Practitioners want to hold the awakening intent of putting the needs of others before personal needs, but identity-fixation is needy-greedy and finds ways to put itself first. Even if practitioners are regarded as inspiring, they know when they are being lazy or distracted. They know when they are falsifying or perverting the results of practice.

> '*… An undercurrent that runs through this slogan is the strong pull of samsara. Lojong practice goes against the grain and threatens our cosy samsaric cocoon, so we try to figure out ways to be dharma practitioners without having to give anything up. We long for transformation, but we really don't want to change anything.*'
> Judith Lief — *Train Your Mind: Lojong Commentary*

Mind Training must be trusted and progress allowed to continue. Practitioners must not develop so far, and then get cold feet. Success must not be recognised as within grasp, and then abandoned. To be partially awake, is to still be asleep. Do not put obstacles in the path of awakening by being false, and perverting Mind Training. Awakening heroes and heroines must indeed be heroic, proclaiming a *Battlecry of Freedom*, and committing to the utmost end of the journey – until awakening is fully achieved.

53

Refrain from being sporadic.

res 'jog mi bya

*Ride and train the mind diligently and wholeheartedly
all the time, not just now and again.*

Ngakpa 'ö-Dzin and I had an idea of moving out of the city in 2011, and buying a place with land where the horses could live with us. Fortunately we were never able to find a place that matched our needs within our budget. The places we could afford were too far from Ngakpa 'ö-Dzin's work, or too small.

I say *fortunately* because I now realise that my image of living with the horses was a rosy fantasy based on the best of owning horses. Whilst Dee and Red lived at livery, even partial livery, I was never wholly responsible for their care. I believe my lack of experience could have been a problem, and the time needed for the horses' total care would have been difficult to accommodate within our other commitments. At the trekking centre they were able to roam thirty acres. This kept them fit without needing regular exercise being ridden. The herd would spontaneously gallop around the fields at least once a day, which was a marvellous sight to witness. A three-acre plot would not have provided the same opportunities.

Horses need daily attention to be happy, healthy, and capable mounts. They do not thrive on sporadic attention, and this is also true of the mind. The mind is trained through the steady and continual application of practice. It needs to be established as an on-going, daily activity. This slogan stresses the need to be committed to the intention of engaging in practice.

When I introduce new people to meditation, I always emphasise the importance of *daily* practice. Consistency of daily practice is as important as the time spent in practice. It is better to practise for a short period *every* day than to practise for longer periods more occasionally. It is more effective to practise ten minutes a day, *every* day, than to practice an hour once a week.

We have a saying for beginners in our meditation group: *have you had your ten a day?* – meaning *have you practised for ten minutes today?*[42] The steady drip of practice gradually erodes habitual patterning. Beginners can sometimes find it difficult to establish a daily practice, and it is important to set realistic and achievable goals. This creates a healthy pattern of stability in daily practice. Once ten minutes a day is being consistently overshot and effortlessly turns into a fifteen or twenty minute session, the duration of a daily commitment can be adjusted. In this way the length of a practitioner's daily practice session can gradually increase.

> *'... once you make a decision to practise mind training, you should stick with it so that it becomes a steady thread throughout your life. Although your circumstances are always changing, your commitment to mind training should be unwavering.'*
> Judith Lief – *Train Your Mind: Lojong Commentary*

Practice should be engaged without expectation. Sometimes practice is inspiring, and this can make it easy to apply. Continuing to practise through periods of dullness and distraction, boredom and frustration, is the mark of a real practitioner. This is when intention has to be resolute and self-discipline firm.

> *'The problem with vacillation—vacillating between two or any number of directions—is that one never gets anywhere with anything. The energy expended in recommencing each alternate involvement takes far more energy than simply continuing – even at a lower level of exertion.'*
> Ngak'chang Rinpoche – in conversation

---

42 This phrase echoes the *5 a Day* campaign. This was launched by the UK National Health Service in March 2003, to encourage people to eat at least five portions of fruit and vegetables every day for better health. Five portions is not actually sufficient to provide a healthy diet, but it is a good starting point. As this campaign is so well-known in the UK, the phrase *'Have you had your 10 a Day'* is immediately recognisable for beginners and usually raises a smile. Ten minutes of meditation a day is a good place for a beginner to start.

Practitioners must reach the point where Mind Training is as natural a part of everyday life as washing, eating, brushing teeth, exercising, and so forth. The intention to practice with regularity and commitment must be held. Then the natural result of Mind Training will manifest. The mind will begin to awaken.

54

Check how much you are gripped by training.

dol tshod du sByang

Riders who ride the trail in the rain, the cold, and the wind; and who prioritise the needs of the horse over their own, are truly gripped by equestrianism.

Horse owners can be extraordinarily selfless in relation to their horses. They are so in love with equestrianism, that they devote their free time and their disposable income to their horses. The reward for this is the joy of riding, and the joy of the relationship with their horses.

This relationship is deeper and more intimate than the relationship with a pet, such as a dog or cat. Riders ride their horses, and move through the landscape upon them. Riders develop the capacity to influence their horses through their intention and their body, and their horses willingly cooperate. Harnessing the power, suppleness, and capacity of such large animals through the intimate cooperation of riding on their backs, is an extraordinary experience.

Through riding, physical activities can be experienced that are beyond the capacity of human beings, but without employing a mechanical vehicle. The feats of horse capacity are experienced by riders through riding. They enjoy exhilarating experiences through their intimate connection with their horses, such as moving at speed, gracefully dancing a dressage exercise, or soaring over a jump. The relationship between engaged horses and riders is unique and unsurpassed.

Through this deep relationship with another species, riders can also come to know themselves in an extraordinary manner. Riding requires the shift in focus from self to horse. Riders must be present and able to be leaders for their horses, and at the same time receptive and sensitive to the character and power of their horses.

The rider is both emptiness and form – the receptive empty presence in the saddle, and the authoritative leader. The horse is also emptiness and form – the receptive and sensitive being that yields to the rider's requests, and the powerful animal that responds with energy and capability.

> *'Train uninterruptedly in Mind Training*
> *until it becomes your nature.'*
> Shamar Rinpoche – *The Path to Awakening*, p. 158

Anyone who has experienced the union of horse and rider in this way, cannot help but be transfixed by the experience. It is impossible to fail to be captivated by such a relationship of harmony and cooperation. The relationship with Mind Training must develop the same intimacy and intensity. The practitioner must become transfixed, captivated, entranced, enthralled, fascinated, engrossed, enraptured, and gripped by Mind Training.

The power, suppleness, and capacity of the trained mind must be ridden. The more the mind is trained, the greater is the experience of extraordinary cooperation with awakening.

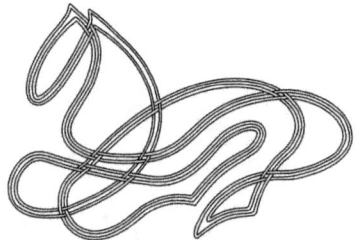

55

Escape duality through investigation and analysis.

brTags dPyad gNyis kyis thar bar bya

Investigate riding without stirrups to discover emptiness of stirrups.
Investigate riding with stirrups to discover the form of stirrups.
Escape duality by riding with stirrups
— as if riding without stirrups.

We would regularly have lessons in Grade III without stirrups and without reins. We crossed our stirrups over in front of our saddles so that they did not bang against the horses, or against the riders' legs. Usually we practised rising trot in lessons, but without stirrups we would experience a sitting trot. This was an excellent method to learn to sit deeply in our saddles, to feel the shape of our horses, and to learn to balance with the movement of the horses. I remember spending lessons of over an hour riding without stirrups at walk, trot, and canter. This could be quite challenging, and demanded both attention, and relaxation.

When riding without reins, they would be knotted and placed onto the horses' necks. The horses often dropped their heads down low, stretching their necks and relaxing when the reins were dropped. This could create a rather disconcerting feeling a bit like vertigo, of having nothing in front of you. This exercise would encourage an upright posture, less reliance on the reins for control, and more confidence with leg aids.

In the beginning of meditation practice, practitioners let go of thought because the usual experience is of thought dominating the mind.[43] Letting go of thought is like dropping the reins or crossing the stirrups. The security of thought is given up in order to discover mind-without-thought.[44]

Riding without stirrups or reins is not normal riding. It is a method to improve normal riding. In the same way, mind-without-thought is not a natural state, but it is a useful state to experience and stabilise.

---

43 The word *thought* is used here to describe *that which arises in the mind*. The Tibetan term is *namthog* (*rNam rTog*, Skt. *vikalpa*). Commonly namthog means *discursive thought* – but in Dzogchen it means *that which moves in mind*.
44 Mind-without-thought is an experience of the emptiness of mind: nè-pa (*gNas pa*), the fruit of the practice of shi-nè (*zhi gNas*) – remaining uninvolved.

Through being able to dwell in stabilised mind-without-thought, practitioners discover emptiness. Then from the basis of the experience of emptiness, thought can be allowed to arise again, and be examined in the context of mind-without-thought.[45] Thought is observed arising, abiding, and dissolving. The content of thought is not involved in the examination, merely the movement.

> *'Thought cannot examine itself in any ultimate sense – it is a closed system. Thought can no more examine its own nature than a knife cut itself, or an eye see itself. The only way an eye can see itself is to avail itself of a mirror. The nature of that mirror—vis-à-vis thought—is the natural reflective capacity of Mind, which is beyond thought. To investigate the nature of thought – we need to use some capacity other than thought.'*
> Khandro Déchen and Ngak'chang Rinpoche – Shock Amazement, p. 46

When, after a period of sitting trot without stirrups, the stirrups are taken back, they feel too short. The depth of sitting has been developed, and the muscles of the hips and legs allowed to lengthen and relax, so that the stirrups need to be lengthened to be comfortable. When the reins are taken back after a period of riding without them, the contact with the horse's mouth is felt more sensitively. The rider becomes more aware of the horse rounding its neck and tucking in its head to accommodate contact on the bit. This can enable the rider to have a lighter touch on the reins and treat the contact through the bit with greater care and respect.

When mind-without-thought has been experienced as a period of stable emptiness, thought—form—is allowed to re-emerge. Previously thought was a continual noise in the mind, undifferentiated and unobserved. Now thought is experienced from a new perspective. The movement of thought can be observed without getting lost in its content. If attention is lost, the practitioner returns to mind-without-thought until that is stable again.

---

45 Lhatong (*lha mThong*) – further vision; Skt. *vipassana*.

Through the discovery of emptiness, the relationship with thought has changed – just as the relationship with stirrups and reins changed through riding without them. The rider does not get caught up with analysing why the legs feel longer and the seat deeper in the saddle, or how the reins feel lighter and more connected to the horse. The rider simply enters into the dimension of the difference in the experience of riding.

In Dzogchen, the investigation of the movement of thought is described as observing a jumping fish. There is a still lake. The fish jumps out of the still lake, and then disappears back into the lake. The lake becomes still once more. The observer engages with the movement of the fish without allowing the mind to snag on looking for the details of the fish.

> *'No comment is made on the namthogs. There are no judgements as to whether the jumping fish are beautiful or grotesque – presence of awareness is simply found in their movement. One allows oneself to become identified with* that which moves.'
> Khandro Déchen and Ngak'chang Rinpoche – Shock Amazement, p. 52

The practitioner moves between emptiness and form – the practices of remaining without thought, and observing the movement of thought. The investigation and analysis of what is the same about these two experiences, becomes the means to escape duality.[46]

> *'Simultaneous awareness of the* clear lake *and the* leaping fish *is the first glimpse of nondual experience. This is the discovery of nyi'mèd – and the vivid portal of Dzogchen.'*
> Khandro Déchen and Ngak'chang Rinpoche – Shock Amazement, p. 63

---

46 Nyi'mèd (*nyi 'med*) – not two.

56

Avoid boastful behaviour.

yus ma sGom

Avoid boasting about the achievements of riding the mind,
as if they have been accomplished alone.
Every achievement in Mind Training is dependent on others.

In the summer months, whilst she lived at the riding school, Dee was turned out at night in a large paddock next to the arena. I always thought of this as Dee's paddock. There were a number of logs in this paddock and it was sometimes used for jumping lessons. One log in particular was rather large and usually ignored in lessons because it was so high and wide. On one occasion, however, at the end of the Grade III lesson, the instructor was encouraging us to jump the huge log. The instructor was herself an experienced and capable show jumper and owned a beautiful stallion. We had two trainee instructors with us that day, plus the regular group of adults.

None of the other regular group members would attempt jumping the huge log. I think this was a reasonable response, knowing how the school horses could behave in jumping lessons. The two trainee instructors were expected to jump it and they were riding able horses. They jumped it with no problems. And then there was me, on Dee. I knew that if she turned and approached the log at a good pace that she would jump it. I felt that I would know in advance, by a sense of hesitation and reluctance, if she felt the jump was beyond her capability.

I cantered away from the log, turned her, and pointed her at the jump. She approached the log at a good pace without a hint of hesitation. We soared over it. It was the largest jump I have ever taken on any horse before or since. I am glad to have done it, but I know full well that it had very little to do with my capability and everything to do with Dee. I was congratulated by the instructor, but she intelligently congratulated me for the relationship I had developed with Dee, rather than for my capacity as a rider.

I could have become puffed up about having done what none of the other class members would do. This would have been foolish and dangerous.

It would have spoiled the open joyfulness of the moment, ignored the reality of Dee being the essential factor, and potentially created problems for me in future lessons if I believed too much in my capabilities.

> *'I was riding Mr Darcy – a fast moving 16 and a half hand horse at a jump. I was without fear only because I had no concept that Melissa Troupe —my instructor—could be in error about the situation. It was entirely insane to be flying into the air on 1,500 lbs of horse. The situation was outside my comprehension of what was possible – and so I had no way of making any intellectual judgment about what was happening. Melissa told me that although Khandro Déchen was a far better rider – that I was a better jumper. That still vaguely baffles me. I feel that the only factor that kept me safe was that I was unable to think. Mr Darcy did it all. I merely failed to fall.'*
> Ngak'chang Rinpoche describing his jumping experience as *'being open to the insanity of the situation'* – personal communication

When practitioners recognise some success in Mind Training, identity-fixation wants to take the credit. Identity-fixation wants to be congratulated and recognised as the great practitioner. In fact any success in awakening is due to the nondual state sparkling through the web of duality. The nondual state has no conditioned, self-satisfied identity. For identity to assert ownership and credit for progress in Mind Training is like a reflection claiming it is responsible for the capacity of the mirror to reflect.

> *'… avoid thinking, "Oh, I was so kind to that person." Or, "Oh, I practice so well. I try so hard. I'm so good."'*
> Thrangu Rinpoche – *The Seven Points of Mind Training*

To practise Mind Training is a personal choice. Its value is inestimable, and ultimately it is the cause of awakening. Practice commitment is not a trophy or a mark of status. Practitioners are not worthy of greater respect or consideration than non-practitioners – in fact quite the reverse. Practitioners must appreciate their great good fortune in having access to Mind Training, and thereby the means to awaken.

Practitioners must recognise that all other beings and circumstances have been the means of their practising Mind Training. Success in practice should not be the cause of self-aggrandisement, therefore, but the cause of humble appreciation.

> *'... if you have correctly distinguished between enemy and friend,*
> *you understand everyone to be a friend.*
> *Then even when you work for others' welfare,*
> *the jaundice of self-centredness does not arise.'*
> Thupten Jinpa – *Essential Mind Training*

57

Avoid being constricted by jealousy and frustration.

ko long ma sDam

*Do not become frustrated, making comparisons
with other riders, as this will undermine
the quality of riding the mind.*

There was one lady in the Grade III class who was clearly a favourite with the instructors. She was always given one of the best horses, praised more than anyone else, and given special attention. She also took private lessons and was studying to take an equestrian examination, so it was understandable that the instructors knew her well and wished to bring her on.

In contrast, I was always given one of the least agile and responsive horses. After having been given *Saffron*—a particularly difficult mare—week after week, and having questioned this verbally to no effect, I eventually wrote a formal letter of complaint to the riding school. The school was owned by the Council, so they had to take notice and reply properly to this formal approach. Thereafter I was given a range of different horses in the Grade III lessons – but never one of the best horses. The situation was resolved by purchasing Dee, as I was then given her to ride in every lesson for the six months we continued with her living there. I ceased having lessons after that.

I liked the lady who was given the best horses to ride, and received special attention, and I was able to avoid allowing jealousy to spoil my friendly relationship with her. Not being *bound* by jealousy—though certainly experiencing some frustration—I was able to act to address the situation in a calm and sensible manner.

This slogan communicates a strong sense of being limited —*bound*—by nervous energy. The intrinsic energy of accomplishment is limited in its flow and potential by the constriction of identity-fixation, which creates jealousy and frustration. Personal identity wants to keep checking to see that no-one else is doing better. There is suspicion and paranoia about others' motivation and intention. Personal identity is frustrated, wanting the situation to be different to how it actually is. It gets all wound up with the impotent energy of wanting to change it, but being unable to do so.

> 'There is a lot of appreciation in jealousy – it is just that the appreciation has become distorted. We are always jealous of the things that we want for ourselves – things that are desirable for us and therefore appreciated. It is as if we missed our stop on the train and got off at a station too far along. If we can go back to the point of simply appreciating, then the distortion that leads to jealousy will naturally unwind itself.'
> Ngakpa 'ö-Dzin Tridral – *Working with Emotions* retreat, Vienna, June, 2017

It is not possible to rest in alert presence and appreciation, whilst there is jealousy, suspicion, paranoia, frustration. The effort of checking everything—but appreciating nothing—prevents expansive openness. Jealousy will not succeed in creating better luck. Suspicion and paranoia will not create relaxed and friendly relationships with others. Frustration will not force a change in the situation. All these emotions relate to personal identity, and caring more about the self than others.

Mind Training dissolves the investment in identity-fixation as the source of security, and transfers concern for supporting personal identity to concern for helping others. The wish for others to be happy and successful, prevents jealousy arising. In prioritising others, personal identity lets go of concern about the motivation and intent of their actions with regard to itself. If the view is held that everything is perfect as it is, and everything is the perfect opportunity to awaken, there can be relaxation, and frustration dissolves. Mind Training develops awakening view and awakening intention, and embraces reality exactly as it is.

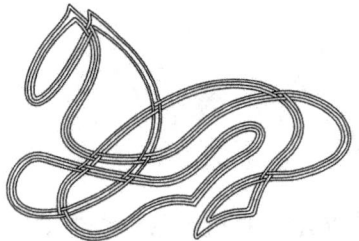

58

Refrain from practising just a little.

yud tsam pa mi bya

*Consistency and commitment create an
empowering relationship when riding the mind.*

Steadiness is most important for a horse rider. The rider must be the leader and the steady support for the horse. The horse's instincts, as a prey animal, are to be wary of everything as a potential predator, and to be ready to flee if necessary. The rider functions as the herd leader – the protector and supporter of the horse, the reassuring presence that enables the horse to overcome its instinct of fight or flight.

Through the qualities given and received by horse and rider, their cooperation enables them both to be greater than they are alone, and to achieve extraordinary feats. A horse may be able to jump a five-bar gate, but it will not usually do so unless it has a reason. If escape from a predator is the reason, the horse will jump the gate. A horse is supple and powerful and can perform extraordinary athletic movements. An exuberant young horse can be seen naturally performing actions that a dressage trainer would name as a pirouette, piaffe, levade, courbette, croupade, and capriole. The rider can engage natural horse capacity, improving power and strength, to develop the capability in the mature horse to perform such actions.

Dedicated, consistent work in the chosen discipline, is needed to achieve the potential of the rider and the horse. Even if all that will be asked of the horse is a gallop through the wood, or the confidence to explore new trails and tackle challenging terrain, there still needs to be a nurtured and developed relationship between the horse and rider.

In the same way, practitioners must nurture the relationship with their practice intention. It is excellent to avoid the sloppiness of sporadic practice and establish a daily practice commitment. It is excellent to successfully accomplish that intention. Now the application of Mind Training *within* that practice commitment is examined.

Is the intention of the session being carried through? Or is it allowed to become dissipated through laziness or distraction? Such dissipation is what is meant by *practising just a little*.

Steadiness and consistency is essential in every practice session. If the intention was to let go of thought – was that the focus of the session? If the intention was to examine the movement of thought – was that the focus of the session?

If the intention was to practice tonglen, lama'i naljor, or visualisation – was that the focus of the session? Or was something else the focus of the mind during the practice session? Practitioners must avoid capriciousness and frivolity in relation to their practice.

> '*Do not change your expression from cheery to depressed at the slightest provocation, because this will only upset your companions.*'
> Thogme Zangpo – *Commentary on the Seven Points of Mind Training*

Similarly the demeanour of being a committed practitioner of Mind Training must be consistent at all times. Moodiness, being temperamental, fickle or oversensitive should be avoided. Waking up in a bad mood should be transformed with practice, and the expression of moodiness avoided. Feeling irritable should not be justified by illness, sadness, or tiredness, and allowed to adversely affect others. Practitioners take responsibility for their mind-state. They do not vomit emotionalism on others.

> '*If bad things happen, we should not get overly upset or depressed; if good things happen, we should not get overly excited and happy. The idea is to be very even-tempered. Whatever happens, good or bad, we should stay on an even keel.*'
> Thrangu Rinpoche – *The Seven Points of Mind Training*

Practitioners must be steady, but steadiness does not mean seriousness, gravity, severity, solemnity, sombreness, or dourness in particular.

Mind Training develops joyfulness, vitality and sparkle. A sense of humour, and delight in humour, is a natural part of that. The recognition that duality is created—actively and wilfully—is humorous. No one is doing this to anyone else – it is not a scene of torture. If there is torture, it is that identity-fixation is torturing itself, by trying to make identity exist beyond the present moment.

It could be viewed as amusing that when sitting, with the intention of allowing the mind to become empty, the mind insists on being full of thought. It could be humorous to know that the intention to cut the flow of an unskilful pattern is resolute, but somehow the pattern keeps happening. It is a choice whether to view these situations as amusing or frustrating. To view them as frustrating would be the moody choice. To view them as amusing would be the awakening choice.

> '*Particularly avoid the Triple S Syndrome:*
> *Sulky, Sullen, and Surly.*'
> Ngak'chang Rinpoche – in conversation

Duality is ludicrous from the perspective of nonduality. Undermining duality should be taken seriously, but the fact of *needing* to undermine the self-creation of duality is humorous.

Practitioners take responsibility for the content of their practice and the content of their minds. Explode that mood. Do not indulge it. Explode laziness and distraction. Do not take a holiday from the demeanour and intention of Mind Training. Focussed intent, and the wish to prioritise others' needs, must be *ever-present*—not just there for a little, and *sometimes-present*. Never allow awakening view and awakening intent to diminish.

> '*Taking Offence is the major popular sport of this era.*
> *People of most Western countries have become highly skilled at it.*'
> Ngak'chang Rinpoche and Khandro Déchen – commenting to their students on the subject of moodiness

59

Do not wish for thanks.

'or che ma 'dod

The rider decides to ride.
Do not expect to be thanked for it.

There was one field at the trekking centre that grew particularly good grass. The owners would not allow the horses into this field until the autumn, so that they could have a feast before the winter, and fatten up a little. One year we happened to be at the livery yard on the day that the herd was being allowed into this pasture. Ngakpa 'ö-Dzin and I were taken down in a Land Rover to a safe vantage point just by the pasture. There we waited until the gate was opened and the stampede began.

We heard the horses long before we saw them. It was an amazing sight. From tiny rescue Shetland ponies and elderly retired horses, to the fittest and largest geldings and mares – they all galloped full pelt to the pasture. It was like watching a tsunami. Arriving at the pasture they cascaded out around the field like a wave breaking and settling, and began to happily graze.

I believe that horses enjoy their excursions with their riders. I think for some their relationship with being ridden is similar to many humans' relationship with taking exercise. Horses would quite like to be left alone, grazing in the field, and mooching about, but in fact they thrive on being asked to work and through embracing their potential. Riders choose horses that display a natural capacity in particular disciplines. I was once told by a lady who competed at a high level, that show jumping horses could tend to be either brave or be careful, and to find one that had both qualities was exceptional. Dee had both qualities, and I know that Dee loved to jump. No-one ever forced Dee to take a jump. It was her natural capability and a pleasure for her.

My experience of horses is that they cannot be forced to do anything, but that it is their natural temperament to enjoy giving what is asked. The rider judges the potential of the horse, and sees what it enjoys, and engages that.

> *'I used a side-pull bosal[47] on Malachi in Montana, but I cut out the rawhide strap and replaced it with a leather band. I did this to prevent hurting the thin-skinned horse. Of course, this plain leather band gave me no control at all: Malachi simply obliged me in my requests. It was all fine until he wanted to take the short trail home. I tried to turn him – but each time I did so he just backed me into a tree. I knew I could not force him. One cannot use strength against a horse because the horse will win. Anger has never been an option in my repertoire – and so I decided that I would simply keep riding him forward and gently attempting to turn him. I would do that all day and into the night if necessary.*
> *On the fifth attempt Malachi made a movement with his head as if to say "Oh—alright then—if it's what you really want…"*
> *Strangely enough—after that—our relationship became entirely problem free.'*
> Ngak'chang Rinpoche – private communication

During the three months when Dee could not be ridden, but still needed to be exercised, I would occasionally set up a jump for her in the manège. I would take her in and remove her headcollar. It was an inexpressible joy to watch Dee taking the jump again and again of her own free will. She took the jump for the sheer joy of jumping.

I am grateful to everything that every horse gave me as a rider. I jumped on Dee more than on any other horse I rode throughout my life. I am grateful to her for those experiences. I did not, however, expect Dee to be grateful to me. Why would I? Everything we did together I asked of her. She never asked anything of me. She gave generously and fully. Every horse that allows a rider on its back, and responds to the requests of the rider is giving. Every rider must be grateful to the horse. It would be ridiculous to expect the horse to be grateful to the rider.

---

47 An American bitless bridle that functions through the pressure of a hard rawhide strap across the horse's nose.

> *'I think devotion is more like the tremendous gratitude*
> *that comes from having a glimpse of one's own enlightened nature*
> *and understanding at the same time that this happened*
> *as a result of the Lama.'*
> Ngakma Shardröl – *Essential Characteristics of Vajrayana: Devotion,*
> aroencyclopaedia.org

Mind Training is the greatest opportunity it is possible to be given in life. Mind Training is the path to awakening – to realise nonduality, to dwell in rigpa. Practitioners should not ask to be congratulated and thanked for training their minds.

> *'Don't expect applause.'*
> Chögyam Trungpa Rinpoche – *Training the Mind,* p. 205

If it is felt that thanks and applause are deserved, then there is still a lot of work to be done. Such an attitude is not awakened view, but rather, is somewhat ridiculous. Practitioners may feel slightly embarrassed if they notice that they would actually quite like a standing ovation. Wryly recognise the wish for approval and appreciation, smile at the recognition – and return to practice.

The reward of practice is the capacity for more practice. Ultimately the reward of more practice is awakening.

Part III
practising Mind Training

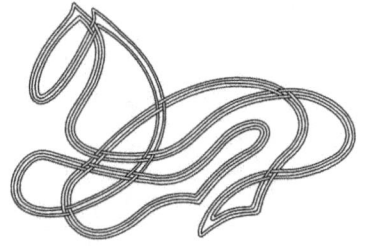

1 – Progression through the Seven Points of Mind Training

The Seven Points of Mind Training are:

1. Preliminary practice, the foundation of the teaching.
2. Awakened mind, the purpose and basis of training.
3. Transforming bad circumstances into the path of awakening.
4. Applying the essential practice and teaching to the whole of life.
5. Evaluating Mind Training.
6. The commitments of Mind Training.
7. Advice on Mind Training.

Preliminary practices are the subject of Point One of Mind Training. These practices offer a glimpse of awakening, the fruit of practice. Awakening is examined in Point Two. Then in Point Three, the methods of Mind Training are introduced. These first three points express the fundamental principles of the vehicles of Buddhism: the base, fruit, and path.

Through embracing the principles of the Buddhist vehicles, practice is engaged, which gives rise to capacity. Practitioners develop experience of Mind Training and begin to embrace awakening. This manifesting capacity is expressed in Point Four as the five powers: confidence, energy, presence, alertness, discriminating awareness.

Through continuing to practise Mind Training, and applying the five powers, the intelligent practitioner evaluates progress. This is Point Five. From that evaluation a firm and determined commitment arises.

The commitments of Mind Training are examined in Point Six. Finally Point Seven offers advice for deepening and maintaining commitment.

Living the view is the fundamental practice of Mind Training. The entire context of life becomes practice. There are periods of formal daily practice, and retreat – and then there is the rest of life. In daily life, the experience and insight gained through formal practice and retreat is applied. Living the view takes the understanding of *awakening* into every moment of existence. View is refined and cultivated, and then simply applied.

Living the view does not mean carrying a conceptual framework with which to filter experience. This would destroy spontaneity. Living the view is a felt experience as much as a practice of recollection and application. Capacity to awaken through daily life grows through continual interaction with the teacher, the path, and the naturally arising circumstances of life as opportunities for practice.

Capable and experienced riders do not have to run through the manual on aids in their mind, to know where to apply their legs, or how to shift their balance, or whether to tighten the reins. Riders enter the dimension of riding through the experience of being on horses' backs. Living the view is riding the horse of mind.

Mind Training offers a comprehensive and approachable method of living the view. The slogans continually return the practitioner to the principles of practice, to the purpose of practice, to the methods of practice. Mind Training warns of the downfalls and hindrances to practice, and describes the benefits. It is both profound and pragmatic, inspirational and sobering, subtle and simple. If fully embraced, it offers a complete path to awakening.

> *'Easy to understand, it is not corrupted.*
> *Easy to practice, it is entered with enthusiasm.*
> *Yet it is profound, so buddhahood is attained.'*
> Jamgon Kongtrul – *The Great Path of Awakening*, p. 2

Point One: Preliminary practice – the foundation of the teaching.

First, train in the preliminaries.
(slogan 1)

Point One contains this single slogan. Preparation is necessary before embarking on any journey. Preliminary practices are the starting point, from where the journey can begin. From this starting point, the methods of the path of that vehicle can then be employed, and *potential travellers* become *actual travellers*.

Every practitioner in any discipline that is approached, will engage in some form of preparatory practices. For a musician this will be learning how to hold or sit at the instrument, how to produce a pleasant sound, practising scales, and so forth. For a horse rider this will be learning how to approach the horse, mount the horse, adjust the stirrups, hold the reins, and eventually learning how to catch, groom, and tack the horse.

In Buddhism the preliminary practices will depend on how and where the beginner commences. They will depend on the teacher and community who are approached, and the vehicle in which their style of practice is based. Chekhawa does not specify the preliminary practices, but emphasises their crucial importance.

Arrival at the destination of any journey, is dependent on setting out. Starting can be the hardest step. As soon as the traveller begins, momentum is gained and progress becomes easier. Once the journey has started, arriving at the destination is immediately a possibility. In the Seven Points, this is indicated by Chekhawa moving, without hesitation, straight to the destination of Mind Training in Point Two. The destination is awakened mind.

Point Two: Awakened Mind – the purpose and basis of training.

Awaken by regarding all phenomena as dreamlike,
and discovering the nature of unborn primordial awareness.
Then allow the method to self-liberate into the natural condition of
the mind, and rest in that condition, regarding the
phenomena of daily life as illusory.
Awaken through fixing the breath on the practice of alternately
sending and receiving. Then examine the three objects of perception,
and the three poisons, to enable them to be transformed into three
roots of goodness. Remember to practise with slogans in
daily life in all activities and situations, and to begin
the practice of sending and receiving with oneself.
(slogans 2 – 10)

Point Two of Chekhawa's Seven Points introduces ultimate awakened view and relative—or relational—awakened intention. It presents the fundamental aspects of view and activity from the perspective of awakening.

Consider all phenomena as dreamlike. (slogan 2)

First the practitioner looks at the appearances of the mind, and recognises that they are dreamlike.

Examine fundamental unborn awareness. (slogan 3)

Secondly the mind itself is examined to see whether it exists. Through this examination, unborn primordial awareness is recognised.

> '*We might then wonder whether the mind itself is real,*
> *so the root text says: Examine the nature of unborn awareness.*'
> Thogme Zangpo – *Commentary on the Seven Points of Mind Training*

Method—examination and analysis—has been employed to directly experience the phenomena of the mind and to discover the natural condition of the mind.

Even the remedy self-liberates into its own natural condition.
(slogan 4)

Next, the instruction is to allow method—examination—to dissolve. Examination and analysis is ceased, so that the natural condition of the mind is experienced.

> *Remain in the dimension of kun-zhi, the essence of the path.* (slogan 5)

The practitioner is instructed to rest in that state. Resting in that state, the realisation is taken into daily life, and all phenomena are viewed as illusory.

> *Everything that arises in daily life is illusory.* (slogan 6)

These five slogans introduce awakening view.

The next five slogans of Point Two move on to introduce the principles of awakening intention. The focus of awakening intention is *other* – that is, everything that is not personal identity.

Firstly the primary method of awakening intention is introduced.

> *Train in alternately sending and receiving;*
> *fix these two on the breath.* (slogan 7)

Here the very *nature of being alive* is harnessed to awaken intention for the purpose of benefitting others. Breathing is utilised as the means, so that the rhythm of life itself becomes the cause of awakening. This impales the intention of being defined by the needs of *other* on every breath.

Having introduced this primary method of awakening intention, Chekhawa then turns the practitioner's mind to the barriers to awakening intention. These are deluded perception and deluded response:

> *Three objects, three poisons, three roots of goodness.* (slogan 8)

Deluded perception is referred to as the three objects, and deluded response is referred to as the three poisons.

Deluded perception and response are corrected through the view expressed in slogans 2 to 6, combined with the focus on others of slogan 7:

> *Regarding all phenomena as dreamlike,*
> *unborn primordial awareness is discovered.*
> *Allowing the method to self-liberate, the natural condition*
> *of the mind is present. Rest in that condition.*
> *Remain in the natural condition of the mind in daily life by*
> *regarding all phenomena as illusory.*
> *Be defined by the needs of others through impaling*
> *taking and giving on the breath.*
> (slogans 2 – 7)

Through awakening perception and response, the three objects and three poisons are transformed into the roots of goodness – into the means of awakening intention.

> '*Dzogchen means* utter totality, *and refers to the natural liberated condition of the individual. This state of innate enlightenment is always there, in its utter totality – simply waiting to be uncovered.*'
> Ngak'chang Rinpoche and Khandro Déchen – *Dzogchen Long-dé*,
> aroencyclopaedia.org

The practitioner now has everything that is needed to glimpse awakening, the fruit of practice. It is possible to begin to awaken view and intention. Chekhawa stresses that Mind Training must be practised at all times and in all situations. It must become a way of life.

> *In all activities, train with slogans.* (slogan 9)

Mind Training is not simply a practice for the meditation room and the meditation cushion. Practitioners must continually return to awakening view and intention whatever their situation.

The last slogan in Point Two indicates that it is not helpful or desirable for practitioners to be in pain.

> *Begin the sequence of sending and receiving with oneself.* (slogan 10)

Riding the breath is utilised in tonglen to awaken the intention to benefit others. The rhythm of life becomes harnessed to benefit others. Breathing in is receiving; breathing out is giving. Breathing in is dissolving form into emptiness. Breathing out is compassionate form arising.

The intention of tonglen is to switch the focus from self-orientation to other-orientation, but practitioners are best able to help others when healthy themselves. Hence, when it is practitioners themselves who are experiencing pain and dissatisfaction in the course of their lives, the practice of tonglen can be employed to help. When practitioners suffer illness, loss, and painful circumstances, these can be addressed through using themselves as the focus for the practice of taking and giving.

Practitioners breathe in and dissolve the experience of pain. Practitioners remember and ignite the joy and inspiration experienced through practice, and breathe this out. In this way, practitioners can relieve their own pain, and refresh their connection with practice. This will help liberate the joy and energy to practise wholeheartedly, that could be constricted by personal pain.

Practitioners develop the capacity to practise deeply at all times and in all situations in order to benefit everyone—including themselves—and everything, everywhere.

Point Three: Transformation – transforming bad circumstances into the path of awakening.

*When all experience is painful, recognise its single cause,
and be grateful to everyone and everything, everywhere
as the method of transforming experience.
Embrace the indivisibility of emptiness, energy and form,
recognising that emptiness protects the mind
from deluded perception and response.
Practise the four highest methods, immediately grasping all
opportunities as the means to awaken.*
(slogans 11 – 17)

The traveller has arrived at the starting point, and learned about the destination. The traveller has embraced the fundamental principles of the vehicle of travel. The journey has begun. Point Three of Mind Training looks at the path of transformation. Here, real engagement with Mind Training has commenced. These six slogans address the practitioner personally, and explain how to practice.

When the world and life is full of malice and bad circumstances, transform it into the path of awakening. (slogan 11)

Point Three begins by acknowledging that life is experienced as unsatisfactory – there is pain, there is malice, there are disturbing emotions. The oscillation between hope and fear, gain and loss, meeting and parting, praise and blame, is recognised as ordinary everyday experience.

Then the single cause of this experience of dissatisfaction is examined and recognised as the mistaken view of inherent personal identity.

Drive all blames into one. (slogan 12)

The protection and nurturing of personal identity is the major cause of all pain.

Transformation of dissatisfaction becomes possible by moving the focus away from the support and protection of identity, and toward benefitting others. Rather than focussing on personal pain and dissatisfaction, the pain and dissatisfaction of others is addressed.

> *'Lojong introduces a different attitude toward unwanted stuff:*
> *if it's painful, you become willing not just to endure*
> *it but also to let it awaken your heart and soften you.'*
> Pema Chödrön – *Always Maintain A Joyful Mind*, p. viii

Diversion of intention away from self to others, has the power to undermine the dominance of personal identity. Focus on others, therefore, becomes the means of awakening. Recognising this, gratitude spontaneously arises. Without others, and external circumstances, there is no basis for the transformation of duality into nonduality.

Practise gratitude to everyone and everything, everywhere. (slogan 13)

Practitioners cultivate this attitude of gratitude, embracing it as a method of awakening.

Through paying attention to the focus on the self as a cause of pain, and focussing on others as a cause of awakening, the nonduality of self and other is then examined. Nonduality is introduced by Chekhawa through examining the inseparability of the three spheres of being.

Meditating on the delusions as the four spheres, emptiness is unsurpassable protection. (slogan 14)

Emptiness is denied by the deluded mind that grasps at identity for security. Familiarity with emptiness is the greatest protection from this delusion. It reduces the dominance of identity, and the need to define all experience through substantiating identity.

Point Three then introduces the method to transform ordinary experience and grasping at an inherent identity.

Apply the four highest methods. (slogan 15)

Ordinary method embraces whatever supports identity, and rejects whatever threatens or challenges identity.
The first two of the Four Highest Methods reverses this ordinary method. First, practitioners embrace all activity that supports others and allows identity to be empty. Secondly, practitioners let go of activity that ignores the needs of others and supports inherent identity.

The third and fourth of the Four Highest Methods address practitioners' relationships with all phenomena. Whatever difficulties are encountered are welcomed as an opportunity to practise transformation. Nothing is rejected. Everything is accepted. Welcomed *as it is,* everything is viewed as a perfect opportunity for transformation. These perfect opportunities are then embraced and transformed through Mind Training.

Engagement with the Four Highest Methods is awakening.

The final instruction of Point Three emphasises that Mind Training must be practised at once, in the present moment.

> *Immediately join whatever you meet with meditation.* (slogan 16)

Everything that is encountered must be immediately embraced as an opportunity and *joined* with the awakening methods of Mind Training.

> *'Continual practice of meditation and attention to everyday conduct go together – they are two aspects of practice rather than two unrelated activities.'*
> Ken McCloud – Translator's Introduction, p. xvii,
> *The Great Path of Awakening*

Through the practice of transformation and developing experience of emptiness, mistaken view becomes increasingly transparent, and intention and activity become increasingly clear and luminous. Appreciation, kindness, a loving and grateful attitude toward everyone and everything, everywhere begins to sparkle into being. This is the path which will awaken the mind.

Point Four: The Five Powers – applying the essentialised practice and teaching to the whole of life.

> *Apply the five perfect powers.* (slogan 17)
> *The five powers are the only crucial manner of conduct.* (slogan 18)

Through Points One, Two, and Three, the base, the fruit, and the path of Mind Training have been presented. If the slogans have indeed been embraced, the traveller is now a practitioner. In the remaining four points of Mind Training, Chekhawa assumes that the practice has indeed been adopted. From here onward, he is addressing awakening practitioners.

Through practising Mind Training, the five powers—or strengths—begin to manifest. Point Four examines the capacity that naturally arises from practising.

> '*The two slogans of Point Four are a blanket approach: you are blanketing your entire life with exertion. It takes exertion to live properly and it also takes exertion to die properly.*'
> Judith Lief – *Train Your Mind: Lojong Commentary*

The five powers indicate certainty and confidence in Mind Training. Practitioners willingly and energetically apply themselves, with alertness, presence, and intelligent discrimination.

Practitioners are so rooted in Mind Training that they will continue to develop and apply the five powers, not only for the rest of their lives, but also into death and rebirth.

Such immersion and certainty in Mind Training enables practitioners to accurately assess their progress and capacity, which is the fifth of the Seven Points.

Point Five: Evaluation – evaluating Mind Training.

Seeing that fundamentally all teachings agree,
always maintain a joyful mind, embrace the primary of the two
witnesses, and recognise that if capable of practising even when
distracted, the mind is well trained.
(slogans 19 – 22)

All the teachings of Buddhism express a single principle: the nonduality of emptiness and form – this is the point at which all teachings agree. This can also be expressed as the nonduality of wisdom and compassion, of openness and kindness, of subject and object, of self and other, of existence and non-existence. How nonduality is expressed depends on the teacher, and the vehicle of practice. In Dzogchen, the nonduality of emptiness and form is primary.

Nonduality has been addressed in Points Two and Three of the Seven Points. If the practitioner has started to recognise that all teachings agree and point to this fundamental principle, this is a sign that practice is having an effect. Acknowledging this insight, joy spontaneously arises in the mind. Chekhawa instructs practitioners to maintain a joyful mind – which is another way of saying: *continue to practise*. If Mind Training continues, moments of insight increase in frequency, and joy arises. Always maintaining a joyful mind does not deny the reality of moments of pain, and difficult circumstances. However if such experiences are *joined with meditation*, the possibility of joy is ever-present. Joy becomes the ground of being a practitioner

> *'This means that Dharma practice is meaningless (no matter how much one does) unless it functions as an antidote to self-grasping.'*
> Thogme Zangpo – *Commentary on the Seven Points of Mind Training*

When the focus is removed from identity-fixation, and transferred to others, intention begins to awaken. Experiencing awakening intention is a cause of joy. It is joyful to help others.

It is joyful to be free of the effort and complication of trying to maintain personal identity in a manner in which it cannot exist. It is joyful to know the cause of pain and dissatisfaction. It is joyful to allow the cause to dissolve. A joyful mind naturally arises, and as long as Mind Training continues, joy will continually arise.

Joyfully recognising that all teachings agree, through a common principle and purpose – practitioners practise. Practice is established. It then becomes important for practitioners to honestly examine for themselves whether identity is becoming increasingly transparent, and whether real concern for the welfare of others is a continual focus.

Practitioners must continually refer back to the first four of Chekhawa's Seven Points in their evaluation. Is taking and giving impaled on the breath? Are all blames being driven into the one cause? Is the capacity to embrace emptiness increasing? Are the Four Highest Methods engaged? Are the five powers of confidence, energy, presence, alertness, and discriminating awareness functioning? In short, are the teachings of the first four points of Mind Training being engaged?

Practitioners who are able to honestly assess their practice in this way will recognise when mistakes are made, and when they have allowed themselves to be distracted. They will also have the capacity to assess their ability to remain with Mind Training at such times. They will see that practice is not lost when things go wrong, or when life is painful. They continually return to practice, and persevere. This is the last consideration in Point Five.

Through correctly assessing that awakening is sparkling through delusion, practitioners become fully committed to Mind Training. Commitment is the topic of the Point Six.

Point Six: Commitment – the commitments of Mind Training.

Embrace commitment to Mind Training by continually engaging the three general principles, and by being determined to practise transformation, whilst remaining natural.
Committed practitioners refrain from talking about weak limbs, or dwelling on the opinion of others, and focus on the strongest of their afflicted emotions first.
Committed practitioners give up all expectations of the fruit of practice, abandon poisonous food, and rely on the root text with a good nature.
Committed practitioners are not agitated by past grievances, do not wait in ambush, or bring out others' secret state. They carry the burden of responsibility, not transferring a dzo's load to an ox. Committed practitioners do not hurry to reach the summit, pervert the meal, or turn gods into demons, and never look for happiness in others' pain.
(slogans 23 – 38)

Mind Training is incredibly skilful and embraces the reality of life *as it is*. Every situation that is encountered, or could be encountered, is recognised as an opportunity to practise, to transform the mind – to awaken. Chekhawa's slogans of Mind Training recognise ordinary human downfalls in a straightforward manner. These hindrances are faced and abandoned, or transformed into goodness.

> *'The word "commitment" ... is often regarded as something extremely dangerous and risky. Commitment is definitely something you need to observe, respect, and adhere to, but you need not fear it. A commitment is given by the teacher to ensure that disciples follow the right course, avoiding hindrances and side-tracks, to proceed in a way that is good and beneficial. It is the teacher's responsibility to make sure of that and the word commitment refers to this.'*
> Thrangu Rinpoche – *The Seven Points of Mind Training*

The principle of progression through the slogans is not so evident in Point Six of the Seven Points.

The slogans of this point have more the sense of brainstorming how to be a committed practitioner – attitudes and activities to embrace, and those to avoid.

Point Six begins by introducing the principles of a committed practititioner's attitude and demeanour:

> *Continually train in the three general principles.* (slogan 23)

The principles of honour, dignity, and impartiality are the natural demeanour of a committed practitioner of Mind Training. The evident *naturalness* of these qualities are an indication of committed practice:

> *Be determined to practise transformation, but remain natural.* (slogan 24)

Ordinary life, however, may present a different view of what is *natural*. Attitudes that are common and considered normal and reasonable, may appear to be natural, but nevertheless need to be abandoned on the path of awakening. These attitudes are brought to the attention of the committed practitioner in Point Six , so that any necessary adjustments can be made.

> *Refrain from talking about weak limbs.* (slogan 25)
> *Do not dwell on the opinion of others.* (slogan 26)
> *Do not be agitated by past grievances.* (slogan 31)
> *Do not wait in ambush.* (slogan 32)
> *Do not bring out others' secret state.* (slogan 33)
> *Never look for happiness in others' pain.* (slogan 38)

This point also examines the way in which practice is approached.

> *Focus on the strongest afflicted emotion first.* (slogan 27)
> *Give up all expectations of the fruit of practice.* (slogan 28)
> *Abandon poisonous food.* (slogan 29)
> *Rely on the root text with a good nature.* (slogan 30)
> *Do not hurry to reach the summit.* (slogan 35)
> *Do not pervert the meal.* (slogan 36)
> *Do not turn gods into demons.* (slogan 37)

Perhaps one of the most important aspects of commitment is taking responsibility:

> *Do not put a dzo's load on an ox.* (slogan 34)

The willingness to take responsibility for personal behaviour and demeanour, and to also be willing to take responsibility for the welfare of others, are primary aspects of awakening.

> *'Whenever you don't want to practice—stamp on that, and then practice. Whenever any bad circumstance comes up that might put you off—stamp on it.'*
> Chögyam Trungpa Rinpoche – *Training the Mind*, p. 191

Mind Training is a lifetime commitment. Practitioners must be patient and simply continue, even when the destination seems too far distant and progress painfully slow.

Mind Training is extraordinary. Practitioners must let go of ordinary, long-held beliefs in fairness and unfairness, praise and blame, and embrace the more expansive view of awakening.

Mind Training is vast and all-embracing. Practitioners must appreciate their great good fortune in being able to practise transformation, and cheerfully grasp the scope of their responsibility.

Mind Training is precious and precise. Practitioners must take care not to become careless or complacent and risk undermining the value and purity of Mind Training.

Through committing to Mind Training in this way, awakening will most certainly manifest.

Point Seven: Advice – advice on Mind Training.

*Practise all the teachings with the single intention of
benefitting others, reversing all misfortunes.
Begin and end well, being patient with whatever occurs,
and guard awakening view and intention,
even at the risk of your life.
Train in the three difficulties, and embrace the three principal causes
of awakening, ensuring that they never deteriorate.
Keeping body, speech, and mind inseparable,
train deeply and pervasively in all areas without prejudice,
and once Mind Training is perfected,
cherish everyone and everything, everywhere.
Always practise with whatever makes you boil, and refrain from
being distracted by external circumstances.
This time make practice the priority,
without falsifying and perverting, and practise consistently,
completely immersed in Mind Training.
Escape duality through investigation and analysis,
without being boastful, jealous or frustrated, practising diligently
for its own sake without wishing for thanks.*
(slogans 39 – 59)

The path of Mind Training is fully embraced and the practitioner is fully committed. In Point Seven—the final point of Mind Training—Chekhawa offers practical advice and subtle adjustments to keep the practitioner completely on the path of awakening. This point encompasses serious and committed intent, with light-hearted recognition of ordinary downfalls – the perfect balance for training the mind.

To begin, Chekhawa reminds practitioners of the primary motivation for practice, which is the intention to benefit and cherish others:

Practise all the teachings with a single intention. (slogan 39)

This reiterates the principles of Mind Training expressed in Points Two and Three – that the emphasis of all practice must be to divert attention away from personal identity, and toward focussing on everything that is *other*. This intention will enable practitioners to overcome and transform all difficulties.

> *Reverse all misfortunes with a single intention.* (slogan 40)

The next four slogans of Point Seven address the attitude to practice and the methods:

> *Both first and last, two things to do.* (slogan 41)
> *Whichever of the two occurs, practise patience.* (slogan 42)
> *Guard the two, even at the risk of your life.* (slogan 43)
> *Train in the three difficulties.* (slogan 44)

These encompass the approach that is needed for a committed practitioner. View and intention must be examined and aligned with awakening, and then this aspiration guarded as more important than life itself.

The next two slogans acknowledge that the teacher is central to any method of practice. It is the teacher who introduces the methods, and is familiar with the fruit of practice. The capacity for sustained practice relies on the teacher, embracing the methods of practice provided by the teacher, and appreciating the circumstances that make it possible to practise. The importance of these three is expressed:

> *Embrace the three principal causes.* (slogan 45)
> *Practise so that the three do not deteriorate.* (slogan 46)

Then Chekhawa offers nine slogans which advise practitioners how to adjust their priorities, to ensure consistency and continuing commitment in practice.

> *Keep the three inseparable.* (slogan 47)
> *Train without prejudice in all areas, deeply and pervasively, and once perfected, cherish everyone and everything, everywhere.*
> (slogan 48)

Meditate continually on whatever makes you boil. (slogan 49)
Refrain from being influenced by external circumstances. (slogan 50)
This time make practice the priority. (slogan 51)
Refrain from misunderstanding and perverting. (slogan 52)
Refrain from being sporadic. (slogan 53)
Check how much you are gripped by training. (slogan 54)
Escape duality through investigation and analysis. (slogan 55)

Practitioners must examine whether *the* three—mind, energy, and body—are inseparable in being harnessed for practice. Has Mind Training become a way of life? Is it inconceivable that Mind Training could be given up? Have they fallen in love with Mind Training? Does Mind Training define them? Is there freedom from doubt, and wholehearted devotion to practice? Is there the joyful recognition that awakening is possible, and the aspiration to achieve this?

If the answer to these questions is '*Yes!*' then practitioners are indeed truly gripped by Mind Training.

The final four slogans of the advice in Point Seven, addresses practitioners who are committed, with a reminder to just practice.

Avoid boastful behaviour. (slogan 56)
Avoid being constricted by jealousy and frustration. (slogan 57)
Refrain from practising just a little. (slogan 58)
Do not wish for thanks. (slogan 59)

If practice is good, they are not boastful. If practice seems slow, or not so good, and others seem to be doing better, they are not jealous or frustrated. They avoid vacillation, practising here and there, now and then. And if practitioners are energetically committed, and truly dedicated , they do not expect anyone to thank them for practising Mind Training.

I find these final four slogans particularly delightful in their humour, warmth, and recognition of the patterns of delusion. Chekhawa Yeshé Dorje certainly had a sense of humour, and an extraordinary insight into the human psyche. After working hard, and committing to practice, don't boast. Don't make comparisons with others – just get on with it. What might the excellent practitioner expect? The answer is to expect nothing. Do not crave for thanks, recognition, or appreciation. Do not expect applause.

> *'Exertion is like the minute before you wake up on a holiday trip: you have some sense of trusting that you are going to have a good time, but at the same time you have to put your effort into it. So exertion is some kind of celebration and joy, which is free from laziness.'*
> Chögyam Trungpa Rinpoche – Training the Mind, p. 132

Mind Training is pragmatic, straightforward, and yet profound. Understand the meaning of awakening. Understand the motivation for awakening. Embrace the path of awakening. As capacity develops, hold to commitment, evaluate progress, and address deluded attitudes and views. Make subtle adjustments as necessary, holding on to the principles of Mind Training, and then awaken, in order to benefit everyone and everything, everywhere.

2 – How to Use the Slogans

To accompany this book there is a set of slogan cards that provide the essence of the presentation of the Seven Points of Mind Training.[1] These fifty-nine cards each contain the slogan, translated from the Tibetan, and a succinct explanation – as presented at the beginning of each slogan in Part II of this book. The cards also include an indication of where the slogan fits within the Seven Points and the whole set of 59 slogans.

Mind Training is a most powerful method of practice for committed and experienced practitioners. The Seven Points and the slogans span Sutra, Tantra, and Dzogchen and offer great depth and subtlety of view. Mind Training with slogans can be introduced as a method for beginners, but it will be necessary to find a teacher and receive further teaching on Mind Training methods to make great progress.

The previous chapter looked at the fifty-nine slogans as a progression through the Seven Points of Mind Training. It is useful to engage with the Seven Points in this way, and become thoroughly familiar with which slogans are in which point. This may enhance the experience of working with the slogans as a method of daily practice.

As a daily practice, the slogans are approached individually. With this in mind, I have tried to ensure that the commentary for each slogan in Part II is self-contained. The commentaries in that section do not refer to other slogans, the position of slogans within the Seven Points, or to the progression of the Seven Points. This means that when a card is drawn, the commentary for that slogan can be read if wished, and it will stand alone as an individual focus on the aspect of Mind Training that slogan addresses.

---

1   Please see the copyright page for information on acquiring slogan cards.

Thorough familiarisation with the slogans and their meaning, will greatly help in approaching the slogans as a daily practice. This is particularly true of the more succinct slogans, where the subject matter may not be immediately obvious. Examples of such slogans are:

Three objects, three poisons, three roots of goodness. (slogan 8)
Apply the four highest methods. (slogan 15)
Continually train in the three general principles. (slogan 23)
Embrace the three principal causes. (slogan 45)
Keep the three inseparable. (slogan 47)

For those working with slogan cards I have tried to offer an indication of the meaning of the more oblique slogans in my pithy comments. This means that the commentaries do not necessarily need to be looked up every time.

Practising with the fifty-nine slogans individually, using the slogan cards, can be approached in different ways. This can be a daily practice, changing the card each day. Alternatively, a card can be a focus for a longer period of time, until it feels appropriate to move on to another slogan. With these two approaches in mind, here are three methods of drawing slogan cards:

1. starting with the first card, work through the slogans in order, from one to fifty-nine;

2. shuffle the cards, and work through all fifty-nine slogans in the random order that arises from shuffling;

3. shuffle the cards and use the slogan that comes to the top as the focus of practice; then, when the decision is made to change the slogan card, shuffle the cards again and work with the new card that comes to the top.

The first approach—working through the slogans in order—is a useful way to get to know them. This approach is also useful for becoming familiar with the Seven Points as a complete teaching.

It takes time to become really familiar with the slogans, studying one a day, as each card will only be seen six times in the course of a year.

The second approach—shuffling the cards and working through them in the generated random order—is interesting in a different way. Practitioners may experience the sensation of the *right* slogan having appeared at just the time it was needed. Again, as a daily method, this would only mean a slogan would be seen six times in a year. Further study may be required to embrace the teaching as a whole, and for the individual slogans to become really well known.

In the third approach—shuffling the cards each time a card is selected—it cannot be guaranteed that every slogan will actually be seen in a year of daily practice with slogan cards. I would not recommend this as the first method for working with slogan cards, as it will not be useful for familiarisation with all the slogans.

The third approach does, however, offer another interesting experience – that certain slogans may appear again and again, and perhaps others are never seen. This can be taken as meaningful by the practitioner if they wish it to be meaningful. But meaning is not certain. Chaos must also be considered. There can be meaning, but there is also chaos. To deny chaos, and rely on meaning, would be to stray into predetermination which is antithetical to the Buddhist teachings.[2]

---

2   Interpreting something as meaningful when it could simply be chaotic is called eternalism. This is one of the philosophical extremes that are denied in Buddhist view. The four are: monism and dualism, nihilism and eternalism. Monism denies individuality in proclaiming everything is one. Dualism denies the oneness of the experience of emptiness. Nihilism denies any meaning in experience, and eternalism denies the lack of meaning. Each extreme can be true *in the moment*, but not as an inherent continuity.

Part IV
appendices

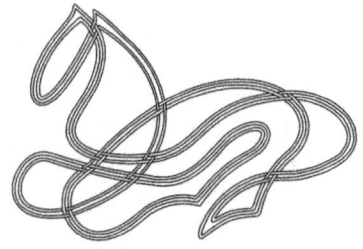

1 – The Bodhisattva's Garland of Jewels

In the language of India: *Bodhisattvamanyāvalī*
In the language of Tibet: *changchub sempé norbü trengwa*[1]
In the English language: *The Bodhisattva's Garland of Jewels*[2]

Homage to great compassion!
Homage to the deities who inspire faith and devotion!
Homage to the masters!

Be done with doubt and indecision,
And embrace your practice with all your heart.
Shake off lethargy, dullness and laziness,
And strive always with enthusiasm and joy.

Mindful, vigilant and careful,
Guard the doorways of your senses at every moment.
Three times each day, three times at night,
Again and again, examine your thoughts.

Make plain your own failings,
But don't look for faults in others.
Make known the good points of others,
But keep quiet about your own best qualities.

Let go of craving for gain and honour,
And give up the urge for profit or fame.

Cultivate love and compassion,
And make your bodhicitta stable.
Avoid the ten unwholesome actions,
And make your faith and confidence be strong.

With few wants, be content with what you have,
And with gratitude repay any kindness you receive.

---

1 *Byang chub sems dPa' nor bu 'Phreng ba.*
2 Attributed to *Jo bo rJe dPal ldan A ti sha* (Tib.) *Atiśa Dīpamkara* (Skt.).

Overcome anger and arrogance,
And let humility rule your mind.
Give up any unwholesome kind of living,
And pursue a livelihood in keeping with the Dharma.

Do away with your addiction to material things,
And adorn yourself with the riches of the Āryas.[3]

The wealth of faith, of discipline,
Generosity and learning,
Decency, self-control,
And wisdom—such are the seven riches.
These most sacred forms of wealth
Are seven treasures that never run out.
Do not speak of this to those who are not human.

Leave all busyness and distraction behind,
And dwell instead in seclusion and solitude.

Refrain from meaningless chatter,
And always keep a check on what you say.

Whenever you see your master or preceptor,
Offer to serve them with devotion and respect.
Those who possess enlightened vision
And those first setting out upon the path—
Regard them both as your spiritual teachers.

Whenever you see any sentient beings,
Regard them as your parents or your children.
Don't befriend those who act in harmful ways;
Instead rely on true spiritual friends.

Drop any feelings of hostility or ill will,
And be happy, wherever you choose to go.

Avoid getting attached to anything at all,
And stay free from craving and desire.
Attachment not only keeps you from happy births,
It kills the very life of liberation.

---

[3] Āryas (Skt.), Tib. pakpa (*'phags pa*) – noble beings or saints.

Should you find a way to peace and happiness,
Strive constantly to put it into practice.
Whatever task you set out to do,
Accomplish that very thing first.
This way, everything will turn out well;
If not, nothing will succeed.

Never take pleasure in acts that harm.
And when thoughts of superiority creep in,
There and then, deflate your self-importance,
And recall your master's personal advice.
Or whenever you feel discouraged or inadequate,
Raise your spirits and encourage yourself.
And always meditate on emptiness.

Should the objects of attachment or aversion appear,
View them as no more than illusions or projections.
Should you hear unpleasant words,
Consider them nothing more than echoes.
Should you suffer physical harm,
See it as the result of your past actions.

Keep entirely to solitude, far away from town,
And, like the carcass of some wild animal,
Stay hidden in nature by yourself,
Free of all entanglement and attachment.

Always keep up your pledges and commitments,
And should laziness or procrastination strike,
Immediately take note of your errors, one by one,
And remind yourself of the heart of your discipline.

Whenever you meet another person,
Speak calmly, sincerely and truthfully.
Take care not to frown or glare,
And always wear a cheerful smile.

And when you're with those you see every day,
Don't be stingy, but be happy to give,
And banish all feelings of envy.

So as to protect others' peace of mind,
Stay clear of quarrels of any kind,
And be patient and always forbearing.

Don't flatter, or be a fickle friend,
But be steadfast and reliable all the time.
Never disparage or belittle other people,
But treat everyone with respect.

When giving advice or instructions,
Do so with compassion and a genuine wish to help.
Be sure never to criticize the teachings.
Set your sights on what inspires you most,
And, through the ten forms of Dharma practice,
Exert yourself in sessions, day and night.

Among others, keep a check on your speech;
When alone, keep a check on your mind.

Whatever virtues you amass in the past, present and future,
Dedicate them all towards great, unsurpassable awakening,
Share your merit among all sentient beings,
And with the seven branch practice,
Continually make great prayers of aspiration.

Practising like this, you will complete
Accumulations of both merit and wisdom,
And eliminate the two forms of obscuration.
You will make this human life meaningful,
And, in time, gain unsurpassable awakening.

This concludes the Bodhisattva's Garland of Jewels, composed by the great Indian pandita Dīpamkara Śrījñāna.

Rigpa Translations, 2008. Revised 2012.

2 – sNying mDo – The Heart Sutra

Chenrézigs—absorbed in the contemplation of unconventional wisdom—perceived duality as empty.

On seeing this directly, he turned to Shariputra saying: *"Form is emptiness, and emptiness is form."* Then—in order to clarify—he continued: *"Form is not different from emptiness – emptiness not different from form. That which appears as emptiness is form – and that which appears as form is emptiness. You will not find emptiness apart from form – nor form apart from emptiness.*

The psychology of duality, sensation, sense connections, thought, and consciousness – these are also emptiness and form. So Shariputra – you can only characterise form in terms of emptiness – and emptiness in terms of form.

The phenomena of reality are neither existent nor non-existent. They are neither pure nor impure. They neither increase nor decrease. Psychological attributes are neither existent, nor non-existent. The perceptions of eyes, ears, nose, tongue, body, and mind – are both reality and illusion. Likewise form, sound, colour, taste, touch, and objects. Likewise the dimension of vision and awareness.

There is neither understanding, nor absence of understanding. There is no suffering, old age, or death – nor do they end. There is neither merit, nor accumulation of merit.

There is no annihilation, no path, and no wisdom. There is neither realisation nor non-realisation. There is neither attainment nor absence of attainment. Because the liberated Mind-warrior's awareness is characterised by this unconventional wisdom – even the four philosophical extremes are not perceived as dualism.

Likewise all those who realise nonduality—in the past, present, and future—dwell in the knowledge of unconventional wisdom, which is none other than rigpa.

So—Shariputra—relax. Relax in the knowledge that unconventional wisdom is the great mantra, the mantra of completion, the mantra of totality, the mantra which expresses everything. Unconventional wisdom dissolves all struggles. It is true, simply because it lacks the complication of falsity. This is the essence of unconventional wisdom."

Om Ga-té, Ga-té, Para Ga-té,
Para-sam Ga-té, Bodhi Svaha

A: Ga-té, Ga-té, Para Ga-té,
Para-sam Ga-té, Bodhi Svaha A:[1]

---

1 This is the Aro gTér Lineage version of the Heart Sutra, translated by Ngak'chang Rinpoche and Khandro Déchen. Both the commonly known and Aro gTér Heart Sutra mantras are included at the end.

3 – Commentary comparisons

The many works offering teaching on The Seven Points of Mind Training seem to be consistent in the expression of the Seven Points. However there is a wide variety with regard to the list of 59 slogans, their placement within the Seven Points, and in their wording and interpretation. This appendix offers an overview of the wording of the individual slogans of Mind Training from the texts included in the bibliography, and from which quotations are given in the main body of the book.

> *'... An examination of various root texts reveals that adjusting the root lines is, in fact, something of a time-honoured tradition among lojong teachers who make these alterations in order to reflect their own understanding of the teachings and their own understanding of what constitutes the most pedagogically efficient method of transmitting these teachings.'*
> Lara Braitstein – translator's introduction, p. viii, *The Path to Awakening*

The 59 slogans in *Battlecry of Freedom* are taken from the Tibetan texts provided in the books of Könchok Yenlak, and Shamar Rinpoche.[1] Although these differ occasionally, they provide a good basis for the structure of this book. I have based the wording of each slogan on my translation from these Tibetan texts, rather than using the wording found in other commentaries. The following tables indicate the differences in wording of slogans, and in their order within the Seven Points, including which slogans some commentaries omit, and additional slogans.

---

1   See bibliography, p. 361.

Point One – preliminary practices

Slogan 1 – *First, train in the preliminaries.*

Chögyam Trungpa	*First, train in the preliminaries.*[2]
Dilgo Khyentse	*First, study the preliminaries.*
Jamgon Kongtrul	*First, do the groundwork.*
Kelsang Gyatso	*First learn the preliminaries.*
	Adds a slogan: *Show the secret to the one who has achieved firmness.*
Khenchen Thrangu	*First, train in the preliminaries.*
Könchok Yenlak	*First, train in the preliminaries.*
Kunzig Shamar	*Train in the preliminaries.*
	Also includes slogan 2 here: *Think that all phenomena are like a dream.*
Thogme Zangpo	*First, train in the preliminaries.*
Thupten Jinpa	*First, train in the preliminaries.*
Wikipedia: Chekawa[3]	*Initially, train in the preliminaries.*

Point Two – awakening

Slogan 2 – *Consider all phenomena as dreamlike.*

Chögyam Trungpa	*Regard all Dharmas as dreams.*
Dilgo Khyentse	*Consider all phenomena as a dream.*
Jamgon Kongtrul	*Look at all experience as a dream.*
Kelsang Gyatso	*Think that all phenomena are like dreams.*
Khenchen Thrangu	*Regard all phenomena as dreams.*
Könchok Yenlak	*Think that all phenomena are like a dream.*
Kunzig Shamar	*– included in point one.*
Thogme Zangpo	*Consider all dharmas as dreamlike.*
Thupten Jinpa	*Train to view all phenomena as dream-like.*
Wikipedia: Chekawa	*Consider phenomena to be like a dream.*

2 Pema Chödron and Judith Lief's slogans are all identical to those of Chögyam Trungpa Rinpoche, and therefore not included in these lists.
3 The spelling of *Chekhawa* in Wikipedia differs to that used in this book.

Slogan 3 – *Examine fundamental unborn awareness.*

Chögyam Trungpa	*Examine the nature of unborn awareness.*
Dilgo Khyentse	*Analyse the unborn nature of awareness.*
Jamgon Kongtrul	*Examine the nature of unborn awareness.*
Kelsang Gyatso	*Analyse the unborn nature of cognition.*
Khenchen Thrangu	*Investigate the nature of unborn awareness.*
Könchok Yenlak	*Examine the unborn nature of awareness.*
Kunzig Shamar	*Analyse the unborn nature of mind.*
	– places slogan 27 here.
Thogme Zangpo	*Examine the nature of unborn awareness.*
Thupten Jinpa	*Examine the nature of the unborn awareness.*
Wikipedia: Chekawa	*Analyse the nature of ungenerated awareness.*

Slogan 4 – *Even the remedy self-liberates into its own natural condition.*

Chögyam Trungpa	*Self-liberate even the antidote.*
Dilgo Khyentse	*The antidote will vanish of itself.*
Jamgon Kongtrul	*Let even the remedy release naturally.*
Kelsang Gyatso	*Even the opponent oneself is free of existing from its own side.*
Khenchen Thrangu	*Even the antidote is released in its ground.*
Könchok Yenlak	*The remedy too liberates itself naturally.*
Kunzig Shamar	*Even the remedy naturally liberates itself.*
Thogme Zangpo	*Let even the antidote be freed in its own place.*
Thupten Jinpa	*The remedy too, is freed in its own place.*
Wikipedia: Chekawa	*Even the antidote itself is naturally free.*

Slogan 5 – *Remain in the dimension of kun-zhi, the essence of the path.*

Chögyam Trungpa	*Rest in the nature of alaya, the essence.*
Dilgo Khyentse	*The nature of the path rests in the alaya.*
Jamgon Kongtrul	*The essence of the path: rest in the basis of all experience.*
Kelsang Gyatso	*Place the actual path on the basis of all.*

Khenchen Thrangu	*Rest within the all-basis, the essential nature.*
Könchok Yenlak	*The essence of the path is to settle the nature of alaya, the ground of all experience.*
Kunzig Shamar	*Rest in the essence of mind, the basis of everything.*
Thogme Zangpo	*Rest in the ālaya, the essence of the path.*
Thupten Jinpa	*Place your mind on the basis-of-all, the actual path.*
Wikipedia: Chekawa	*Focus on the nature of the basis of all, the entity of the path. Having attained stability, be shown the secret.*

Slogan 6 – *Everything that arises in daily life is illusory.*

Chögyam Trungpa	*In post-meditation, be a child of illusion.*
Dilgo Khyentse	*In post meditation, consider phenomena as illusory.*
Jamgon Kongtrul	*In daily life, be a child of illusion.*
Kelsang Gyatso	*Between sessions, consider all phenomena as illusory.*
Khenchen Thrangu	*In post meditation, regard all beings as illusions.*
Könchok Yenlak	*Between sessions, be someone who is in tune with illusion.*
Kunzig Shamar	*In post meditation, know that all phenomena are illusory.*
	– places slogan 28 here.
Thogme Zangpo	*Between sessions, be a conjurer of illusions.*
Thupten Jinpa	*In the intervals be a conjurer of illusions.*
Wikipedia: Chekawa	*Between sessions be an illusionist.*

Slogan 7 – *Train in alternately sending and receiving; fix these two on the breath.*

Chögyam Trungpa	*Sending and taking should be practised alternately. These two should ride the breath.*
Dilgo Khyentse	*Train to give and take alternately.*
Jamgon Kongtrul	*Train in taking and sending alternately. Put them on the breath.*
Kelsang Gyatso	*Train alternately in giving and taking.*
Khenchen Thrangu	*Alternately practice sending and taking; these two should ride the breath.*
Könchok Yenlak	*As for the former, practise sending and taking alternately.*
Kunzig Shamar	*Practice alternating the two, giving and taking.*

Thogme Zangpo	*Train in the two—giving and taking—alternately.*
	These two are to be mounted on the breath – is given as a separate slogan.
Thupten Jinpa	*Train alternately in the two—giving and taking.*
	Place the two astride the breath is given as a separate slogan.
Wikipedia: Chekawa	*Train alternately in the two, taking and giving.*
	Mount the two upon the breath.

Slogan 8 – *Three objects, three poisons, and three roots of goodness.*

Chögyam Trungpa	*Three objects, three poisons and three seeds of virtue.*
Dilgo Khyentse	*Three objects, three poisons and three seeds of virtue.*
Jamgon Kongtrul	*Three objects, three poisons and three seeds of virtue.*
Kelsang Gyatso	*Three objects, three poisons and three virtuous roots are the brief instruction for the subsequent attainment.*
Khenchen Thrangu	*Three objects, three poisons and three roots of virtue.*
Könchok Yenlak	*Three objects, three poisons and three roots of goodness.*
Kunzig Shamar	*Three objects, three poisons and three roots of virtue.*
Thogme Zangpo	*Three objects, three poisons & three sources of virtue.*
Thupten Jinpa	*There are three objects, three poisons, and three roots of virtue.*
Wikipedia: Chekawa	*There are three objects, three poisons, and three roots of virtue.*

Slogan 9 – *In all activities, train with slogans.*

Chögyam Trungpa	*In all activities, train with slogans.*
Dilgo Khyentse	*In all your actions, train yourself with maxims.*
Jamgon Kongtrul	*Use reminders in everything you do.*
Kelsang Gyatso	*To remember this, train in every activity by words.*
Khenchen Thrangu	*In all your activities, train with these words.*
Könchok Yenlak	*Use bywords to train in every kind of activity.*
Kunzig Shamar	*Train your conduct by means of the slogans.*
Thogme Zangpo	*In all activities, train by applying slogans.*
Thupten Jinpa	*In all your actions, train by means of the words.*
Wikipedia: Chekawa	*Train yourself with the verses during all activities.*

Slogan 10 – *Begin the sequence of sending and receiving with oneself.*

Chögyam Trungpa	*Begin the sequence of sending and taking with yourself.*
Dilgo Khyentse	*Begin the training sequence with yourself.*
Jamgon Kongtrul	*Begin taking with you.*
Kelsang Gyatso	*Begin the sequence by taking from your own side.*
Khenchen Thrangu	*Begin the sequence of sending and taking with yourself.*
Könchok Yenlak	*When taking, begin with yourself.*
Kunzig Shamar	*– omitted.*
Thogme Zangpo	*Begin the process of taking with yourself.*
Thupten Jinpa	*– omitted.*
Wikipedia: Chekawa	*Begin taking with yourself.*

Point Three – transformation

Slogan 11 – *When the world and life is full of malice and bad circumstances, transform it into the path of awakening.*

Chögyam Trungpa	*When the world is filled with evil, transform all mishaps into the path of bodhi.*
Dilgo Khyentse	*When all the world is filled with evils, place all setbacks on the path of liberation.*
Jamgon Kongtrul	*When misfortune fills the world and its inhabitants, make adversity the path of awakening.*
Kelsang Gyatso	*When the container and the contents are filled with evil, transform adverse conditions into the path of enlightenment.*
Khenchen Thrangu	*When the whole world is filled with negativity, transform adverse conditions into the path of awakening.*
Könchok Yenlak	*When the whole world is filled with iniquity, transform adverse circumstances into the path of awakening.*
Kunzig Shamar	*When beings and the world are filled with evil, convert adversities into the path of awakening.*
Thogme Zangpo	*When all the world is filled with evil, transform adversity into the path of enlightenment.*
Thupten Jinpa	*When the world and its inhabitants boil with negativity, transform adverse conditions into the path of enlightenment.*

| Wikipedia: Chekawa | *When the vessel and its contents are filled with negativities, transform these unfavorable conditions into the path to enlightenment.* |

Slogan 12 – *Drive all blames into one.*

Chögyam Trungpa	*Drive all blames into one.*
Dilgo Khyentse	*Lay the blame for everything on one.*
Jamgon Kongtrul	*Drive all blame into one.*
Kelsang Gyatso	*– omitted.*
Khenchen Thrangu	*Drive all blame into one.*
Könchok Yenlak	*Of all that is blameworthy, focus on one thing only.*
Kunzig Shamar	*Hold one fault accountable for all misfortunes.*
Thogme Zangpo	*Drive all blames into one.*
Thupten Jinpa	*Banish all blames to the single source.*
Wikipedia: Chekawa	*Put all the blame on the one.*

Slogan 13 – *Practise gratitude to everyone and everything, everywhere.*

Chögyam Trungpa	*Be grateful to everyone.*
Dilgo Khyentse	*Reflect upon the kindness of all beings.*
Jamgon Kongtrul	*Be grateful to everyone.*
Kelsang Gyatso	*– omitted.*
Khenchen Thrangu	*Be grateful to everyone and everything.*
Könchok Yenlak	*Cultivate deep gratitude towards everyone.*
Kunzig Shamar	*Reflect on the great kindness of all beings.*
Thogme Zangpo	*Meditate on the great kindness of all.*
Thupten Jinpa	*Toward all beings contemplate their great kindness.*
	Adds the slogan: *With the three views and treasury of space, the yoga of protection is unexcelled.*
Wikipedia: Chekawa	*Meditate on everyone as kind.*

Slogan 14 – *Meditating on the delusions as the four kayas, emptiness is unsurpassable protection.*

Chögyam Trungpa	Seeing confusion as the four kayas is unsurpassable shunyata protection.
Dilgo Khyentse	Voidness is the unsurpassed protection; thereby illusory appearance is seen as the four kayas.
Jamgon Kongtrul	The ultimate protection is emptiness; know what arises as confusion to be the four aspects of being.
Kelsang Gyatso	– omitted.
Khenchen Thrangu	Seeing delusive appearances as the four kayas is the unexcelled protection emptiness gives.
Könchok Yenlak	Meditate on appearances arising from confusion as being the four kayas: emptiness is the supreme protection.
Kunzig Shamar	Cultivate deluded appearance as the Four Kayas; emptiness is the unsurpassed protection.
	Adds a slogan: *Three views are like the treasury of the sky, the unsurpassed protection of the yoga.*
Thogme Zangpo	Meditating on delusory perceptions as the four kāyas. Is the unsurpassable śūnyatā protection.
Thupten Jinpa	By meditation on illusions as the four buddha bodies, emptiness is protection unsurpassed.
Wikipedia: Chekawa	– omitted.
	Adds a slogan: *The measure of being trained is to no longer regress. To be trained is to possess the five signs of greatness.*

Slogan 15 – *Apply the four highest methods.*

Chögyam Trungpa	Four practices are the best of methods.
Dilgo Khyentse	The best way is to use the four practices.
Jamgon Kongtrul	The best way is to use the four practices.
Kelsang Gyatso	Applying the four preparations is the supreme method.
Khenchen Thrangu	The best method entails four practices.
Könchok Yenlak	The supreme method is composed of the four activities.
Kunzig Shamar	Mastering the four practices is the supreme method.
Thogme Zangpo	The fourfold practice is the best of methods.
Thupten Jinpa	The fourfold practice is the most excellent method.
Wikipedia: Chekawa	Possess the four preparations, the supreme method.

The third of the four highest methods: *welcoming bad circumstances as the opportunity to practise transformation* is commonly couched in the words *offering to the döns*.[4] A *dön* is a negative force or negative influence – the experience of ill will, or of bad circumstances in life. Traditionally offerings can be made in the sense of formal physical offerings such as *torma*.[5]

More importantly perhaps, offering can be made in the sense of welcoming negativities, opening the door to them. Then, through having allowed the negativities the space to be examined, allow them to dissolve through practising transformation. Everything is embraced as an opportunity for practice.

The last of these four practices is commonly couched in the words *offering to the dharmapalas*.[6] The dharmapalas are beings who protect the teachings and practitioners. Having welcomed the döns, offerings are made to the protectors as a reminder to embrace and neutralise the döns with transformative practice.

Slogan 16 – *Immediately join whatever you meet with meditation.*

Chögyam Trungpa	*Whatever you meet unexpectedly, join with meditation.*
Dilgo Khyentse	*To bring the unexpected to the path, begin to train immediately.*
Jamgon Kongtrul	*Work with whatever you encounter immediately.*
Kelsang Gyatso	*Apply meditation to whatever circumstances you meet.*
Khenchen Thrangu	*Whatever you meet, instantly join it with meditation.*
Könchok Yenlak	*Join unexpected events with your practice.*
Kunzig Shamar	*Whatever you encounter in the present, use it in your meditation.*
Thogme Zangpo	*Whatever you encounter, apply the practice.*
Thupten Jinpa	*Relate whatever you can to meditation right now.*
Wikipedia: Chekawa	*Immediately apply whatever you meet to meditation.*

4   *gDon*
5   *gTor ma* – dough offerings created in various shapes and colours used as offerings in tantric ceremonies.
6   *Dharmapala* (Skt.) Tib. *chö-kyong (chos sKyong)* – the protectors.

Point Four – the five powers

Slogan 17 – *Apply the five perfect powers.*

Chögyam Trungpa	*Practice the five strengths – the condensed heart instructions.*
Dilgo Khyentse	*The pith instructions briefly summarised: put the five strengths into practice.*
Jamgon Kongtrul	*A summary of the essential instructions: train in the five forces.*
Kelsang Gyatso	*This brief essential instruction should be applied with the five forces.*
Khenchen Thrangu	*Practice the five powers, the condensed heart instructions.*
Könchok Yenlak	*The epitome of the pith instructions is the application of the five powers.*
Kunzig Shamar	*The instructions condensed into their essence: Train in the five powers.*
Thogme Zangpo	*The essence of the instruction, briefly stated, is to apply yourself to the five strengths.*
Thupten Jinpa	*Apply yourself to the five powers.*
Wikipedia: Chekawa	*In brief, the essence of the instructions is to apply the five forces.*

Slogan 18 – *The five powers are the only crucial manner of conduct.*

Chögyam Trungpa	*The mahayana instruction for ejection of consciousness at death is the five strengths: how to conduct yourself is important.*
Dilgo Khyentse	*On how to die, the Mahayana teaches these five strengths. It matters how you act.*
Jamgon Kongtrul	*The mahayana instructions for how to die are the five forces. Posture is important.*
Kelsang Gyatso	*The five forces are the most important practice of the instructions of Mahayana transference.*
Khenchen Thrangu	*The Mahayana instructions for transferring consciousness at death are the five strengths; the way you behave matters.*
Könchok Yenlak	*The mahayana instructions for dying are the same five powers. Conduct is essential.*
Kunzig Shamar	*The Great Vehicle teachings on death are the five powers themselves; your conduct is critical.*
Thogme Zangpo	*The mahāyāna advice for transference involves the same five strengths. Conduct is important.*

Thupten Jinpa	*As Mahayana's transference method is the five powers alone, their practice is vital.*
Wikipedia: Chekawa	*The Great Vehicle instructions on transference are those very five forces; cherish this behavior.*

As the five powers are not specified in the Tibetan of the root texts I have given the five powers specified by the great Nyingma practitioner, Kyabjé Düd'jom Rinpoche – Jig'drèl Yeshé Dorje.

Chekhawa was a Nyingma practitioner, and the Nyingma tradition was predominant at the time he was teaching, and composing The Seven Points of Mind Training.

The five powers listed in other commentaries are:

1. determination
2. familiarisation
3. the seeds of virtue
4. remorse or self-reproach
5. aspiration.

This alternative set of five powers will certainly also be present once the methods of Mind Training are engaged. This set of powers express the manner of active engagement with Mind Training from the perspective of Sutra. They are reminiscent of the basic form of monastic scriptural practices. Whereas the five powers specified by Kyabjé Düd'jom Rinpoche – Jig'drèl Yeshé Dorje, are more connected to the practice of Tantra and Dzogchen. They express the qualities that will naturally begin to manifest in the practitioner through Mind Training: confidence, enthusiasm, presence, alertness, and discriminating awareness.

These five powers manifest and strengthen the practitioner, and become the basis for further progress toward awakening. The difference in the two sets of five powers, creates a difference of emphasis in the fourth point of Mind Training.

Determination is connected to the energy of intention and effort – it enables the practitioner to stay on the path. Familiarisation with the methods of Mind Training makes engagement possible.

The *seeds of virtue*, are the activities of developing goodness, of accumulating merit. This presents the gradual view of development through practice – that goodness must grow slowly and gradually like a lotus blossom that eventually emerges from the mire of the lake. This is the view from the perspective of Sutra.

In Sutra, the principle of practice is renunciation. Chekhawa frequently refers to the practice of transformation, which is the principle of Tantric practice. This is the faster practice of changing view and intention in the moment, through transforming perception and response. The text also encompasses the Dzogchen view of self-liberation – that awakening can simply be discovered spontaneously. Awakening can happen in any moment, and is the potential of every moment.

The power of regret or remorse, is the recognition of a missed opportunity, or of a mistake. If an opportunity to help another has been missed, or there was insufficient presence in the moment of perception to prevent an unskilful patterned response, it is appropriate to recognise this and regret it. Remorse is also a reason to feel joyful and celebrate the awareness that enabled recognition of the mistake. Remorse naturally leads to the aspiration to do better, and to truly embrace the path of awakening in each and every moment.

Many of the commentaries on the second slogan of this point include details of how to die well. These may include a position in which to lie at the time of death, breathing exercises, visualisations and so on. The details of such teachings will be specific to different lineages and traditions. The root text simply stresses that applying the five powers is the only crucial manner in which to behave at all times.

'Remorse is healthy. [...]There is nothing wrong with shame, regret, remorse, or guilt. If I have acted in a loathsome manner: shame, regret, remorse, and guilt are healthy responses. It is not healthy to grovel and wallow in a self-referencing slough of these sensations. I need to feel these sensations in the moment – swiftly followed by the determination never to act loathsomely again.'

Ngak'chang Rinpoche – personal communication

Point Five – evaluation

Slogan 19 – *All teachings agree at one point.*

Chögyam Trungpa	*All Dharma agrees at one point.*
Dilgo Khyentse	*All Dharma has a single goal.*
Jamgon Kongtrul	*All instructions have one aim.*
Kelsang Gyatso	*All Dharma is condensed into one purpose.*
Khenchen Thrangu	*All the Buddha's dharma converges on a single point.*
Könchok Yenlak	*All Dharma is united in one objective.*
Kunzig Shamar	*All dharma teachings are for a single purpose.*
Thogme Zangpo	*All teachings share a single purpose.*
Thupten Jinpa	*The intent of all teachings converges on a single point.*
Wikipedia: Chekawa	*Combine all the Dharma into one intention.*

Slogan 20 - *Embrace the primary of the two witnesses.*

Chögyam Trungpa	*Of the two witnesses, hold the principal one.*
Dilgo Khyentse	*Rely upon the better of the two witnesses.*
Jamgon Kongtrul	*Two testimonies: rely on the important one.*
Kelsang Gyatso	*Hold to the principal of the two witnesses.*
Khenchen Thrangu	*Of the two witnesses, attend to the principal one.*
Könchok Yenlak	*Of the two witnesses, heed the most important one.*
Kunzig Shamar	*Rely on the better of the two witnesses.*
Thogme Zangpo	*Of the two witnesses, rely upon the principal one.*
Thupten Jinpa	*Of the two witnesses, uphold the principal one.*
Wikipedia: Chekawa	*Of the two witnesses, rely on the primary one.*

Slogan 21 – *Always be joyful.*

Chögyam Trungpa	*Always maintain only a joyful mind.*
Dilgo Khyentse	*Always be sustained by cheerfulness.*
Jamgon Kongtrul	*A joyous state of mind is a constant support.*
Kelsang Gyatso	*Always rely upon a happy mind alone.*
Khenchen Thrangu	*At all times, rely only on a joyful mind.*
Könchok Yenlak	*An ever-serene mind is the only recourse.*
Kunzig Shamar	*Be sustained continually by a joyful mind.*
Thogme Zangpo	*Always maintain only a joyful attitude.*
Thupten Jinpa	*Cultivate constantly the joyful mind alone.*
Wikipedia: Chekawa	*Always rely on mental happiness alone.*

Slogan 22 – *If you are capable even when distracted, you are well trained.*

Chögyam Trungpa	*If you can practice even when distracted, you are well trained.*
Dilgo Khyentse	*With experience you can practise even when distracted.*
Jamgon Kongtrul	*Proficiency means you do it even when distracted.*
Kelsang Gyatso	*One is trained if one is able to do the practice even when distracted.*
Kelsang Gyatso	Adds a slogan: *The indication of having been trained is reversal.* Adds a slogan: *The sign of having trained is possessing five greatnesses.*
Khenchen Thrangu	*If you can practice even when distracted, you are well trained.*
Könchok Yenlak	*If you are able even when distracted, you have trained well.*
Kunzig Shamar	*You are well trained if you can even withstand distraction.*
Thogme Zangpo	*If this can be done even when distracted, you are proficient.*
Thupten Jinpa	*If this can be done even when distracted, you are well trained.*
Wikipedia: Chekawa	*You are trained when able even if distracted.*

Point Six – commitment

Slogan 23 – *Continually train in the three general principles.*

Chögyam Trungpa	*Always abide by the three basic principles.*
Dilgo Khyentse	*Always train in the three common points.*
Jamgon Kongtrul	*Always train in the three basic principles.*
Kelsang Gyatso	*Always train in the three general points.*
Khenchen Thrangu	*Always train in the three basic principles.*
Könchok Yenlak	*Always train in the three basic principles.*
Kunzig Shamar	*Always abide by the three basic principles.*
Thogme Zangpo	*Train constantly in three basic principles.*
Thupten Jinpa	*Train constantly in the three general points.*
Wikipedia: Chekawa	*Constantly train in the three general points.*

Slogan 24 – *Be determined to practise transformation, but remain natural.*

Chögyam Trungpa	*Change your attitude, but remain natural.*
Dilgo Khyentse	*Change your attitude and maintain it firmly.*
Jamgon Kongtrul	*Change your intention, but behave naturally.*
Kelsang Gyatso	*Remain natural while changing your aspiration.*
Khenchen Thrangu	*Change your attitude and be natural.*
Könchok Yenlak	*Transform your approach while remaining natural.*
Kunzig Shamar	*Remaining natural, transform your attitude.*
Thogme Zangpo	*Change your attitude, but remain natural.*
Thupten Jinpa	*Transform your attitude but remain as you are.*
Wikipedia: Chekawa	*Change your attitude, but remain natural.*

Slogan 25 – *Refrain from talking about weak limbs.*

Slogans 25 and 26 are often difficult to tell apart in commentaries, or are swapped about.

Chögyam Trungpa	*Don't talk about injured limbs.*
Dilgo Khyentse	*Do not discuss infirmities.*
Jamgon Kongtrul	*Don't talk about other's shortcomings.*
Kelsang Gyatso	*Do not speak about degenerated limbs.*
Khenchen Thrangu	*Don't speak ill of others' shortcomings.*
Könchok Yenlak	*Do not speak of others' infirmities.*
Kunzig Shamar	*Do not talk about the defects of others.*
Thogme Zangpo	*Don't speak of injured limbs.*
Thupten Jinpa	*Do not speak of the defects [of others].*
Wikipedia: Chekawa	*Do not think about others' affairs.*

Slogan 26 – *Do not dwell on the opinion of others.*

Chögyam Trungpa	*Don't ponder others.*
Dilgo Khyentse	*Do not have opinions on other people's actions.*
Jamgon Kongtrul	*Don't dwell on others' problems.*
Kelsang Gyatso	*Never think about others' faults.*
Khenchen Thrangu	*Don't ponder the affairs of others.*
Könchok Yenlak	*Never judge others.*
Kunzig Shamar	*Whatever the faults of others may be, do not contemplate them.*
Thogme Zangpo	*Don't ponder others' flaws.*
Thupten Jinpa	*Do not reflect on others' shortcomings.*
Wikipedia: Chekawa	*Do not mention [others'] impaired limbs.*

Slogan 27 – *Train with the strongest afflicted emotion first.*

Chögyam Trungpa	*Work with the greatest defilements first.*
Dilgo Khyentse	*Work on the strongest of your defilements first.*
Jamgon Kongtrul	*Work on your strongest reactions first.*
Kelsang Gyatso	*Purify your greatest delusion first.*
Khenchen Thrangu	*Work with the stronger afflictions first.*
Könchok Yenlak	*Purify whichever affliction is the strongest first.*
Kunzig Shamar	– placed after slogan 3.

Thogme Zangpo	*Train first with the strongest destructive emotions.*
Thupten Jinpa	– omitted.
Wikipedia: Chekawa	*Initially, purify whatever affliction is the strongest.*

Slogan 28 – *Give up all expectation about the fruit of practice.*

Chögyam Trungpa	*Abandon any hope of fruition.*
Dilgo Khyentse	*Give up hoping for results.*
Jamgon Kongtrul	*Give up all hope of results.*
Kelsang Gyatso	*Abandon hope for results.*
Khenchen Thrangu	*Send away any hope for results.*
Könchok Yenlak	*Abandon all hope of results.*
Kunzig Shamar	– placed after slogan 6.
Thogme Zangpo	*Abandon any expectations of results.*
Thupten Jinpa	*Discard all expectations of reward.*
Wikipedia: Chekawa	*Give up all hope of reward.*

Slogan 29 – *Abandon poisonous food.*

Chögyam Trungpa	*Abandon poisonous food.*
Dilgo Khyentse	*Give up poisoned food.*
Jamgon Kongtrul	*Give up poisoned food.*
Kelsang Gyatso	*Abandon poisonous food.*
Khenchen Thrangu	*Avoid poisonous food.*
Könchok Yenlak	*Avoid poisoned food.*
Kunzig Shamar	*Abandon poisonous food.*
Thogme Zangpo	*Give up poisonous food.*
Thupten Jinpa	*Discard poisonous food.*
Wikipedia: Chekawa	*Avoid poisoned food.*

Slogan 30 – *With a good nature rely on the root text.*

Chögyam Trungpa	*Don't be so predictable.*
Dilgo Khyentse	*Don't be hidebound by a sense of duty.*

Jamgon Kongtrul	*Don't rely on a sense of duty.*
Kelsang Gyatso	*Do not follow delusions.*
Khenchen Thrangu	*Don't be so constant.*
Könchok Yenlak	*Do not make a point of constancy.*
Kunzig Shamar	*Helping others is not based on returning favours.*
Thogme Zangpo	*Don't be so loyal to the cause.*
Thupten Jinpa	*Do not maintain inappropriate loyalty.*
Wikipedia: Chekawa	*Do not hold a grudge.*

The Tibetan for this slogan seems to be quite straightforward, so I can offer no insight into the variations of interpretation.

Slogan 31 – *Do not be agitated by past grievances.*

Chögyam Trungpa	*Don't malign others.*
Dilgo Khyentse	*Do not meet abuse with abuse.*
Jamgon Kongtrul	*Don't lash out.*
Kelsang Gyatso	*Do not retaliate to verbal abuse.*
Khenchen Thrangu	*Don't get riled by critical remarks.*
Könchok Yenlak	*Avoid the agitation of hurtful talk.*
Kunzig Shamar	*Do not expose the faults of others to irritate them.*
Thogme Zangpo	*Don't lash out in retaliation.*
Thupten Jinpa	*Do not torment with malicious banter.*
Wikipedia: Chekawa	*Do not respond to malicious talk.*

Slogan 32 – *Do not wait in ambush.*

Chögyam Trungpa	*Don't wait in ambush.*
Dilgo Khyentse	*Do not wait in ambush.*
Jamgon Kongtrul	*Don't wait in ambush.*
Kelsang Gyatso	*Do not wait in ambush.*
Khenchen Thrangu	*Don't lie in ambush.*
Könchok Yenlak	*Do not wait in ambush.*

Kunzig Shamar	*Do not wait in ambush.*
Thogme Zangpo	*Don't lie in ambush.*
Thupten Jinpa	*Do not lie in ambush.*
Wikipedia: Chekawa	*Do not wait in ambush.*

Slogan 33 – *Do not bring out others' secret state.*

Chögyam Trungpa	*Don't bring things to a painful point.*
Dilgo Khyentse	*Do not strike at weakness.*
Jamgon Kongtrul	*Don't go for the throat.*
Kelsang Gyatso	*Do not offend others.*
Khenchen Thrangu	*Don't strike at weak points.*
Könchok Yenlak	*Do not focus on others' sore points.*
Kunzig Shamar	*Never strike at the heart.*
Thogme Zangpo	*Don't strike a vulnerable point.*
Thupten Jinpa	*Do not strike at the heart.*
Wikipedia: Chekawa	*Do not strike to the core.*

Slogan 34 – *Do not put a dzo's load on an ox.*

Chögyam Trungpa	*Don't transfer the ox's load to the cow.*
Dilgo Khyentse	*Do not lay the dzo's load on an ox's back.*
Jamgon Kongtrul	*Do not put an ox's load on a cow.*
Kelsang Gyatso	*Do not transfer your own faults or burdens onto others.*
Khenchen Thrangu	*Don't transfer a dzo's burden onto an ox.*
Könchok Yenlak	*Do not burden a cow with an ox's load.*
Kunzig Shamar	*Do not put an ox's load on a cow.*
Thogme Zangpo	*Don't transfer the ox's burden to the cow.*
Thupten Jinpa	*Do not place the load of a dzo onto an ox.*
Wikipedia: Chekawa	*Do not put the load of a dzo on an ox.*

Slogan 35 – *Do not hurry to reach the summit.*

Chögyam Trungpa	*Don't try to be the fastest.*
Dilgo Khyentse	*Do not praise with hidden motives.*
Jamgon Kongtrul	*Don't be competitive.*
Kelsang Gyatso	*Do not aim to be the first to get the best.*
Khenchen Thrangu	*Don't aim to be the fastest.*
Könchok Yenlak	*Do not play to win.*
Kunzig Shamar	*Do not aim to be the best.*
Thogme Zangpo	*Don't be competitive.*
Thupten Jinpa	*Do not sprint to win a race.*
Wikipedia: Chekawa	*Do not aim to win the race.*

Slogan 36 – *Do not pervert the meal.*

Chögyam Trungpa	*Don't act with a twist.*
Dilgo Khyentse	*Do not misuse the remedy.*
Jamgon Kongtrul	*Don't make practice a sham.*
Kelsang Gyatso	*Do not misuse Dharma.*
Khenchen Thrangu	*Don't act with a twist.*
Könchok Yenlak	*Do not misuse magic.*
Kunzig Shamar	*Do not misuse the remedy.*
Thogme Zangpo	*Don't misperform the rites.*
Thupten Jinpa	*Do not abuse this [practice] as a rite.*
Wikipedia: Chekawa	*Do not use perverse means.*

The *meaning* of this slogan is consistent in all commentaries, indicating twisting or perverting the teachings. The word *meal* is not used in the other commentaries' wording of the slogan, although it is indicated in the Tibetan: *lTo* means *a meal*; *log* means *reversed, opposite, wrong, perverted*. In slogan 29—*abandon poisonous food*—Chekhawa employs food as an analogy for the teachings, and I suggest that he returned to the analogy of Mind Training and nourishment in this slogan. Hence I have translated the Tibetan as given: *do not pervert the meal.*

Slogan 37 – *Do not turn gods into demons.*

Chögyam Trungpa	*Don't make gods into demons.*
Dilgo Khyentse	*Do not bring a god down to the level of a demon.*
Jamgon Kongtrul	*Do not turn a god into a demon.*
Kelsang Gyatso	*Do not turn a god into a demon.*
Khenchen Thrangu	*Don't turn gods into demons.*
Könchok Yenlak	*Do not turn a god into a demon.*
Kunzig Shamar	*Do not use gods for evil.*
	Adds a slogan: *Be like a humble servant before all.*
Thogme Zangpo	*Don't reduce gods to demons.*
Thupten Jinpa	*Do not turn the gods into demons.*
Wikipedia: Chekawa	*Do not turn a god into a demon.*

Slogan 38 – *Do not look for happiness in others' pain.*

Chögyam Trungpa	*Don't seek others' pain as the limbs of your own happiness.*
Dilgo Khyentse	*Do not take advantage of suffering.*
Jamgon Kongtrul	*Don't look to profit from sorrow.*
Kelsang Gyatso	*Do not seek happiness by causing unhappiness to others.*
Khenchen Thrangu	*Don't seek others' pain as the limbs of your happiness.*
Könchok Yenlak	*Do not look to make pain part of pleasure.*
Kunzig Shamar	*Do not delight in the suffering of others.*
Thogme Zangpo	*Don't seek others' misery as crutches of your own happiness.*
Thupten Jinpa	*Do not seek misery as a means to happiness.*
Wikipedia: Chekawa	*Do not seek [others'] suffering as a means to your own happiness.*

Point Seven – advice

Slogan 39 – *Practise all the teachings with a single intention.*

Chögyam Trungpa	*All activities should be done with one intention.*
Dilgo Khyentse	*Do everything with one intention.*
Jamgon Kongtrul	*Use one practice for everything.*

Kelsang Gyatso	*Do all yogas by one.*
Khenchen Thrangu	*All practices should be done with one intention.*
Könchok Yenlak	*There is one way to do all practices.*
Kunzig Shamar	*Practise all yogas in one way.*
Thogme Zangpo	*Do everything with a single intention.*
Thupten Jinpa	*Accomplish all yogas through a single means.*
Wikipedia: Chekawa	*Perform all yogas with the one.*

Slogan 40 – *Reverse all misfortunes with a single intention.*

Chögyam Trungpa	*Correct all wrongs with one intention.*
Dilgo Khyentse	*Apply one remedy in all adversity.*
Jamgon Kongtrul	*Use one remedy for everything.*
Kelsang Gyatso	*Perform every suppression of interference by one.*
Khenchen Thrangu	*One practice corrects everything.*
Könchok Yenlak	*Confront all problems with one solution.*
Kunzig Shamar	*Subdue all obstacles by one method.*
Thogme Zangpo	*Counter all adversity with a single remedy.*
Thupten Jinpa	*Overcome all errors through a single means.*
Wikipedia: Chekawa	*Apply the one to all perverse oppressors.*

Slogan 41 – *Both first and last, two things to do.*

Chögyam Trungpa	*Two activities: one at the beginning, one at the end.*
Dilgo Khyentse	*Two things to be done, at the start and at the finish.*
Jamgon Kongtrul	*Two things to do: one at the beginning, one at the end.*
Kelsang Gyatso	*There are two activities: one at the beginning and one at the end.*
Khenchen Thrangu	*At the start and the finish, an activity to be done.*
Könchok Yenlak	*In the beginning, in the end: two things to do.*
Kunzig Shamar	*Two actions to perform: at the beginning and at the end.*
Thogme Zangpo	*Two tasks: one at the beginning and one at the end.*
Thupten Jinpa	*There are two tasks—one at the start and one at the end.*
Wikipedia: Chekawa	*Do the two activities, one at the beginning and one at the end. Be mindful in order to admonish yourself.*

Slogan 42 – *Whichever of the two occurs, practise patience.*

Chögyam Trungpa	*Whichever of the two occurs, be patient.*
Dilgo Khyentse	*Bear whichever of the two occurs.*
Jamgon Kongtrul	*Whatever happens, good or bad, be patient.*
Kelsang Gyatso	*Endure both, whichever arises.*
Khenchen Thrangu	*Whichever of the two occurs, be patient.*
Könchok Yenlak	*Patiently accept whichever of the two occurs.*
Kunzig Shamar	*Be patient with whichever of the two arises.*
Thogme Zangpo	*Whichever of the two occurs, be patient.*
Thupten Jinpa	*Whichever of the two arises, be patient.*
Wikipedia: Chekawa	*Be patient whichever of the two occurs.*

Slogan 43 – *Guard the two, even at the risk of your life.*

Chögyam Trungpa	*Observe these two, even at the risk of your life.*
Dilgo Khyentse	*Even if it costs you your life, defend the two.*
Jamgon Kongtrul	*Keep these two, even if your life is at risk.*
Kelsang Gyatso	*Guard both as you would your life.*
Khenchen Thrangu	*Maintain these two, even at the risk of your life.*
Könchok Yenlak	*Keep both as if your life depended on it.*
Kunzig Shamar	*Guard the two, even at the cost of your life.*
Thogme Zangpo	*Keep the two, even at your life's expense.*
Thupten Jinpa	*Guard the two, even at the cost of your life.*
Wikipedia: Chekawa	*Guard the two at the risk of your life.*

Slogan 44 – *Train in the three difficulties.*

Chögyam Trungpa	*Train in the three difficulties.*
Dilgo Khyentse	*Train yourself in three hard disciplines.*
Jamgon Kongtrul	*Learn to meet three challenges.*
Kelsang Gyatso	*Train in the three difficulties.*
Khenchen Thrangu	*Train in the three difficult points.*
Könchok Yenlak	*Train in the three challenges.*
Kunzig Shamar	*Train in the three difficulties.*

Thogme Zangpo	*Train in the three difficulties.*
Thupten Jinpa	*Train in the three difficult challenges.*
Wikipedia: Chekawa	*Train in the three difficult ones.*

Slogan 45 – *Embrace the three principal causes.*

Chögyam Trungpa	*Take on the three principal causes.*
Dilgo Khyentse	*Have recourse to three essential factors.*
Jamgon Kongtrul	*Foster three key elements.*
Kelsang Gyatso	*Practise the three main causes.*
Khenchen Thrangu	*Take up the three main causes.*
Könchok Yenlak	*Adopt the three principal causes.*
Kunzig Shamar	*Keep the three main causes.*
Thogme Zangpo	*Acquire the three main provisions.*
Thupten Jinpa	*Adopt the three principal conditions.*
Wikipedia: Chekawa	*Obtain the three principal causes.*

Slogan 46 – *Practise so that the three do not deteriorate.*

Chögyam Trungpa	*Pay heed that the three never wane.*
Dilgo Khyentse	*Meditate on three things that must not deteriorate.*
Jamgon Kongtrul	*Take care to prevent three kinds of damage.*
Kelsang Gyatso	*Become acquainted with the three non-degenerations.*
Khenchen Thrangu	*Pay attention that these three things do not diminish.*
Könchok Yenlak	*Unfailingly cultivate three things.*
Kunzig Shamar	*Cultivate the three without diminishment.*
Thogme Zangpo	*Cultivate the three that must not decline.*
Thupten Jinpa	*Contemplate the three that are free of degeneration.*
Wikipedia: Chekawa	*Cultivate the three without deterioration.*

Slogan 47 – *Keep the three inseparable.*

Chögyam Trungpa	*Keep the three inseparable.*
Dilgo Khyentse	*Three things maintain inseparably.*
Jamgon Kongtrul	*Engage all three faculties.*

Kelsang Gyatso	*Possess the three inseparables.*
Khenchen Thrangu	*Keep the three inseparable.*
Könchok Yenlak	*Make sure you have the inseparable three.*
Kunzig Shamar	*Keep the three inseparable .*
Thogme Zangpo	*Keep the three inseparable.*
Thupten Jinpa	*Be endowed with the three inseperable factors.*
Wikipedia: Chekawa	*Possess the three without separation.*

Slogan 48 – *Train deeply and pervasively in all areas without prejudice, and once perfected, cherish everyone and everything, everywhere.*

Chögyam Trungpa	*Train without bias in all areas; it is crucial to do this pervasively and wholeheartedly.*
Dilgo Khyentse	*Train impartially in every field; your training must be deep and all-pervading.*
Jamgon Kongtrul	*Train on every object without preference. Training must be broad and deep.*
Kelsang Gyatso	*Train without bias towards the objects.*
	Adds a slogan: *It is important to train deeply and encompass all.*
Khenchen Thrangu	*Train impartially in all areas; deep, pervasive, and constant training is crucial.*
Könchok Yenlak	*Train impartially in every instance. Once deep and inclusive training has taken place, love everyone.*
Kunzig Shamar	*Practise with impartiality.*
	Adds a slogan: *All training must be pervasive and profound.*
Thogme Zangpo	*Apply the training impartially to all. It is vital that it be deep and all-pervasive.*
Thupten Jinpa	– omitted.
Wikipedia: Chekawa	*Train in purity and impartiality with respect to objects.*

As can be seen in the list, some commentaries split this into two slogans.

Slogan 49 – *Always practise with whatever makes you boil.*

Chögyam Trungpa	*Always meditate on whatever provokes resentment.*
Dilgo Khyentse	*Always meditate on what is unavoidable.*
Jamgon Kongtrul	*Always work on whatever makes you boil.*
Kelsang Gyatso	*– omitted.*
Khenchen Thrangu	*Always meditate on what aggravates you.*
Könchok Yenlak	*Always practise with special cases.*
Kunzig Shamar	*Meditate consistently in every circumstance.*
Thogme Zangpo	*Meditate constantly on those who've been set apart.*
Thupten Jinpa	*Train constantly toward the chosen objects.*
Wikipedia: Chekawa	*Meditate constantly on the special cases.*

Slogan 50 – *Refrain from being influenced by external circumstances.*

Chögyam Trungpa	*Don't be swayed by external circumstances.*
Dilgo Khyentse	*Do not be dependent on external factors.*
Jamgon Kongtrul	*Don't rely on extraneous conditions.*
Kelsang Gyatso	*Do not rely on other conditions.*
Khenchen Thrangu	*Don't be swayed by outer circumstances.*
Könchok Yenlak	*Do not concern yourself with external factors.*
Kunzig Shamar	*Do not depend on external conditions.*
Thogme Zangpo	*Don't be dependent on external conditions.*
Thupten Jinpa	*Do not depend on other conditions.*
Wikipedia: Chekawa	*Cherish all of the encompassing and profound trainings.*

Slogan 51 – *This time make practice the priority.*

Chögyam Trungpa	*This time, practise the main points.*
Dilgo Khyentse	*This time, do what is important.*
Jamgon Kongtrul	*Practice what's important now.*
Kelsang Gyatso	*Apply the principal practice at this time.*
Khenchen Thrangu	*This time practice what is most important.*
Könchok Yenlak	*Put the most important things into practice now.*

Kunzig Shamar	*From now on, practice is the chief priority.*
Thogme Zangpo	*This time, practise what's most important.*
Thupten Jinpa	*Engage in the principal practices right now.*
Wikipedia: Chekawa	*Practice the most important right now.*

Slogan 52 – *Refrain from falsifying and perverting.*

Chögyam Trungpa	*Don't misinterpret.*
Dilgo Khyentse	*Do not make mistakes.*
Jamgon Kongtrul	*Don't get things wrong.*
Kelsang Gyatso	*Do not misinterpret.*
Khenchen Thrangu	*Don't make mistakes.*
Könchok Yenlak	*Do not misconstrue.*
Kunzig Shamar	*Do not be misdirected.*
Thogme Zangpo	*Don't misunderstand.*
Thupten Jinpa	*Do not apply misplaced understanding.*
Wikipedia: Chekawa	*Avoid the distorted understandings.*

Many of the commentaries to this slogan specify six areas with regard to mistakes and misinterpretation. The mistakes are about what to adopt and what to abandon, when to apply a method and when it is inappropriate.

The six areas for attention are:

1. patience or endurance,
2. interest and aspiration,
3. delight and appreciation,
4. compassion,
5. caring and helping,
6. rejoicing.

All six have the same theme: the pain of someone else is easy to bear, but personal pain is unbearable. Looking at this, it becomes possible to assess how much the emptiness of identity is actually a lived reality, and thereby, how much the focus on the needs of others is really felt as a priority.

The six areas are examined in terms of the appropriate engagement with Mind Training:

- Is there patience when things are going well, but not when practice or life is challenging? Is there patience with the pain of others, but no patience with personal pain?

- Is there a yearning for possessions and an easy life, but a lack of yearning for practice and awakening?

- Is delight taken in material comforts, but the benefits of Mind Training are not appreciated or savoured?

- Is there compassionate concern for practitioners who forgo the pleasures of life in order to embrace a life of spiritual practice, rather than concern for those who are experiencing real difficulties?

- Is there energy to help and care for friends and family, but no energy to help those who are unfriendly or distant? Is there enthusiasm to pursue worldly pursuits, and encourage others in this way, but no energy to develop or encourage spiritual practice?

- Is the happiness of friends celebrated, but also the unhappiness of enemies? Is success in misdeeds celebrated – such as giving accolades to someone who has become rich through swindling others?

Slogan 53 – *Refrain from being sporadic.*

Chögyam Trungpa	*Don't vacillate.*
Dilgo Khyentse	*Be consistent in your practice.*
Jamgon Kongtrul	*Don't switch on and off.*
Kelsang Gyatso	*Do not be erratic.*
Khenchen Thrangu	*Don't fluctuate.*
Könchok Yenlak	*Do not be inconsistent.*
Kunzig Shamar	*Do not be inconsistent.*
Thogme Zangpo	*Don't be inconsistent.*

Thupten Jinpa	*Do not be sporadic.*
Wikipedia: Chekawa	*Do not be erratic.*

Slogan 54 – *Check how much you are gripped by training.*

Chögyam Trungpa	*Train wholeheartedly.*
Dilgo Khyentse	*Be zealous in your training.*
Jamgon Kongtrul	*Train wholeheartedly.*
Kelsang Gyatso	*Train with certainty.*
Khenchen Thrangu	*Train with your whole heart.*
Könchok Yenlak	*Practise decisively.*
Kunzig Shamar	*Train uninterruptedly.*
Thogme Zangpo	*Train wholeheartedly.*
Thupten Jinpa	*Train with decisiveness.*
Wikipedia: Chekawa	*Train continuously.*

The Tibetan syllable at the beginning of this slogan—*dol*—means a net or a trap. Shamar Rinpoche and Yenlak Rinpoche's version of the Tibetan disagree for the next syllable. Shamar Rinpoche has *chod* for the second syllable, which means *to cut*. The combination of these two syllables—*dol-chod*—gives the meaning of *focussing without distraction*. Yenlak Rinpoche, however, has *tshod* as the second syllable, which means *to measure or judge*. As Yenlak Rinpoche's translation is the older, and given that Chekhawa seems to enjoy employing evocative imagery in the slogans, I have translated this slogan as: *Check how much you are gripped*—as in netted or trapped—*by (mind) training.*'

Slogan 55 – *Escape duality through investigation and analysis.*

Chögyam Trungpa	*Liberate yourself by examining and analysing.*
Dilgo Khyentse	*Free yourself by analysis and testing.*
Jamgon Kongtrul	*Find freedom by probing and testing.*
Kelsang Gyatso	*Be released by two: investigation and analysis.*
Khenchen Thrangu	*Free yourself through examination and analysis.*

Könchok Yenlak	*Free yourself by examining and analysing.*
Kunzig Shamar	*Liberate by examination and analysis.*
Thogme Zangpo	*Gain freedom through discernment and analysis.*
Thupten Jinpa	*Be released through the two: investigation and close analysis.*
Wikipedia: Chekawa	*Attain liberation with the two, investigation and analysis.*

Slogan 56 – *Avoid boastful behaviour.*

Chögyam Trungpa	*Don't wallow in self-pity.*
Dilgo Khyentse	*Don't take what you do too seriously.*
Jamgon Kongtrul	*Don't boast.*
Kelsang Gyatso	*Do not be boastful.*
Khenchen Thrangu	*Don't make a big deal about it.*
Könchok Yenlak	*Do not make a habit of showing off.*
Kunzig Shamar	*Do not seek recognition.*
Thogme Zangpo	*Don't be boastful.*
Thupten Jinpa	*Do not boast of your good deeds.*
Wikipedia: Chekawa	*Refrain from retaliating.*

Some of the commentaries talk about self-pity in this slogan. Self-pity could be understood as an inverted, or perverted, form of boastfulness. It is a different type of attention-seeking. Self-pity can be a big obstacle to progress, sapping energy and undermining the energy of enthusiastic engagement.

Personal pain can become a big reference point, a painful identity that is not allowed to heal. Because of receiving kindness and attention from others, the pain is held onto and used as a way to gain further kindness and attention. The pain may be continually renewed, rather than being allowed to naturally dissolve, so that others continue to sympathise and feel pity. The kindness and attention are appreciated honestly at first. It is like being given medicine. But the patient becomes addicted to the medicine and unable to heal, because healing would mean an end to the kindly attention.

To heal would be to lose the reason for more medicine. The person becomes trapped in the pain because it has become a definition.

The painful definition becomes uncomfortably comfortable, and easier than entertaining the emptiness of change. It also becomes an excuse for not being able to help others or notice their pain.

> *'Instead of wallowing in your own fascination either with being special or not getting what you deserve, you could practice thinking of others for a while.'*
> Judith Lief – Train Your Mind: Lojong Commentary

Self-pity is needy and greedy, demanding attention in the same way that boastful behaviour seeks attention. The need to be the centre of attention makes Mind Training impossible. Awakening mind and awakening intention makes others the centre of attention.

Slogan 57 – *Avoid being bound by jealousy and frustration.*

Chögyam Trungpa	*Don't be jealous.*
Dilgo Khyentse	*Do not be bad tempered.*
Jamgon Kongtrul	*Don't be hypersensitive.*
Kelsang Gyatso	*Do not get angry.*
Khenchen Thrangu	*Don't let being irritated tie you up.*
Könchok Yenlak	*Do not be irritable.*
Kunzig Shamar	*Do not hold on to anger.*
Thogme Zangpo	*Don't be irritable.*
Thupten Jinpa	*Do not be ill-tempered.*
Wikipedia: Chekawa	*Do not look for other conditions.*

The final word in the Tibetan for this slogan disagree in the texts of Shamar Rinpoche and Könchok Yenlak. Shamar Rinpoche has the last word as *sDom*, whereas Könchok Yenlak has *sDam*. *sDom* means to bind, discipline or stop, and *sDam* means to be bound or fastened. The overall meaning of the slogan remains the same.

Slogan 58 – *Refrain from practising just a little.*

Chögyam Trungpa	*Don't be frivolous.*
Dilgo Khyentse	*Do not be temperamental.*
Thogme Zangpo	*Don't be temperamental.*
Jamgon Kongtrul	*Don't be impulsive.*
Kelsang Gyatso	*Do not be unstable.*
Khenchen Thrangu	*Don't overreact.*
Könchok Yenlak	*Do not be capricious.*
Kunzig Shamar	*Do not be moody.*
Thogme Zangpo	*Don't be temperamental.*
Thupten Jinpa	*Do not be fickle.*
	Adds a slogan: *Do not be boisterous.*
Wikipedia: Chekawa	*Do not act impetuously.*

Slogan 59 – *Do not wish for thanks.*

Chögyam Trungpa	*Don't expect applause.*
Dilgo Khyentse	*Do not expect to be rewarded.*
Jamgon Kongtrul	*Don't expect thanks.*
Kelsang Gyatso	*Do not wish for gratitude.*
Khenchen Thrangu	*Don't expect a standing ovation.*
Könchok Yenlak	*Do not crave thanks.*
Kunzig Shamar	*Do not seek gratitude.*
Thogme Zangpo	*Don't seek acknowledgment.*
Thupten Jinpa	– omitted.
	Adds a slogan: *Through this proliferation of the five degenerations transform [every event] into the path of enlightenment.*
Wikipedia: Chekawa	*Do not wish for gratitude.*

Glossary of Buddhist Terms

Alaya
: *see Kun-zhi.*

Aro gTér Lineage
: The Nyingma Lineage founded by the great yogini Khyungchen Aro Lingma (1886–1923). She received the pure vision gTérma from Yeshé Tsogyel.

Atisha
: Tib. Jo-wo Je Palden Atisha *(Jo bo rJe dPal lDan A ti sha)* Skt. *Atiśa Dīapamkar Śrījñāna* (980–1054). Came to Tibet in 1042 to help reestablish monastic Buddhism.

Awakened hero
: changchub sempa *(byang chub sems dPa')*, Skt. *Bodhisattva* – one who aspires to awaken view and intention.

Awakened mind
: chang chub kyi sem *(byang chub kyi sems)*, Skt. *Bodhicitta* – the mind that has awakened view and intention.

Awakening
: chang chub *(byang chub)*, Skt. *Bodhi* – the purpose of Mind Training. It is the realisation of the nonduality of emptiness and form, self and other, existence and non-existence, and manifests as awakened view and awakened intention.

Bodhicitta
: *see Awakened mind.*

Bodhisattva
: *see Awakened hero.*

Changchub-kyi-sem
: *see Awakening.*

Changchub-sempa
: *see Awakening Hero.*

Chekhawa Yeshé Dorje
'Chad kha ba Ye shes rDo rJe (1101–1175). The teacher who composed the Seven Points of Mind Training – lojong don dun ma (*Lojong don bDun ma*).

Damtsig
dam tshig – vow, commitment.

Dharmakaya
see *Spheres of being*.

Dzogchen
see *Vehicle*.

Eight worldly dharmas
Tib. jig ten chö gye (*jigs rTen chos brGyad*) – experiencing the phenomena of life as an unsatisfactory oscillation between hope and fear, loss and gain, meeting and parting, praise and blame. Other sets of eight may include pleasure and pain, fame and shame.

Emptiness
Emptiness (Tib. tongpa nyi – *sTong pa nyid*, Skt. *shunyata*) – the womb of potential from which all form arises.

Five powers
Tob nga (*sTobs lNga*) – confidence, energy, presence, alert attention, discriminating awareness. These are the powers that are developed through Mind Training.

Four naljors
naljor zhi (*rNal 'byor bZhi*) the preliminary practices of the Aro gTér Lineage: 1. remaining uninvolved – shi-nè (*zhi gNas*), 2. further vision – lhatong (*lhag mThong*), 3. discovering what is the same – nyi'med (*gNyis 'med*), and 4. continuity, spontaneous presence – lhundrüp (*lhun grub*).

Heart Sutra
nying Do (*sNying mDo*), Skt. Prajnaparamita Hridaya Sutra – the Sutra that expounds the essence of Buddhism, that form and emptiness are a nonduality. See Part IV, Appendix 2, p. 311.

Kadampa
bKa' gDams pa – the name given to followers of Atisha in the 11th century.

Kagyüd school
see Sarma.

Kaya
see Spheres of being.

Khorwa
'khor ba, Skt. samsara – the cycle of dissatisfaction that is created through mistaken perception and the deluded response of attraction, aversion, or indifference.

Kun-zhi
Skt. *alaya* – all ground, the ground of all, beginningless awakened mind.

Lama
bLama, Skt. *guru* – the spiritual teacher.

Lama'i Naljor
bLa ma'i rNal 'byor, Skt. *guru yoga* – unifying with the mind of the Lama (spiritual teacher) through visionary practice.

Langdarma
gLang dar ma – ruled Tibet 836–841.

Langri Thangpa
gLang ri Thang pa (1054–1123) Author of the Eight Verses of Mind Training.

Lojong
see Mind Training.

Mind Training
Tib. Lojong (*bLo sByong*) – the practice developed by Atisha and passed down as an oral tradition. It was developed into the text *Seven Points of Mind Training* by Chekhawa Yeshé Dorje.

Nirmanakaya
see Vehicle.

Nyingma
rNying ma – the *Old Translation School*, who practised the original form of Buddhism in Tibet founded by Padmasambhava and Śāntaraksita. This pertains not only to the lineage of practice but to the style of translation. Nyingma translations are not literal word-for-word from Sanskrit, unlike the Sarma translations.

Padmasambhava
Guru Rinpoche, the Lotus-born Lama who founded the yogic stream of Nyingma Vajrayana Buddhism in Tibet in the 8th century.

Paramitas
Tib. *par pyin* (phar phyin) – the transcendences or perfections. They are enumerated as six or ten perfections.

Preliminary practice
ngöndro (*sNgon 'gro*) – practices that prepare for the main body of practice.

Refuge
kyab (*sKyabs*) – the first vow of commitment which asserts that the practitioner is a Buddhist.

Rigpa
rig pa – unborn primordial awareness, the experience of the nonduality of form and emptiness.

Rinchen Zangpo
Rin chen bZang po (958–1055). A Tibetan scholar appointed to oversee the reestablishment of monastic Buddhist practice.

Root misconceptions
Tib. nyon mong-pa dug sum (*nyon mongs pa dug gSum*); Skt. *klesha*. Attraction, aversion, and indifference. Described as the three poisons in slogan 8.

Sakya school
see *Sarma*.

Sambhogakaya
see *Vehicle*.

Samsara
see Khorwa.

Samyé
bSam yas – the great university monastery that was built in the 8th century and restored in the 11th century.

Sang-gyé Yeshé
Sangs rGyas Ye shes – a 9th century yogic practitioner, and disciple of Padmasambhava, who terrified Langdarma by manifesting a scorpion the size of nine yaks, and cleaving a mountain top.

Śāntaraksita
Tib. Shiwa Tso (*Shi ba Tsho*), 725–788. Founded the monastic stream of Nyingma Buddhism in Tibet in the 8th century.

Sarma
gSar ma – the new translation schools of Kagyüd (*bKa' brGyud*) and Sakya (*sa sKya*) that arose when monastic Buddhism was re-established in Tibet in the 11th century.

Serlingpa
gSer gLing pa, Skt *Dharmakīrtiśrī* – 10th century practitioner from Burma who was Atisha's root teacher. *gSer* means gold, or golden, and *gLing* means place, region, or island. Chekhawa refers to him as the *One from the Golden Isle*.

Sharawa Yonten Dag
Sha ra ba Yon tan Grags (1070–1141). A disciple of Langri Thangpa, who taught Mind Training to Chekhawa.

Slogan
A battlecry. An Anglicisation of the Scottish Gaelic and Irish word *sluagh-ghairm* – *sluagh* meaning army or host, and *gairm* meaning cry.

Songtsen Gampo
Srong bTsan sGam po – a king who united the clans of Tibet and ruled 618–649.

Spheres of being

1. Emptiness – the sphere of unconditioned potentiality (Tib. chö-ku – *chos sKu*; Skt. *dharmakaya*).
2. Energy – the sphere of intangible appearances (Tib. long-ku – *longs sKu*, Skt. *sambhogakaya*).
3. Form – the sphere of realised manifestation (Tib. trülku – *sPrul sKu*, Skt. *nirmanakaya*).
4. The essence sphere (ngo-wo-ku or dorje-ku – *ngo bo nyid sKu, rDo rJe sKu*, Skt: *svabhavikakaya*). The inseparability of the first three spheres is expressed as this fourth sphere.

Spiritual Friend

The teacher in Sutra. Tib. **ge-wa'i-she-nyen** (*dGe ba'i bShes gNyen*, Skt. *Kalyanamitra*).

Sutra

see Vehicle.

Sutrayana

From the perspective of the nine vehicle system of the Nyingma school, Sutrayana encompasses the three renunciate vehicles: 1. the Hearers – *Shravakayana*, 2. the Solitary Realisers – *Pratyékayabuddhayana*, and 3. those who dedicate their practice to the liberation of all beings – *Bodhisattvabuddhayana*.

Tantra

see Vehicle.

Theg pa

see Vehicle.

Tonglen

gTong len – the practice of taking and giving described in slogan 7, that is central to Mind Training.

Tri Ralpachen

Khri Ral pa can – ruled Tibet 815–836.

Trisong Détsen

Khri srong lDe bTsan – ruled Tibet 755–797.

Tsenpo

bTsan po – king, ruler, monarch.

Vajra Master

The teacher in Tantra and Dzogchen. Tib. Dorje Löpon (*rDo-rJe sLob-dPon*, Skt. *Vajracarya*).

Vajrayana

From the perspective of the nine vehicle system of the Nyingma Tradition, Vajrayana encompasses six vehicles: the three Outer Tantras – kriya, upa, and yoga; and the three Inner Tantras – maha, anu and ati (Dzogchen). When the word Tantra is used it means the five vehicles prior to Dzogchen.

Vehicle

Tib. thegpa (*theg pa*), Skt. Yana – a complete method of practice that has a base, a path, and a fruit. From the perspective of Dzogchen there are three vehicles: Sutra (do – *mDo*), Tantra (gyüd – *rGyud*), and Mahasandhi (Dzogchen – *rDzogs chen*). Commonly these are referred to as Sutra, Tantra, and Dzogchen. The principle of Sutra is renunciation. The principle of Tantra is transformation. The principle of Dzogchen is self-liberation.

Yana

see Vehicle.

Yeshé Ö

ye shes 'od (c. 959–1040) – the king who invited Atisha to Tibet, ostensibly to *re-establish* Buddhism – but actually to establish his own authority as *spiritual king*. The Nyingma lineages were vital and unbroken: there was nothing to *re-establish*.

Yogic tradition

The tradition of non-celibate practice and mainly non-monastic, and non-institutional practice. Tib. gö kar chang lo'i dé (*gos dKar lCang lo'i sDe*). Practitioners are often called called yogis and yoginis – but these terms can also apply to advanced monks and nuns. Ordained gö kar chang lo practitioners are called ngakmas (*sNgags ma*) and ngakpas (*sNgags pa*), naljormas (*rNal 'byor ma*) and naljorpas (*rNal 'byor pa*).

Glossary of Equestrian Terms

Back-up
: The horse steps backwards in response to the rider's request.

Balance position
: Riders stand in the stirrups with their weight off the horse's back. They are balanced so that they are not thrown forward onto the neck, or back to bounce on the horse's back. This is a comfortable position for horse and rider for an extended canter or a gallop.

Bareback
: Riding without a saddle.

Bay
: A horse that is brown in colour.

Bolt
: When the horse suddenly takes off at a fast pace – usually a flight reaction.

Bosal side pull
: A type of bitless bridle. The side pull places pressure on the horse's nose for control through the reins.

Canter
: A fast, three-beat gait of the horse.

Collection
: The horse's energy is full and rounded, but contained like a spring, through placing more of its weight in the hind quarters.

Comportment
: The carriage and shape of the horse as it moves, such as an arched neck, weight in the hind quarters, back lifted and rounded, head held vertically.

Cross-over bridle
: A bitless bridle that applies pressure to the cheeks, nose and poll of the horse's head, as well as under the jaw where the reins cross each other. I rode Dee in this type of bridle for about 10 years.

Crupper
: An item of tack that goes under the horse's tail and is attached to the saddle, to prevent the saddle moving forward.

Curb bit
: A type of bit that uses a lever action.

Dee
: A Welsh cob mare whom I owned from 2005 to 2017. She was 27 when she died of a heart attack. She was a bay, with a black mane and tail, two white socks, and a white star, 15.2 hands high.

Double bridle
: A bridle with two sets of reins that attach to a curb and a snaffle bit. In the hands of an experienced rider and well schooled horse, the double bridle allows a wide range of contact and control through the bits.

Dressage
: An equestrian sport that embraces the full range of a horse's athletic capacity and grace. The rider's aids should be imperceptible in asking for the movements and paces of a dressage performance.

Endurance riding
: Cross country riding over long distances.

English style
: A style and method of riding that is seen throughout the world. The saddle is flat with a low pommel, and stirrups that hang from leather straps. The reins are held with sufficient tension to maintain contact with the horse through the bit.

Fun ride
: A non-competitive equestrian event. Riders from a wide area may attend to join in the activities. At the trekking centre, fun rides included a hack, and a cross country jumping course.

Gallop
: The fastest pace of a horse. It is a four-beat variation of a canter, with a longer stride.

Gelding
A male horse that has been castrated, or the act of castrating. The purpose of gelding is to create a calmer, quieter, and better behaved horse than might be the case with an ungelded stallion.

Giving the horse its head
Letting go of contact with the bit through the reins. This may be to allow the horse to relax its head down as a break from schooling, or at the end of a ride. Or it may be to allow the horse to lift its head and feel free to move as fast as it wishes.

Gripping with knees
The method of riding that I was taught in the 1960s. The saddle is gripped with the knees over the horse's shoulder to maintain correct posture on the horse. It is out of favour nowadays, and considered to restrict the horse's movement. Leg wrapping is preferred, which gives a longer line to the leg, with the focus of contact more on the thigh and lower leg, than on the knee. In both disciplines, the heel of the foot should be kept down in the stirrup.

Hackamore
A bitless bridle that controls the horse through pressure on the face, nose, and chin, rather than on a bit in the mouth. We rode Red in a hackamore for a couple of years.

Hacking / a hack
Non-competitive riding along trails and horse tracks.

Halt and spring into canter
An exercise where the horse is encouraged to collect its weight into the hind quarters in order to powerfully spring straight from a halt into a canter.

Hand
An ancient method of measuring horses, using the width of the hand to measure the height from the ground to the wither. In the UK, a hand was standardised as being 4 inches (100mm) in 1540 by Henry VIII. If a horse is described as 15.0 hands high, this means that it measures 15 x 4 inches from the ground to the wither. The quarter sections of the hand are indicated by saying 15.1, 15.2, and 15.3 – meaning 15 hands plus 1 inch, 2 inches, or 3 inches respectively.

Head-shy
A horse that is reluctant to have its head touched or handled, and is usually difficult to bridle.

Join up
A natural horsemanship technique where the horse is sent away from a trainer standing in the centre of a round pen. The horse is made to keep moving through the trainer's body language or the use of a long whip. The trainer looks for signs that the horse is ready to accept the trainer as herd leader, such as dropping its head or making chewing movements. The trainer then quietly turns away from the horse and allows the horse to come over and join up with them.

Leg wrapping
A method in which riders maintain balance and correct posture in the saddle, and contact with the horse, through wrapping their legs around the horse, keeping their heels down so the legs are long. Contact with the horse is through the thigh and lower leg.

Leg yield
A lateral movement where the horse is instructed to move forwards and sideways at the same time.

Long reining
see Lunging.

Lunging
Can also be spelt lungeing or longeing. A method of training the horse from the ground on a long rein or reins.

Martingale
A piece of tack attached to the reins and the girth. It is used to encourage the horse to carry its head in the correct position.

Manège
The French term for an arena for schooling horses, usually rectangular. It is often incorrectly written as menage.

Mucking out
Removing soiled bedding from a stable.

Neck rope
A rope around the neck of the horse that can be held for extra security in the saddle, or instead of the reins.

Novice
A rather vague term for a rider with little experience or knowledge. Riding establishments will have their own definitions for riders who are novice, intermediate, and experienced. In a sense I was only ever a novice rider as I had little formal training. I did, however, have a great deal of experience, and in some equestrian establishments this would lead to my being considered more capable than a novice.

Piaffe
A dressage movement where the energy of the horse is highly collected and it trots almost on the spot.

Pirouette
A dressage movement where the horse turns in a circle. The hind legs hardly move, whilst the fore legs create the circle.

Poll
The top of the horse's head, between or just behind the ears.

Pommel strap
A strap that clips onto the front of an English saddle that can be held by the novice rider for extra security in the saddle, or instead of the reins.

Quarter mark patterns
Decorative grooming marks on the haunches—quarters—of the horse. They are often used to enhance the appearance of a horse's coat in competition. A template may be used, or skilful use of grooming tools.

Red – High Jinks
A 16.2 hands, bay, thoroughbred/cob cross. His official name was High Jinks, but he was always known as *Red* because of the beautiful deep red colour of his coat. He had a black mane and tail, one white sock, and a delightful snip on his nose.

Riding aids
> The rider's method of instructing the horse. Aids may include use of the leg, seat, hands, and voice.

Rising trot
> *see Trot.*

Rug/rugging
> Horses may be given a rug for various reasons. In the winter a rug may be used for warmth. In the summer a horse may be rugged to give them protection from flies. After hard work a horse may be given a cooling rug so that they do not catch a chill. There is a large range of styles, types, and weights of rug available. Rugs are called blankets in America.

Schooling
> Working on the relationship between horse and rider within the riding discipline being used. This is to practice riding aids, to introduce new movements to the horse, and to increase suppleness and performance of horse and rider.

Show jumping
> Jumping fences in an arena at competition. The jumps will vary in height, width, and combination.

Shying
> A sudden, usually sideways, movement of the horse, away from a sound or sight that has startled it. Also known as spooking.

Sitting trot
> *see Trot.*

Snaffle bit
> A bit that places direct pressure on the horse's mouth without a lever action. It is one of the most commonly used bits.

Snip
> A white mark on a horse's face between and below the nostrils.

Sock
> When describing a horse's markings, the sock is the part of a horse's leg above the hoof and below the knee.

Spooking
see Shying.

Trot – collected, working, and extended; rising and sitting.
The trot is a two-beat gait of the horse, where diagonal legs move together. In the *collected trot* the horse is asked for a short, but energetic stride. The *working trot* is an easy, comfortable working pace for horse and rider. The *extended trot* is more demanding for the horse with a longer stride. All three paces of trot will be used in dressage. In English style riding it is usual to *rise to the trot*, as opposed to *sitting the trot*. This is called posting in Western riding. In the rising trot the rider rises slightly out of the saddle on every other beat of the trot. When riding in a circle, or in an arena, it is necessary for the rider to coordinate the sitting beat with when the horse's outer foreleg and inner hind leg are back, and the inner foreleg and outer hind leg are forward. This helps keep the horse balanced and energetic. In sitting trot, the rider does not rise on each alternate beat of the trot, but sits for the whole movement. Sitting trot is usually a schooling exercise in English style riding, and a dressage movement. In Western style riding sitting to the trot is usual.

Turn out
To allow the horse freedom to graze in a field. The first livery yard we used only turned the horses out at night in the summer, and for a few hours during the day in the winter. At the trekking centre the horses lived out all the time. After an evening feed they were turned out. If a horse was reluctant, it would be allowed to remain in the stable overnight. In all the years Dee lived at this centre, she only asked to stay in the stable overnight twice. All the horses wanted to live out, and were keen to be turned out as soon as they had finished a feed.

Western style riding
This refers to the tack and riding aids used in traditional American ranch riding. The saddle, stirrups, girth, and bridle, are all of a different style from those used in English riding. One of the principles of the Western style of riding is to be able to work with cattle from horseback.

Whiskey
The only significant pony in my early years of riding. He was a six-year-old, bay gelding, 13.2 hands high.

Withers
: The ridge between the shoulder blades, which is the highest point of the horse's body. Dee had particularly high withers.

Worming
: A schedule of treatment to keep a horse free of worm parasites. The worming schedule was always managed by the livery manager, so that all horses were wormed at the same time.

Wrangler
: A person experienced in riding and handling horses. It is a term commonly associated with Western riding.

Bibliography

Books

A Concise Lojong Manual, Könchok Yenlak the 5th Sharmapa, translated by Pamela Gayle White, Bird of Paradise Press, 2014, 3rd printing, ISBN 978-0-9881762-6-3.

A Tibetan-English Dictionary, Sarat Chandra Das, Motiulal Banarsidass, 1976.

Always Maintain A Joyful Mind – and other Lojong Teachings on Awakening Compassion and Fearlessness, Pema Chödrön, Shambhala, 2007, ISBN 978-1-59030-460-0.

Emailing the Lamas from Afar, Ngakpa Chögyam and Khandro Déchen, Aro Books Inc, 2009, ISBN 978-0-96539-485-7.

Enlightened Courage, Dilgo Khyentse Rinpoche, Snow Lion Publications, 1993 and 2006, ISBN 978-1-55939-253-2.

Entering the Heart of the Sun and Moon, Ngakpa Chögyam and Khandro Déchen, Aro Books Inc, 2009, ISBN 978-0-96539-483-3.

Essential Mind Training, Thupten Jinpa, Wisdom Publications, 2011, Kindle edition, ISBN 978-0-86171-714-9.

Illusory Advice, Ngakma Nor'dzin and Ngakpa 'ö-Dzin, Aro Books worldwide, 2016, ISBN 978-1-89818-537-6.

Rays of the Sun, Ngakpa Chögyam, Aro Books worldwide, 2011, ISBN 978-1-89818-506-2.

Roaring Silence, Ngakpa Chögyam and Khandro Déchen, Shambhala, 2002, ISBN 978-1-57062-944-0.

Shock Amazement, Khandro Déchen and Ngakpa Chögyam, Aro Books worldwide, 2018, ISBN 978-1-89818-545-1.

The Great Path of Awakening – the Classic Guide to Lojong, a Tibetan Buddhist Practice for Cultivating the Heart of Compassion, Jamgon Kongtrul, translated by Ken McLoud, Shambhala Classics, 1987 and 2005, ISBN 978-1-59030-214-9.

The Nyingma School of Tibetan Buddhism – its Fundamentals and History, by Dudjom Rinpoche Jigdrel Yeshe Dorje, Wisdom Publications, 1991, ISBN 978-0-86171-199-4.

The Seven Points of Mind Training, The Venerable Khenchen Thrangu Rinpoche Geshe Lharampa, Namo Buddha Publications, 2004, Kindle edition, ISBN 978-1-931571-01-5.

Wisdom Eccentrics, Ngakpa Chögyam, Aro Books Inc, 2011, ISBN 978-0-96539-486-4.

The Path to Awakening, Shamar Rinpoche, edited and translated by Lara Braitstein, Delphinium Books, 2014, ISBN 978-1-88328-559-3.

Tibet, a History, Sam Van Schaik, Yale University Press, 2011, ISBN 978-0-30015-404-7.

Training the Mind – Cultivating Loving Kindness, Chögyam Trungpa, Shambhala, 1993, ISBN 978-0-87773-954-8.

Universal Compassion – Inspiring Solutions for Difficult Times, Geshe Kelsang Gyatso, Tharpa Publications, first published 1988, ISBN 978-0-94800-672-2.

Online Sources

https://en.wikipedia.org

http://www.aroencyclopaedia.org/

http://www.lotsawahouse.org/

https://tricycle.org/trikedaily/train-your-mind-lojong-commentary-judy-lief/

https://treasuryoflives.org/biographies/

http://nitartha.pythonanywhere.com/

www.ingramcontent.com/pod-product-compliance
Lightning Source LLC
Chambersburg PA
CBHW051627230426

43669CB00013B/2202